T0320724

# Examining the Socio–Technical Impact of Smart Cities

Fenio Annansingh
*York College, City University of New York, USA*

A volume in the Advances in Human
and Social Aspects of Technology
(AHSAT) Book Series

Published in the United States of America by
    IGI Global
    Information Science Reference (an imprint of IGI Global)
    701 E. Chocolate Avenue
    Hershey PA, USA 17033
    Tel: 717-533-8845
    Fax:  717-533-8661
    E-mail: cust@igi-global.com
    Web site: http://www.igi-global.com

Library of Congress Cataloging-in-Publication Data

Names: Annansingh, Fenio, 1974- editor.
Title: Examining the socio-technical impact of smart cities / Fenio
   Annansingh, editor.
Description: Hershey, PA : Information Science Reference, [2020] | Includes
   bibliographical references and index. | Summary: "This book explores the
   theoretical understanding of the socio-technical impact of smart cities
   by promoting the conceptual interactions between social and governmental
   structures (people, task, structure) with new technologies"-- Provided
   by publisher.
Identifiers: LCCN 2020002710 (print) | LCCN 2020002711 (ebook) | ISBN
   9781799853268 (hardcover) | ISBN 9781799853275 (paperback) | ISBN
   9781799853282 (ebook)
Subjects: LCSH: Smart cities. | Information technology--Social aspects.
Classification: LCC TD159.4 .E93 2020  (print) | LCC TD159.4  (ebook) | DDC
   303.48/33--dc23
LC record available at https://lccn.loc.gov/2020002710
LC ebook record available at https://lccn.loc.gov/2020002711

This book is published in the IGI Global book series Advances in Human and Social Aspects of Technology (AHSAT) (ISSN: 2328-1316; eISSN: 2328-1324)

British Cataloguing in Publication Data
A Cataloguing in Publication record for this book is available from the British Library.

All work contributed to this book is new, previously-unpublished material.
The views expressed in this book are those of the authors, but not necessarily of the publisher.

For electronic access to this publication, please contact: eresources@igi-global.com.

# Advances in Human and Social Aspects of Technology (AHSAT) Book Series

ISSN:2328-1316
EISSN:2328-1324

**Editor-in-Chief:** Mehdi Khosrow-Pour, D.B.A., Information Resources Management Association, USA

## MISSION

In recent years, the societal impact of technology has been noted as we become increasingly more connected and are presented with more digital tools and devices. With the popularity of digital devices such as cell phones and tablets, it is crucial to consider the implications of our digital dependence and the presence of technology in our everyday lives.

The **Advances in Human and Social Aspects of Technology (AHSAT) Book Series** seeks to explore the ways in which society and human beings have been affected by technology and how the technological revolution has changed the way we conduct our lives as well as our behavior. The AHSAT book series aims to publish the most cutting-edge research on human behavior and interaction with technology and the ways in which the digital age is changing society.

## COVERAGE

- End-User Computing
- Digital Identity
- Technology and Freedom of Speech
- Public Access to ICTs
- Philosophy of technology
- Cyber Bullying
- Technology and Social Change
- ICTs and social change
- Human Development and Technology
- Human Rights and Digitization

IGI Global is currently accepting manuscripts for publication within this series. To submit a proposal for a volume in this series, please contact our Acquisition Editors at Acquisitions@igi-global.com or visit: http://www.igi-global.com/publish/.

# Titles in this Series

*For a list of additional titles in this series, please visit:* http://www.igi-global.com/book-series

*Human-Computer Interaction and Technology Integration in Modern Society*
Hakikur Rahman (Institute of Computer Management and Science, Bangladesh)
Engineering Science Reference • © 2021 • 347pp • H/C (ISBN: 9781799858492) • US $195.00

*Information Technology Applications for Crisis Response and Management*
Jon W. Beard (Iowa State University, USA)
Information Science Reference • © 2021 • 310pp • H/C (ISBN: 9781799872108) • US $195.00

*ICT Solutions for Improving Smart Communities in Asia*
Noor Zaman (Taylor's University, Malaysia) Khalid Rafique (AJK Information Technology Board, Pakistan) and Vasaki Ponnusamy (Universiti Tunku Abdul Rahman, Malaysia)
Engineering Science Reference • © 2021 • 377pp • H/C (ISBN: 9781799871149) • US $235.00

*Information Technology Trends for a Global and Interdisciplinary Research Community*
Francisco J. García-Peñalvo (University of Salamanca, Spain)
Information Science Reference • © 2021 • 374pp • H/C (ISBN: 9781799841562) • US $195.00

*Latin American Women and Research Contributions to the IT Field*
Adriana Peña Pérez Negrón (Universidad de Guadalajara, Mexico) and Mirna Muñoz (CIMAT - Unidad Zacatecas, Mexico)
Engineering Science Reference • © 2021 • 459pp • H/C (ISBN: 9781799875529) • US $195.00

*Present and Future Paradigms of Cyberculture in the 21st Century*
Simber Atay (Dokuz Eylül University, Turkey) Gülsün Kurubacak-Meriç (Anadolu University, Turkey) and Serap Sisman-Uğur (Anadolu University, Turkey)
Information Science Reference • © 2021 • 246pp • H/C (ISBN: 9781522580249) • US $185.00

701 East Chocolate Avenue, Hershey, PA 17033, USA
Tel: 717-533-8845 x100 • Fax: 717-533-8661
E-Mail: cust@igi-global.com • www.igi-global.com

# Table of Contents

**Preface**.................................................................................................................xii

**Chapter 1**
Collaborative Governance: A New Paradigm Shift for the Smart Cities..............1
    *Gedifew Sewenet Yigzaw, Bahir Dar University, Ethiopia*

**Chapter 2**
E-Scooter Systems: Problems, Potentials, and Planning Policies in Turkey .......36
    *Betül Ertoy Sariişik, Gazi University, Turkey*
    *Ozge Yalciner Ercoskun, Gazi University, Turkey*

**Chapter 3**
Learning Cities as Smart Cities: Connecting Lifelong Learning and
Technology........................................................................................................68
    *Leodis Scott, DePaul University, USA & Teachers College, Columbia*
        *University, USA*

**Chapter 4**
Large Technical Systems: Artificial Intelligence and Future Applications in
Smart Cities......................................................................................................91
    *Muhammed Can, University of Minho, Portugal*
    *Halid Kaplan, University of Texas at San Antonio, USA*

**Chapter 5**
Using Big Data Analytics to Assist a Smart City to Prevent Cyber Security
Threats.............................................................................................................107
    *Fenio Annansingh, York College, City University of New York, USA*

**Chapter 6**
Smart New York City: The Emergence of Sustainable Technological
Innovations.............................................................................................................125
    *Wesley Palmer, York College, City University of New York, USA*

**Chapter 7**
Smart Parking: The Cornerstone of a Smart City.............................................138
    *Fenio Annansingh, Department of Business and Economics, York*
        *College, City University of New York, USA*

**Chapter 8**
Smart Cities, ICT, and Small Businesses in the USA.......................................155
    *Lloyd Amaghionyeodiwe, York College, City University of New York,*
        *USA*

**Chapter 9**
Review of the Role of the Internet of Things (IoT) on the Consumer Market:
Focusing on Smart Tourism, Healthcare, and Retailing....................................180
    *Yong Kyu Lee, York College, City University of New York, USA*

**Compilation of References** ........................................................................... 199

**About the Contributors** ................................................................................ 228

**Index**................................................................................................................ 230

# Detailed Table of Contents

**Preface**................................................................................................................. xii

**Chapter 1**
Collaborative Governance: A New Paradigm Shift for the Smart Cities............... 1
    *Gedifew Sewenet Yigzaw, Bahir Dar University, Ethiopia*

In this 21st century, collaborative governance has got a great attention to resolve socio-economic problems and assure sustainable development goals. It is a new form of governance in which multi-stakeholders, such as the public agencies, private sectors, civil society organizations and international public organizations are working together to build trust in government, resolve societal challenges, assure economic prosperity and development, and bring institutional transformation. This book chapter describes the theoretical and conceptual perspectives of collaborative governance. The author believed that giving some insights on the collaborative governance; conceptual understanding, the dynamics and importance of collaborative governance for building the smart cities, its nexus with development, and measurement parameters for checking its effectiveness, could produce a theoretical and conceptual asset for the other authors who want to make an in-depth investigation on the areas of governance.

**Chapter 2**
E-Scooter Systems: Problems, Potentials, and Planning Policies in Turkey ....... 36
    *Betül Ertoy Sariişik, Gazi University, Turkey*
    *Ozge Yalciner Ercoskun, Gazi University, Turkey*

Transportation planning, as one of the essential parts of city planning, has the potential to solve many problems on a global scale. These problems can be listed as traffic congestion, air pollution, fossil-fuel consumption, accessibility problems, global warming, climate change, and psychological problems affecting human lives. In recent years, transportation planning studies have come to the fore within the concept of sustainable urban mobility. The focus of this research is e-scooter systems, one of the micromobility options within the scope of urban mobility. The study explores how the availability of this micro transport mode can affect the time, cost, and ease of travels. In order to get information about the applications in Turkey, provider representatives were interviewed, and mobile applications and expert opinions were consulted.

**Chapter 3**
Learning Cities as Smart Cities: Connecting Lifelong Learning and
Technology.................................................................................................................68
    *Leodis Scott, DePaul University, USA & Teachers College, Columbia
        University, USA*

The purpose of this chapter is to explore the connections between technology and lifelong learning and the respective initiatives of smart cities and learning cities. The Pew Research Center reports that place-based learning remains vital for pursuing knowledge especially from digital technology. This means that although learning occurs in traditional places (home, work, or community), the use of technology further enhances learner engagement across the entire society. As such, learning cities is a placed-based initiative for implementing education and lifelong learning. Smart cities, similarly, expand the implementation of education and lifelong learning, but through a broader medium of digital technology and the internet. The important connection between lifelong learning (as learning cities) and technology (as smart cities) is the aim for providing access to every individual in society. This chapter offers an analysis of two concepts representing these two cities' initiatives.

**Chapter 4**
Large Technical Systems: Artificial Intelligence and Future Applications in
Smart Cities.............................................................................................................91
    *Muhammed Can, University of Minho, Portugal
    Halid Kaplan, University of Texas at San Antonio, USA*

In recent years, artificial intelligence has become a new normal in the modern world. Even though there are still limitations and it remains to be premature both in terms of applications and theoretical approaches, AI has a huge potential to shift various systems from healthcare to transportation. Needless to say, smart cities are also significant for AI's development. IoT, big data applications, and power networks bring a new understanding of how we live and what the future will be like when AI is adapted to smart cities. However, it is highly misleading to focus on AI itself in this manner. Rather, it should be considered as a part of the 'Large Technical System'. In this vein, the chapter will ask the following questions: To what extent might AI contribute the power networks of smart cities? How can LTS theory explain this evolution both in terms of technical aspects and technopolitics?

**Chapter 5**
Using Big Data Analytics to Assist a Smart City to Prevent Cyber Security
Threats..................................................................................................................107
*Fenio Annansingh, York College, City University of New York, USA*

The concept of a smart city as a means to enhance the life quality of citizens has been gaining increasing importance in recent years globally. A smart city consists of city infrastructure, which includes smart services, devices, and institutions. Every second, these components of the smart city infrastructure are generating data. The vast amount of data is called big data. This chapter explores the possibilities of using big data analytics to prevent cybersecurity threats in a smart city. It also analyzed how big data tools and concepts can solve cybersecurity challenges and detect and prevent attacks. Using interviews and an extensive review of the literature have developed the data analytics and cyber prevention model. The chapter concludes by indicating that big data analytics allow a smart city to identify and solve cybersecurity challenges quickly and efficiently.

**Chapter 6**
Smart New York City: The Emergence of Sustainable Technological
Innovations.............................................................................................................125
*Wesley Palmer, York College, City University of New York, USA*

This study is an examination of the integration of information, telecommunications, mobile technology, and artificial intelligence (AI) technology in New York City's (NYC) infrastructure to maximize development and to improve the services provided to residents and their quality of life. Efficiency in service delivery is enhanced through smart technologies, and embracing innovation makes city systems efficient. The study is based on Barlow and Levy-Bencheton's smart cities theory. The research questions concern how the integration of smart technology improves the quality of life for residents and provides economic benefits for the city. The researcher surveyed 425 New York City residents to analyze the impact of smart technology on the city's systems. The findings indicated that 96% of residents experienced positive effects from smart technology on their quality of life. Smart cities have digitalized systems to enhance water supply, transportation, waste management, safety, public awareness, and health service delivery, among other essential services.

**Chapter 7**
Smart Parking: The Cornerstone of a Smart City.............................................138
*Fenio Annansingh, Department of Business and Economics, York*
*College, City University of New York, USA*

With the increase of urban population and traffic congestion, smart parking is a strategic, economic, environmentally friendly solution for cities looking to remain connected. A sustainable parking system parking is connected in some way to every facet of the city that is water, waste, energy, and transportation. With the information and communication technology evolution and the development of the internet of things, drivers can more efficiently find satisfying parking spaces with smart parking services. This research adopts a survey approach by employing the use of questionnaires. From the questionnaire, descriptive data analysis is used to synthesize, analyze, and interpret the data. The result elicits user requirements and constraints for the development of a mobile app solution that will eliminate unnecessary traffic and ensure the maximum utilization of municipal parking facilities. These user requirements will determine the design and development of a mobile application that saves time, reduce the environmental impact, and improve the quality of life.

**Chapter 8**

Smart Cities, ICT, and Small Businesses in the USA........................................155
    *Lloyd Amaghionyeodiwe, York College, City University of New York,*
        *USA*

The phenomenon of smart cities is not new in the literature, and one of the definitions emphasizes the use of information and communication technologies (ICTs) to improve quality of life and efficiency of services. To this end, IT systems become crucial and essential to a city's quest to be "smart." Thus, many organizations including SMEs have developed and utilized networks to facilitate their operations, transactions, and business functions. Given the role of small businesses in an economy and their quest operate in a smart environment and using surveys from organization, this study examines how smart these small businesses are by looking at their ICT usage. The study found that inasmuch as these small businesses improved in their usage of ICT, they are now faced with the risk of cyberattack, and while many of these businesses are virtually doing nothing to curb this, it becomes pertinent for an awareness to be put in place to help these small businesses realize the need for risk management especially as it relates to cyberattacks.

**Chapter 9**
Review of the Role of the Internet of Things (IoT) on the Consumer Market:
Focusing on Smart Tourism, Healthcare, and Retailing .................................... 180
*Yong Kyu Lee, York College, City University of New York, USA*

This chapter reviews the internet of things (IoT) as a key component of a smart city and how it is applied to consumers' daily lives and business. The IoT is a part of information and communication technology (ICT) and is considered a powerful means to improve consumers' quality of life. The "thing" could be any object which has internet capability, such as wearable devices and smart TVs/phones/speakers. Several studies have identified driving factors that have led consumers to adopting them, but also concerns of consumers' resistance to IoT devices. The three major fields of application of IoT technologies were selected to review the role of the IoT in consumers' daily lives and business.

**Compilation of References** ............................................................ 199

**About the Contributors** .............................................................. 228

**Index** ........................................................................ 230

# Preface

Smart cities are becoming a priority for municipals, local authorities, government, research, and educational institutions. The increase in urbanization and development across the globe presents significant opportunities for smart cities, and information and communication technology (ICT), mainly broadband network, provides the underlying infrastructure. These technologies have exerted a growing and pervasive influence on the nature, structure, and execution of urban infrastructure, management, economic activity, and daily activities. Cities have taken a leading role in developing and utilizing pervasive and ubiquitous computing and digitally instrumented devices to monitor, manage and regulate city flows and processes by engaging with mobile devices that many urban individuals already own and employ to navigate the city.

This book *Examining the Socio-Technical Impact of Smart Cities* provides insights into the practical utilization of the Internet of Things (IoT), cloud computing, cybersecurity, and big data integration into smart city applications. These developments provide socio-economic development opportunities resulting in more comfortable, safe, functional, competitive, and sustainable cities.

Chapter 1 seeks to provide a conceptual and theoretical understanding of collaborative governance and the advancement of smart cities. It highlights the role of deliberate, collaborative governance as a reform approach to build smart cities, shows its nexus with sustainable development, describes the role of coordination and collaboration in bringing good urban governance.

Chapter 2 examines the demand for environmentally friendly vehicles. It investigates electric scooter (e-scooter) systems as an urban transportation tool by reviewing the potential benefits and challenges. It looks at the regulatory and the city planning policies for this transportation mode using a smart city in Turkey.

Chapter 3 considers the socio-technical impact of smart cities on lifelong learning. The chapter discusses the connection between lifelong learning (learning cities) and technology (smart cities). While smart cities rely heavily on technology, infrastructure, and organizational systems, learning cities focus on communication, interaction, and learning. It seeks to provide the bridge the gap between learning cities and smart cities.

Chapter 4 investigates emerging technologies and the impact on societies, geopolitics, economies. Using large technical systems theory to provide theoretical lenses to understand what lies behind the complex large technological systems, the chapter examines the development in machine learning techniques and AI and the implications on society-state relations or individual-society dimensions.

Chapter 5 explores the possibilities of using big data analytics to prevent cybersecurity threats in a smart city. It also analyzes how practitioners and researchers can use big data tools and concepts to solve cybersecurity challenges and detect and prevent attacks. It concludes by indicating that big data analytics allow a smart city to identify and solve cybersecurity challenges quickly and efficiently.

Chapter 6 is based on Barlow and Levy-Bencheton's smart cities theory. It looks at integrating information, telecommunications, mobile technology, and artificial intelligence (AI) technology in a smart city infrastructure to maximize development and improve residents' services and quality of life. The chapter provides insight into the benefits of smart technology in NYC and for other city management.

Chapter 7 introduces the concept of developing a sustainable parking system. It exploits the information and communication technology evolution and the development of the Internet of Things (IoT) as the underlying framework for developing a parking application that identifies and utilizes parking spaces more efficiently.

Chapter 8 looks at the adoption of ICT technologies by small businesses to enhance their productivity and competitiveness by making them smarter. It examines small business reliant and utilization of technology, especially in an era of ongoing digital transformation. The chapter shows that small businesses are vulnerable to cyberattacks with the adoption of new technologies. However, they are often ill-equipped to handle these threats.

Chapter 9 reviews the role of the IoT on consumers' daily lives and business in three major areas—smart tourism, healthcare, and retailing. These application fields are closely connected to the development of the smart city, and their markets increase with the IoT technologies. The chapter helps researchers and practitioners understand the role of IoT in overcoming obstacles and challenges, especially in a consumer market.

# Chapter 1
# Collaborative Governance:
## A New Paradigm Shift for the Smart Cities

**Gedifew Sewenet Yigzaw**
*Bahir Dar University, Ethiopia*

## ABSTRACT

*In this 21st century, collaborative governance has got a great attention to resolve socio-economic problems and assure sustainable development goals. It is a new form of governance in which multi-stakeholders, such as the public agencies, private sectors, civil society organizations and international public organizations are working together to build trust in government, resolve societal challenges, assure economic prosperity and development, and bring institutional transformation. This book chapter describes the theoretical and conceptual perspectives of collaborative governance. The author believed that giving some insights on the collaborative governance; conceptual understanding, the dynamics and importance of collaborative governance for building the smart cities, its nexus with development, and measurement parameters for checking its effectiveness, could produce a theoretical and conceptual asset for the other authors who want to make an in-depth investigation on the areas of governance.*

## 1. INTRODUCTION

No organization of government possesses sufficient authority, resources, and knowledge to effect the enactment and achievement of policy intentions. Instead, policies require the concerted efforts of multiple actors, all possessing significant

DOI: 10.4018/978-1-7998-5326-8.ch001

capabilities but each dependent on multiple others to solidify policy intention and convert it into action. Indeed, it is often difficult for anyone actor, or group of actors, to manage, or manipulate the flow of problems and solutions onto the political agenda in the first place. (Bressers, O'Toole, & Richardson, 1995)

The concept of governance has become very fashionable development agenda over the past several decades in the political science and public administration areas. The term has been widely used by policy makers, politicians, governance practitioners, international organizations, and other different stakeholders. One of the key characteristics of using a governance lens is the recognition that there is a wide range of actors involved in governance, such as various government organizations, business sectors, civil society organizations, for example, non-governmental organizations (NGOs) and community groups and the private sectors (Devas, 2001). When we take a snapshot concept of governance, Yohannes (2017) has described governance as "a new process of governing or a changed condition of ordered rule or the new method by which society is governed. He has also added that governance deals with the methods by which citizens participate in decision making, how government is accountable to its citizens and how the society obliges its members to be governed by its rules and laws. From this instance, it is considered as a ruling system consisting of delegation of authority, power decentralization, people's participation, and group/stakeholder dynamism in level of participation, idea sharing and decision-making. From these all perspectives, one can infer that the issue of governance embraces all of the methods- good and bad that societies use to distribute power and manage public resources and problems. Hence, it is the relationship and collective decision-making process contracted between and/or among the civil society and the state, between rulers and ruled; the government and the governed. In a broadest sense of the term, it comprises the mechanisms, processes and institutions, through which citizens and groups articulate their interests, exercise their legal rights, meet their obligations and mediate their differences. Moreover, Aluko (2010) also defines governance as the act or process of governing a nation, state, or legal entity. It is the activity of governing a country, controlling, ruling, managing, regulating, influencing, or directing a place. Governance recognizes that power exists inside and outside the formal authority and institutions of government.

The formation of governance as a new model of arrangement recognizes government, civil society and the private sector as the key actors in the administration apparatus and providing services to citizens. At the local level, these groups can be further specified to include central government, state or provincial government (where applicable), local authorities, non-governmental organizations (NGOs), community-based organizations (CBOs), and the private sector. In the urban context, governance is the sum of many ways; individuals and institutions plan and manage the common affairs of the city (Adegun, 2011). This understanding lens consists of governance as a concept that recognizes the power existence inside and outside the formal authority and institutions of government, and governance emphasizes as a process. Besides, it recognizes that decisions are made based on complex relationships between many actors with different priorities.

It is through this governance arrangement that one can clearly understand these actors and the relationships between them. Because governance is an important administration approach of employing collective decision-making process and practices in order to address societal problems (Förster, 2016). In this sense, governance has become collaborative in nature that clearly shows the coordination and network of different stakeholders to resolve the societal problems and bring the transformational paradigm shift from a type of relationship where one side governs the other [that is, the government] to a set of relationships where mutual interaction takes place in order to make desirable choices for the citizens. Now days, it is a collaborative governance and/ or collective action which plays a key role to build trust in the government, assure accountability and transparency, bring quality service delivery to the people, and thereby ensure sustainable development in order to reduce extreme poverty from the landscape of the world. As a result, collaborative governance as a new model of governance arrangement has received significant attention in recent years in order to build the smart cities. The issue of building cities which are smart in terms of people (smart people), governance (smart governance), environment (smart environment), and smart technology is the primary task of urban governments today than ever before.

In this regard, collaborative governance which has been emerged as a response to failures of implementation of policies and programs at the urban centers, and community level, would play a key role in order to build smart cities. Hence, the implication of this chapter is to provide a conceptual and theoretical understanding on collaborative governance on the advancement of the smart cities, to highlight the role of deliberate collaborative governance as a reform approach so as to build smart cities, to show its nexus with sustainable development, to describe the role of coordination and collaboration in bringing good urban governance, and finally, to explore some key challenges of collaborative governance facing in the urban areas. Besides, the author has tried to describe the application and impacts public-private partnership model on building the smart cities. Some scholars described the definition of collaborative governance in the narrowest perspective, and others defined it in the broadest perspective. In this section, the author, depending upon different literatures, has defined collaborative governance in the broadest vein which is much more beyond than public-private partnership in which both of them are mutually beneficial and include structures, processes, actions and reactions. Finally, the author has explored some future trends or possible research areas in which in-depth investigations could be conducted and concluding remarks of the author has been finally addressed in the last section of this chapter.

## 2. COLLABORATIVE GOVERNANCE: DYNAMICS AND IMPORTANCE FOR BUILDING SMART CITIES

### 2.1. The Dynamics of Collaborative Governance

In this globalized world, a new paradigm shift of governance has emerged to replace adversarial and managerial modes of policy making and implementation. During the last two/three decades, a new strategy of governing called "collaborative governance" brings public and private stakeholders together in collective forums with public agencies to engage in consensus-oriented decision making in the urbanity. This governance model was emerged as a response to failures of nation states' implementation of policies and programs at the community level. In addressing these failures, collaborative governance attempts to create, interpret, and apply policy through the participation of multiple stakeholders. Van Buuren et al. (2007) describe collaborative governance as "a reaction to traditional planning and policy-making approaches that are primarily top-down oriented, focusing on the government instead of the governed, mainly technocratically oriented and adversarially organized." As an interactive and iterative process, collaborative governance engages multiple actors with different and complementary knowledge and experience. Put in another way, this mode of governance brings multiple stakeholders together in common forums with public agencies to engage in consensus-oriented decision making. Similarly, it has emerged as a response to the failures of downstream implementation and to the high cost and politicization of regulations. It has developed as an alternative to the adversarialism of interest group pluralism and to the accountability failures of managerialism (Plotnikof, 2015; Ansell & Gash, 2008).

One may argue that trends toward collaboration have arisen from the growth of knowledge and institutional capacity. This mode of governance is currently practicing and developing in public organizations to involve stakeholders in co-creating solutions for shared problems such as policy and service innovation. Moreover, it is initiated by policy makers or public managers with the hope of bringing together stakeholders to explore new solutions and thereby co-create public value and innovation (Ansell & Gash, 2008; O'leary & Vij, 2012).

In the public management perspective, collaborative governance is the process of facilitating and operating in multi-organizational arrangements to solve problems that cannot be solved, or easily solved, by single organizations. It manifests itself in various initiatives and practices of inter-organizational collaborations and comprises both long- and short-term events such as roundtable discussions, networks, partnerships and community programs. The following table clearly summaries the concept of collaborative governance.

*Table 1. The definition of collaborative governance*

| No. | Description | Author/s |
|---|---|---|
| 1 | The relationship involving public agencies and non-stakeholders describing it as "an arrangement where one or more public agencies directly engage non-stakeholders in a collective decision-making process that is formal or consensus-oriented and deliberative and that aims to make or implement public policy or manage public programs or assets. | Ansel and Gash (2008) |
| 2 | An amalgam of public, private and civil-society organizations engaged in some joint effort. | Donahue (2004) |
| 3 | The processes and structures of public policy decision making and management that engage people constructively across the boundaries of public agencies, levels of government, and/or the public, private and civic spheres in order to carry out a public purpose that could not otherwise be accomplished. | Emerson et.al (2011) |
| 4 | The process of establishing, steering, facilitating, operating, and monitoring cross-sectoral organizational arrangements to address public policy problems that cannot be easily addressed by a single organization or the public sector alone". These arrangements are characterized by joint efforts, reciprocal expectations, and voluntary participation among formally autonomous entities, from two or more sectors —public, for profit, and nonprofits —in order to leverage the unique attributes and resources of each sector. | Tang and Mazmanian (2010) |

Moreover, collaborative governance captures a fuller range of emergent forms of cross-boundary governance, extending beyond the conventional focus on the public manager or the formal public sector. Besides, it is also possible to see collaborative governance in a wider spectrum. It is a strategy used to planning, regulation, policy making and public management to coordinate, adjudicate and integrate the goals and interests of multiple stakeholders. Collaborative governance does not, in principle, require transformative effects on any one class of partner. Governments can continue to represent the public interest through democratic processes. Civil society and labor organizations can be party to collaborative governance while maintaining their heterogeneous perspectives and complex, dynamic, organic, value-based accountability. In the same way, business can be involved in new governance models while continuing to seek to maximize financial returns to the owners of capital with management held to account through the rule of law, and the self-interested oversight of the investment community (Ansell, 2012; Silvia, 2011). It is used as a technique to bring citizens and other stakeholders together for common projects or agendas, to construct democracy along less adversarial and managerial lines, and to restore trust in government and expand democratic consent by widening citizen participation and deliberation in the agendas and affairs of the public. Thus, this new governance paradigm typically emphasizes on collaboration and partnership between and among the public, private, and interested stakeholders.

Scholars argued that collaborative governance is a governing arrangement in which decision-making power is shared among multiple organizations, it is a tool for managing uncertainty, it rhetorically seems to serve as a means of managing political and economic risks associated with high societal expectations, combining fears and concerns with diverse and substantial demands (Scott, 2015; Hutter, 2016). Cross-organizational collaboration enables managers to incorporate diverse types of knowledge into a process and to understand how stakeholders might respond to a policy decision. The life cycle of collaborative governance contains two key elements or phases. In the first cycle, the design of public policy increasingly involves business and civil society inputs, including specialized knowledge and, crucially, lobbying to secure specific outcomes. The implementation of public policy habitually requires the explicit support of non-state actors in terms of resources and implementation pathways. With the growing importance of multiple actors during the implementation phase, their leverage also tends to increase over policy design. It is a response to a failure of traditional mechanisms for allocating resources, and setting and enforcing rules to effectively secure key public goods. Its logic is framed by the institutional interests of those involved, notably government, business, and civil society organizations. Of these participants, business, above all, has legitimized interests in private gain, and so treats public goods instrumentally to that end (Zadek, 2006).

According to the collaborative governance regime framework (Emerson & Nabatchi, 2015), which is based on one of the most comprehensive reviews of the collaboration literature, collaborative governance is composed of three interacting elements, or "dynamics" that together yield changes in the world both proximate outputs, like learning and managerial capacity, and longer-term effects on the environment. The first element, "the principled engagement", is the process by which participants engage with one another, especially the use of deliberation and interest-based negotiation to make joint decisions. The second, "shared motivation," is the affective stance of individual participants to one another and to the process as a whole, i.e., whether they trust the other participants, feel like their interests are respected by the group, and view the collaborative process as legitimate. The third, "capacity for joint action," involves the structure and resources necessary to support engagement, including facilitation, leadership, and scientific information (Emerson & Nabatchi, 2015). These three dynamics form the crux of collaboration (Ulibarri, 2019). In this stand point, collaborative governance creates and fosters an environment of participation among regional actors, governments, and the private sector. This facilitates new networks for further enhancement of the trust base, and the ongoing sharing of ideas. The involvement of diverse actors contributes to a heightened investigation of policies and programs in the region (Ansell & Gash, 2008; Bevir &Richards, 2009). Thus, it is collaborative governance which reveals how the collaborative approach can be used to tap the resourcefulness and entrepreneurship of the private sector, and improvise fresh and flexible solutions to today's most pressing public challenges in the world.

## 2.2. Collaborative Governance for Building Smart Cities

The urban development has resulted in a change of paradigm in the $21^{st}$ century, and the resource activities for smarter cities have become the priority task with the direct involvement from different stakeholders such as practitioners, political parties, academicians, government organizations, business sectors and civil society organizations (Ermia et al., 2017). In the struggle to be innovative and competitive in the city market, new products and solutions are increasingly developed in collaborative settings within value networks or entire value chains that involve more than one organization. Cities have always been about shared space, human interaction and encounter, and the exchange of goods and services through marketplaces and moneylending. A successful city needs good governance and collective civic structures to facilitate and regulate the interface between the shared public realm and private interests, and to enable effective and fair sharing of resources and opportunities (McLaren & Agyeman, 2015). From the ideal-typical perspective with the focus on governance, smart cities are defined as cities with smart collaboration (Meijer & Bolívar, 2016). Considering the organizational changes, smart city initiatives aim to increase the efficiency and effectiveness of public administration as well as aspects that promote smart governance to encourage greater collaboration between stakeholders (Chourabi et al., 2012) and improve the provision of information and services.

A collaborative urban government can apply collective city intelligence for innovative solutions to problems, and it can also provide shared governance that ultimately fosters the trust and confidence of citizens in governments (Chun et al., 2012). In positive collaborative governance model, data, information, and information communication technology (ICT) are crucial components of a smart city. This can be measured in terms of data management capacity and quality, information processing, creation of smart environment with smart people and information sharing, which are the key aspects for promoting collaboration and inter-organizational communications in the cities (Gil-Garcia et al., 2015). The significance of data and information in the smart cities using digital technology, in the cooperative governance atmosphere, is the most important in order to improve and speed up the decision-making processes of urban policies (Charalabidis et al., 2012). Cities that implement collaborative strategies have the capacity to construct public policies based on the contribution of different points of view and social actors, precisely identifying local problems and improving public investment. In addition, it creates the capacity to think in the long term, having as a principle the transparency and the division of responsibilities in the structuring of sustainability policies. Finally, the collaborative governance enables the empowerment of citizens, making the city a public space for social participation. Active democracy requires new governance models, which must be collaborative and produce positive results for the society and for sustainability (Conti et al., 2019).

Besides, Scholl and Scholl (2014) argued that smart collaborative governance can be seen as basis to smart, open and participatory government. These concepts play a key role in the growing discourse on smart cities, so we may expect that Information and Communication Technologies (ICTs) play a key role in smart government as part of wider models of smart collaborative governance. Smart cities are related to ICT-based urban innovation, i.e., intelligent use of ICTs to deliver better urban services, dealing with growing urban problems due to increasing urbanization, without the proper establishment of policies focused on well-being. One of the main objectives of smart cities is increasing the quality of life in the city. Testoni and Boeri (2015) suggest that to manage the dynamics of smart cities, a new model of governance is needed along with strong coordination by the local government to support in managing complex co-operation processes with a variety of stakeholders, in particular citizens. This scenario requires reshaping the role of governments, citizens, and other social actors, as well as exploring the new and emergent information technologies to frame a new governance model, including new relationships, new processes, and new government structures. In this regard, the use of ICT simplifies and improves the internal administrative operations of urban government, facilitates public service interaction between government and all stakeholders, enables citizen participation, and ensures inclusiveness and equal opportunities for all (Castelnovo et al., 2015). Thus, it is through collaborative model of governance that the wide ranges of societal problems can be solved and smart cities (i.e., a technology-intensive city, with extensive use of sensors and interconnected devices to gather and analyze data in real time to deliver public services more efficiently and effectively) can be built. Consequently, smart cities require smart collaborative governance arrangements to make cost-effective use of the technology and to bring the digital transformation in the city. It is important to say that the success of collaborative governance depends not only on the strategy of including non-governmental actors in the management of a city but also of a mobilized society. This happens because the engagement and mobilization of different actors can directly impact social transformation and sustainability issues (Bryson et al., 2014).

## 2.3. Deliberative Collaborative Governance: A Reform Approach to Build Smart Cities

A process which is termed as a deliberative collaborative governance (DCG) that enables more meaningful public participation in issues that matter, with greater decision-making transparency, accountability and perceived legitimacy, has been demonstrably effective in helping to redress the governance gaps (Weymouth & Hartz-Karp, 2015). This is the most important in structuring and building smart cities in this contemporary world. Because the deliberate participation and collaboration of different stakeholders in crafting city policies, installing information communication technologies, developing cleaned and smart city environment, and in fostering the interrelationship between people as well as advancing city economy could play paramount importance in order to make cities smart and smarter. Existing government structures, siloed, technocratic and hierarchical, have been incapable of effectively addressing wicked problems, and of meeting the public's expectation that it is government's job to resolve such issues. This apparent lack of capability further erodes public trust, which makes it even harder to address the challenges - and so the governance gap widens. In order to reduce these governance gaps, the new model of collaborative governance structure was introduced and started application. This in turn, will increase public trust in government and hence, cultivate a willingness and capacity to take part in future collaborative responses to wicked problems aggravated in the urban centers. Wicked problems are ranging from domestic issues, such as the impoverishment of education, health care, and justice systems; the crumbling of transportation, utility, energy, and other infrastructure systems; and recurring crises in housing, financial, and industrial markets to international and global issues, such as climate change, food and water shortages, infectious disease, human trafficking, and the illegal arms trade (Emerson & Nabatchi, 2015). The newly coined concept of DCG reframes deliberative democracy to focus on the transformative reform that is envisaged – a new form of collaborative governance that is solidly grounded in discursiveness and descriptive representativeness (i.e., resembling a representative sample of the population). DCG unites elements of the broad field of collaborative governance with that of deliberative democracy.

Furthermore, Gollagher and Hartz-Karp (2013) have proposed a particular collaborative governance approach they have termed it as DCG which they contend as likely to be the most effective in resolving wicked problems in the cities, and they have described sustainability examples from across the globe that exhibit at least some of the characteristics of this approach. Moreover, the concept of DCG was devised to address some of the key critiques of two related approaches – Deliberative Democracy and Collaborative Governance. The theory and practice of deliberative democracy incorporates inclusive, deliberative, and influential participation in policy development and decision-making. The most problematic critique of deliberative democracy as it relates to sustainable collaborative governance is its lack of success in reforming existing democratic institutions. This critique notes that although proliferating rapidly, the deliberative democracy movement has failed to secure institutionalization in the existing governance structure in all but a few places around the world, and hence, has failed to "democratize democracy" (Pateman, 2012). This failure may manifest in political elites, like media commentators and politicians (Boswell, Niemeyer, & Hendriks, 2013), viewing deliberative democratic processes as unworkable, or a revolutionary movement intending to overthrow the existing system. This reform has the capacity to change the existing system dynamics in regional governance to create a virtuous cycle, where greater collective ownership of wicked problems and potential solutions will decrease unrealistic expectations of what government can and cannot do, and increase the likelihood of more effective outcomes (Weymouth & Hartz-Karp, 2015).

In relation with this, Ansell and Gash (2008) argued collaborative governance as an arrangement where one or more public agencies directly engage non-state stakeholders in a collective decision-making process that is formal, consensus-oriented, and deliberative, and that aims to make or implement public policy or manage public programs or assets effectively. This concept involves an actor deliberately participating with other organized actors in the governance structure (unions, government departments, NGO's…etc.) that results in genuine attempts at partnership to formulate policies and create recommendations. However, as Gallagher and Hartz-Karp argue, the key to more effectively addressing wicked problems is the holistic understanding of the system involved, and achieving this will also require the "practical wisdom" of everyday people (Gollagher & Hartz-Karp, 2013). Thus, urban scholars such as Nijkamp and Kourtit (2013) emphasize that the city is a social fabric based on interaction, participation, and collective responsibility.

In this regard, cities around the world are struggling to find smart solutions to the above mentioned wicked urban problems and looking to learn new strategies from successful techno-governance practices in other cities (Meijer, 2016). Becoming a smarter city is not an optional policy agenda but is a mandatory policy strategy for the cities of the world today. In this perspective, DCG is an important device in order to make cities smarter in terms of people, infrastructures, economy, environment and governance through the use of deliberation and cooperation. This could improve convenience, facilitate mobility, create efficient and effective processes, improve air and water quality, enable to identify urban problems (such as congestion, theft, housing affordability issues, environmental wastes, pollution…etc.), bring better data access and information, and deploying of urban resources to enable collaboration across different parts of the cities. From this, one can conclude that deliberative collaborative governance is important to build smart cities. This can be achieved through coordinative and collaborative efforts with multiple stakeholders in deliberation and facilitation. To sum up, DCG is essential to capture how the shared responsibility, authority, and power are coupled with a pragmatic problem-solving orientation to wicked problems that emphasizes deliberative analysis, fact finding, and policy evaluation can move the communities towards resilience and smartness of the cities (Gallagher & Hartze-Karp, 2013).

## 3. COLLABORATIVE GOVERNANCE AND SUSTAINABLE DEVELOPMENT

It is difficult and challenging to separate collaborate governance from development and vice versa. Development in the absence of cooperation and coordination is collaborative governance in the absence of development. In this vein, it is possible to say that development and prosperity can be strongly achieved through the collaboration between and among different stakeholders, such as the government which represents the public institutions and citizens, the business sector [the market], civil society organizations and international organizations. From this, collaborative governance, sometimes, termed as networked governance, is the must for ensuring and achieving sustainable development goals. The concept of governance is concerned directly with the management of the development process, involving both the public and the private sectors. It encompasses the functioning and capability of the public sector as well as the rules and institutions that create the framework for the conduct of both public and private business, including accountability for economic and financial performance, and regulatory frameworks relating to companies, corporations, and partnerships (Islam, 2017). Fair and effective governance is critical to ensuring that development benefits both people and the planet. In this vein, governance should entail processes, decisions, and outcomes that sustain natural resources alleviate poverty and improve the quality of life. A governance lens offers a powerful impetus for promoting reforms in policies and programs for sustainable development. These include open and transparent opportunities for poor and disadvantaged citizens to access information and secure their rights over land, forest, and energy resources and to encourage governments to adopt policies that are more friendly to people and the environment (Weber, 2015).

The International Monetary Fund (IMF) in 1996 acknowledged that promoting good governance in all its aspects by ensuring the rule of law, improving the efficiency and accountability of the public sectors, bringing public-private partnership, and tackling corruption are essential elements of a framework within which economies of both developed and developing countries can prosper (IMF, 2005). It is in this and other perspectives that collaborative governance expresses the power which is exercised in the management of state, civil society and private sector to work in cohesion for accelerated economic growth and greater human development. If the standards of governance remain poor, it becomes inevitable for the government to implement sound development management. To have the desired effect on people's lives, they must improve their socioeconomic conditions and alleviate poverty. It is good to encourage the private sector to invest and develop infrastructure, minimize financial constraints and to create an enabling environment for economic growth. Focusing upon collaboration and partnership in the affairs of the country is a prime economic and societal mover as well as driver of technological and political change in the country because collaboration implies that non-state stakeholders will have real responsibility for policy outcomes. In collaborative governance (Ansell & Gash, 2008), stakeholders will often have an adversarial relationship to one another, but the goal is to transform adversarial relationships into more cooperative ones.

The key roles of non-government actors, including business sectors, have more confirmed in the United Nations (UN) declaration of achieving sustainable global development goals. The UN Sustainable Development Summit adopted a new framework to guide development efforts between 2015 and 2030, entitled "Transforming our world: the 2030 Agenda for sustainable development." Humanity has the ability to make development sustainable to ensure that it meets the needs of the present without compromising the ability of future generations to meet their own needs. Meeting essential needs requires not only a new era of economic growth for nations in which the majority are poor, but an assurance that those poor get their fair share of the resources required to sustain that growth. Such equity would be aided by political systems that secure effective citizen participation in decision making and by greater democracy in international decision making (UN, 2015; FAO, 2017). It is a fact that sustainability issues involve complex interactions between social, economic, and environmental factors that are often viewed quite differently by disparate stakeholder groups.

The Sustainable Development Goals (SDGs) are a universal set of goals and targets agreed by 194 UN member states to guide their development policies and initiatives over the next 15 years. The SDGs apply equally to developed and developing countries, and the framework of targets and indicators provides the basis for stimulating initiative, monitoring performance and levering compliance. The SDGs address, in an integrated manner, the social, economic and environmental dimensions of development, their interrelations, aspects related to peaceful societies and effective institutions, as well as means of implementation. The 2030 Agenda focuses on the elimination of hunger and reduction of poverty and inequality (opportunity, resource access, gender, and youth) in all their forms. It is associated with a financing framework that recognizes the need not just for innovation and business development but also social protection. It commits to support the Paris

Agreement on Climate Change, by promoting and facilitating energy efficiency and clean energy. It seeks to increase resilience – to climate change, weather and natural disaster, market volatility and political instability. And it seeks to reduce the pressure of human economic activity on the natural environment by stressing the need not just for habitat and ecosystem protection, but also increased resource use efficiency, and sustainable production and consumption – thereby spreading collective responsibility for delivering sustainability across all economic players (UN, 2015).

When the world's governments adopted the SDGs in 2015 to achieve by 2030, they opened the window to a massive expansion of a new form of governance that has been growing on the global stage for some two decades. Obviously, they called multi-stakeholder initiatives, public–private partnerships, or cross-sector collaborations; these partnerships across governments, civil society, and the private sector are changing how we conceive of governance and public policy (Florini & Pauli, 2018). The Goal 17 of SDGs in UN is an instrument which is barking on the world to "strengthen the means of implementation and revitalize the global partnership for sustainable development." This is argued that enhancing the global partnership for sustainable development, complemented by multi-stakeholder partnerships that mobilize and share knowledge, expertise, technology, and financial resources, to support the achievement of the SDGs in all countries, in particular developing countries and encouraging and promoting effective public, public–private, and civil society partnerships, building on the experience and resourcing strategies of partnerships are clearly described to achieve sustainable development goals through eradicating poverty, hunger and famine. This shows that the new form of governance, which is collaborative, has strong nexus with sustainable development of one's country. Accordingly, the 2030 Agenda provides a high-level policy and monitoring framework designed to stimulate and coordinate the activities of national governments, the UN and other intergovernmental organizations, civil society organizations and other institutions - in pursuit of sustainable development, with the specific aim of eradicating extreme poverty and hunger (UN, 2015). It fosters collaborative governance in which revitalization of Global Partnership for Sustainable Development, based on a spirit of strengthened global solidarity, focused in particular on the needs of the poorest and most vulnerable and with the participation of all countries, all stakeholders and all people.

Moreover, in 2015, governments all around the world agreed on a set of SDGs in which they are universal, connected and undividable. The goals and the document, Agenda 2030, is unique and taken together, they can be seen as a global consensus on the goals for sustainable development. One of the seventeen goals is directly related to cities and urban development (UN, 2015). The Goal 11 of SDGs is "making cities and human settlements inclusive, safe, resilient and sustainable." The world is becoming increasingly urban. The level of urbanization is rapidly changing with

60 percent of the world's population expected to live in cities by 2030 and nearly 70 percent by 2050. The rapidly increasing dominance of urban areas places the process of urbanization among the most significant global trends of the 21st century. The transformative force of urbanization and the role that cities can play have far reaching implications beyond demographic change. While urbanization includes rural urban migration, proportional increases in the urban population, and the spatial expansion of cities, it also has other very important social, behavioral, political, economic, and environmental dimensions. As a result, urban life influences consumption and production patterns as well as levels and rates of urban socio-economic activities, growth and development. Furthermore, urban life refers to cognitive processes; the changing of mind-sets in ways that profoundly influence social development and innovation (UN, 2014).

In addition, in this 21st century, our world is going through massive urbanization, and sustainable urbanization is considered as a mechanism to protect the interest of all stakeholders during this urbanization process (Liu et al., 2016). In this perspective, it is possible to say that the smart cities can be measured in line of urbanization. So that the author has described that to what extent the rate of urbanization positively or negatively affects the cities. According to a report of the UN Habitat (2012), 54% of the world's population lives in urban areas, with an expected increase to 66% in 2050. However, this increasing population is not equally concentrated among the different parts of the world as the same report states that a larger portion of urban people will be increased in the cities and towns of less developed countries. In this regard, the estimated population growth in Asia is 1.4 billion, 0.9 billion in Africa, and is 0.2 billion in Latin America and the Caribbean by 2050 (Satterthwaite, 2007). In 2014, 30% of urban residents lived in slum-like settings; in sub-Saharan Africa, this number was 55%, which was the largest of any region. Moreover, more than 880 million persons worldwide resided in slums until 2014. Additionally, megacities are the main contributors of carbon emissions and weather changes. Therefore, it is hardly surprising that governments and business leaders are now keenly focused on cities and their effects on economic development and public well-being, to climate variation and sustainability (KPMG International Cooperative, 2012).

Most of the cities are suffering from extreme level of poverty, unhygienic housing conditions, and poor livability even after the impressive improvement since 2000 (Ellis & Roberts, 2015). Thus, developing cities in a sustainable way is a large endeavor in these developing countries. Building cities safe and sustainable which is confirming access to safe and cheap housing, improving slum settlements, investing in public transportation, forming green public spaces, and refining urban planning and supervision in a way that is both participatory and comprehensive is a mandatory collective responsibility of countries in the world (World Bank (WB), 2016). By endorsing a stand-alone goal on cities (Goal 11), known as the "urban SDG"– make cities and human settlements inclusive, safe, resilient and sustainable– the international community recognized urbanization and city growth as a transformative force for development. This first-ever international agreement on urban-specific development acknowledges sustainable urban development as a fundamental precondition for sustainable development.

Over the last two and more decades, there have been a number of international agreements and declarations regarding sustainable developments. The SDGs ascertain the influence of urbanization in speeding up prosperity and welfare, and provide cities with a vibrant starring role in this renovation. Sustainable development cannot be accomplished without renovating the method of how we build and cope with our urban spaces (WB, 2016). The key aim of Goal 11 is to build cities and human settlements that are all-encompassing, harmless, resilient, and sustainable. Given the high urbanization rates in many countries and the envisaged future share of urban dwellers in the total population, SDG 11 and the question of sustainable urbanization is of importance for most of the countries. SDG 11 addresses directly the urban level with 10 targets and 15 indicators developed by the UN (UN, 2015). Those strongly link to potential urban transformations to sustainability.

*Table 2. Targets of Sustainable Development Goal 11*

| Targets |
| --- |
| 11.1. By 2030, ensure access for all to adequate, safe and affordable housing and basic services and upgrade slums; |
| 11.2. By 2030, provide access to safe, affordable, accessible and sustainable transport systems for all, improving road safety, notably by expanding public transport, with special attention to the needs of those in vulnerable situations, women, children, persons with disabilities and older persons; |
| 11.3. By 2030, enhance inclusive and sustainable urbanization and capacity for participatory, integrated and sustainable human settlement planning and management in all countries; |
| 11.4. Strengthen efforts to protect and safeguard the world's cultural and natural heritage; |
| 11.5. By 2030, significantly reduce the number of deaths and the number of people affected and substantially decrease the direct economic losses relative to global GDP caused by disasters, including water-related disasters, with a focus on protecting the poor and people in vulnerable situations; |
| 11.6. By 2030, reduce the adverse per capita environmental impact of cities, including by paying special attention to air quality and municipal and other waste management; |
| 11.7. By 2030, provide universal access to safe, inclusive and accessible, green and public spaces, in particular for women and children, older persons and persons with disabilities; |
| 11.a. Support positive economic, social and environmental links between urban, per-urban and rural areas by strengthening national and regional development planning; |
| 11.b. By 2020, substantially increase the number of cities and human settlements adopting and implementing integrated policies and plans towards inclusion, resource efficiency, mitigation and adaptation to climate change, resilience to disasters, and develop and implement, in line with the Sendai framework for disaster risk reduction 2015–2030, holistic disaster risk management at all levels; and |
| 11.c. Support least developed countries, including through financial and technical assistance, in building sustainable and resilient buildings utilizing local materials. |

Source: UN Sustainable Development Goals, 2015a

## 3.1. Collaboration and Coordination in The New Urban Age

The term urban has become a keyword of early twenty-first-century economic, political, and cultural discourses. However, as its reverberation has intensified in social science and in the public sphere, the conceptual and cartographic specificity of the urban has been severely dulled. Accordingly, urban growth in the world is taking place in a context which has changed significantly over the last decade. The era of globalization has proved to be a major driving force in shaping urban development. The factor which presses pressures for increased coordination was the emergence of difficult problems that could not readily be solved through the actions of any individual public sector organization. These wicked problems in urban areas require substantially greater coordination and collaborative efforts than do relatively domestic problems that fall precisely into the domain of a single government organization. Building smart cities requires coordination and collaboration to work together. The smart cities are defined as cities with smart collaboration (Meijer & Bolívar, 2016). Governments around the world are facing complex problems, and solving them requires government agencies, non-profit and private organizations to work together (Pardo et al., 2010). In this sense, collaboration is an important concept. Collaboration can be defined as a process or a set of activities in which two or more agents work together to achieve shared goals (Chun et al., 2012). Margerum (2011) has also defined collaboration as an approach used to solve complex problems in which a diverse group of autonomous stakeholders deliberates to build consensus and develop networks for translating consensus to results.

Thus, urban governance which can be defined as interaction and collaboration between different stakeholders in decision making processes plays a paramount contribution for sustainable urban development and building smart city governance (Alonso & Lippez-De Castro, 2016). One of the critical issues of concern to most national governments world over is the need to stem the rate of urbanization induced by the incidence of globalization, industrialization and an unprecedented population growth rate in the cities (Jiboye, 2005; Osasona et al., 2007). This concern has led to several global summits organized at various level of government, international agencies including the United Nations, such as the Millennium Development Goals Summits, the 2002 World Summit in Johannesburg and the 2005 La-Havana UN Sustainable Cities Documentation of experience program among several others. In each of these summits, member nations restate the need for good and effective governance as a means of achieving sustainable development in the cities (Oladunjoye, 2005; UN-Habitat, 2007; UNDPI, 2008; Jiboye, 2011a). A WB Report in 2000 and another of the IMF in 2006 had indicated that about 66 percent of the world's population lived in the countryside in the early 1950s; however, current estimate by the United Nations has put the world population at 6.572 billion people, of which 3 billion (about 50%) now live within the urban areas, and by 2030, about 61 percent of the world population is projected to live in the cities; and this growth is expected to occur mainly in developing countries (UN, 2004; UNCHS, 2007; UNFPA, 2007; Daramola & Ibem, 2011). The United Nation's Habitat had estimated that almost a billion people already live-in slum conditions around the world and that slums are growing dramatically within the world's poorest cities, particularly, in Sub-Sahara Africa and Asia (UN-Habitat, 2012).

With the increasing population explosions and massive rural-urban migration accompanying the urbanization process in the developing countries; global economic integration, increased international trade, capital flows, telecommunication, new waves of technologies, and shifts in the comparative advantage of production continue to play a central role in integrating major urban centers and shaping the spatial organization of the cities (Jiboye, 2005). The reality of this scenario is congestion resulting from overpopulation and proliferation of slums in the cities (Ravalin, 2007; Jiboye, 2009). Governance is a neutral concept in which the actors, mechanisms, processes and institutions can produce positive or negative results, hence, the notion of "good urban governance" is emphasized. As indicated in the UNDP policy document, good governance is a necessary ingredient to achieve equitable and sustainable growth and development. The UN-Habitat launched the Global Campaign on Urban Governance in 1999. The Campaign's goal is to contribute to the eradication of poverty through improved urban governance. It aims to increase the capacity of local governments and other stakeholders to practice good urban governance and to raise awareness and advocates for good urban governance around the world. This is the new urban agenda in the world today. The New Urban Agenda (NUA) incorporates a new recognition of the correlation between good urbanization and development. It underlines the linkages between good urbanization and job creation, livelihood opportunities, and improved quality of life, which should be included in every urban renewal policy and strategy. This further highlights the connection between the NUA and the 2030 Agenda for Sustainable Development, especially Goal 11 on sustainable cities and communities. By 2050, the world's urban population is expected to nearly double, making urbanization one of the twenty-first century's most transformative trends. Populations, economic activities, social and cultural interactions, as well as environmental and humanitarian impacts are increasingly concentrated in cities, and this poses massive sustainability challenges in terms of housing, infrastructure, basic services, food security, health, education, decent jobs, safety and natural resources, among others (UN, 2017).

Consequently, good urban governance (GUG) is vital to improving the quality of life in cities. At the global and regional level, the index is expected to facilitate comparison of cities based on the quality of their urban governance. At the local level, the index is expected to catalyze local action to improve the quality of urban governance by developing indicators that respond directly to their unique contexts and needs. GUG requires collective and collaborative decision-making architecture. Thus, it explains the fact that the decision-making process has become characterized by interdependent networks of actors (government, private sector, NGOs, Civic organizations, community-based organizations and civil society actors). As a result, the concept of governance indicates a new style of government which is a non-hierarchical control model characterized by formal and informal rules, structures, and processes in a context of a greater degree of cooperation and interaction between public and private actors (Kooiman, 1993; Rhodes 1997). Moreover, GUG is participatory, consensus oriented, accountable, transparent, responsive, effective and efficient, equitable and inclusive and follows the rule of law. It assures that corruption is minimized, the views of minorities are taken into account and that the voices of the most vulnerable in society are heard in decision-making. It is also responsive to the present and future needs of society (UNDP, 1997; Jiboye, 2011b).

However, a World Bank Research in 2002 had demonstrated that good governance correlates with positive development outcomes. The survey concluded that the result of good governance is development which gives priority to the poor, advances the cause of women, sustains the environment, and creates needed opportunities for employment and other livelihood opportunities (UN-Habitat, 2004; Jiboye, 2011b). Furthermore, the societal culture and diversity, when it is accommodated in a good way, could play a positive role for the achievement of urban development goals. Henceforth, the NUA acknowledges that culture and cultural diversity are sources of enrichment for humankind and provide an important contribution to the sustainable development of cities, human settlements and citizens, empowering them to play an active and unique role in development initiatives. The NUA further recognizes that culture should be taken into account in the promotion and implementation of new sustainable consumption and production patterns that contribute to the responsible use of resources and address the adverse impact of climate change (UN, 2017).

Consequently, urbanization has the ability to transform the social and economic fabric of nations. Cities are responsible for the bulk of production and consumption worldwide, and are the primary engines of economic growth and development. Roughly three-quarters of global economic activity is urban, and as the urban population grows, so will the urban share of global Gross National Product (GNP) and investments. The right to development for low-income and middle-income countries can only be realized through sustainable urbanization that addresses the needs of both rural and urban areas. It must also be recognized that cities are home to extreme deprivation and environmental degradation with one billion people living in slums. In many countries, the number of slum dwellers has increased significantly in recent years, and urban inequality is deepening. The dynamism of cities represents a major sustainable development opportunity. By getting urban development right, cities can create jobs and offer better livelihoods; increase economic growth; improve social inclusion; promote the decoupling of living standards and economic growth from environmental resource use; protect local and regional ecosystems; reduce both urban and rural poverty; and drastically reduce pollution (UN Habitat, 2013).

To achieve better urban development through coordination and cooperation, a sound urban development which could able to accelerate progress towards achieving SDGs, including the end of extreme urban poverty, is a precondition policy instrument in this urbanized world. According to Nam and Pardo (2011), the collaboration among different functional sectors, private and public organizations, and among different levels of government within a geographical region is fundamental to see the urban performance. The smart city concept is integrated by a set of integration of infrastructures and technology-mediated services, social learning for strengthening human infrastructure, and governance for institutional improvement and citizen engagement. From this perspective, the implementation of a smart city governance infrastructure that should be democratically accountable, responsive, legitimate and transparent is an important good urban governance concept in the NUA.

## 4. THE IMPACT OF PUBLIC PRIVATE PARTNERSHIP ON BUILDING SMART CITIES

Private-Public Partnership (PPP) was coined and popularized in the 1970s when neo-liberal ideas began questioning the previously dominant Keynesian paradigm and the role of the state in the context of poor economic performance. Instead of ascribing poor economic performance to the failures or inadequacies of the market, government failure or inefficiency was blamed (UNDP, 2015). The New Public Management (NPM) became an important concept and played a great role in the partnership discourse in this 21$^{st}$ century. It is a public sector management mechanism which is employed to describe how management techniques from the private sector are now being applied to public services. The NPM (including the reinvention movement and the new managerialism) has played a great role in PPP doctrine. The doctrines of public sector management encompassed by NPM focused on a shift towards greater competition both between public sector organizations, and between public sector organizations and the private sector (Hood, 1995; Lane, 2000). In this context, PPP was invoked as alternatives to bureaucratic public services and inefficient state-owned enterprises, frequently, for the promotion of privatization (Cavelty & Sute, 2009). It was argued that handing over public tasks to private actors (i.e., to privatize them, or to contract them out, or at least to carry them out in partnership with private businesses) was the main means to downsize the role of the state, to enhance the efficiency of the public administration and public service provision, and to reverse previously alleged crowding out of the private sector by state owned enterprises (Savas, 1982).

Many governments around the world have engaged in PPPs with the aim of improving infrastructure and enhancing public service delivery. Building and operating infrastructure facilities as well as the delivery of basic services have predominantly been the responsibility of the public sector as they involve huge investment costs and take long time for the returns on investment to be realized. However, it has proved very difficult for many governments to meet the growing demand for infrastructure facilities and basic services by themselves. The inability of the public sector (government) to provide infrastructure and deliver services affects the promotion and expansion of businesses in communities. As a result, governments in several countries have been increasingly engaging the private sector in the provision of infrastructure facilities, investments in operation and maintenance of facilities as well as the delivery of basic services through PPP arrangements (UNDP, 2015; Asubonteng, 2011).

The concept of PPP has been defined differently in different contexts and there is no broad international consensus on what constitutes PPP. The following table clearly shows the definition of PPP; this would enable us to make comparison.

The world is changing and revolutionizing the models that we use to manage and operate urban infrastructures, whether they be transportation, water, energy or communications. Along with the digitalization of infrastructure and the emergence of smart cities, there is a worldwide trend of increasing the involvement of the private sector in the financing and direct operation of urban infrastructures and public services (Iossa & Martimort, 2015; Roumboutsos, 2015; Rouhani et al., 2016). Large transportation investments, such as metro systems, commuter railways or rapid bus systems, are being developed with an active involvement of the private sector (Chen et al., 2016). As a result, the PPP model of governance is important to provide public administrations throughout the world with support in the organization, management and development of projects involving collaboration between the public and private sectors in the smart cities arena (Cruz & Sarmento., 2017). it helps cities around the world to transform themselves into smart and sustainable cities by embracing the SDGs of the UN. It is very vital to achieve the goal 11 of the UN- "make cities and human settlements inclusive, safe, resilient and sustainable." Moreover, the PPP or otherwise termed as the P-3 governance arrangement provides smart city infrastructure (i.e., the physical supporting urban infrastructure systems, such as roads, water systems, railways, metros, solid waste management...etc.) and thereby can contribute to the advancement of the smart cities. The smart infrastructure (described as the application of technology to deliver a more effective and efficient infrastructure service) provides the evidence for informed decision-making and responds intelligently to changes in its environment, including user-demands and

*Table 3. The concept of PPP*

| No. | Description | Author/s |
|---|---|---|
| 1 | It refers to a collaborative arrangement between government or the public sector, and a private entity for better provision of public infrastructure and services. It is a voluntary and collaborative relationship between various parties, both state and non-state, in which all participants agree to work together to achieve a common purpose or specific task, and share risks and responsibilities, resources, and benefits. | UNDP, (2015); Hodge & Greve (2011) |
| 2 | An arrangement between a public body and a private party or parties (including community beneficiaries) for the purpose of designing, financing, building and operating an infrastructure facility that would normally be provided by the public sector. In other words, PPP is a contractual agreement between a governmental organization and a private party whereby the latter performs whole or certain parts of the government organization's service delivery, infrastructure provision or administrative function, and assumes the associated risks. | Jomo et al., (2016); Asubonteng, (2011); Hodge & Greve (2011) |
| 3 | It is on-going agreements between government and private sector organizations in which the private organization participates in the decision-making and production of a public good or service that has traditionally been provided by the public sector and in which the private sector shares the risk of that production. | Forrer et al. (2010); Roehrich et al (2014) |
| 4 | A relationship that consists of shared and/or compatible objectives and an acknowledged distribution of specific roles and responsibilities among the participants which can be formal or informal, contractual or voluntary, between two or more parties. The implication is that there is a cooperative investment of resources, joint risk-taking, sharing of authority, and benefits for all partners. | Lewis (2002) |
| 5 | A long-term contract between a private party and a government agency, for providing a public asset or service, in which the private party bears significant risk and management responsibility. It describes a range of possible relationships among public and private entities in the context of infrastructure and other services. | World Bank Institute (2012); Carter, Kaga, & da Rosa (2014) |
| 6 | A cooperative venture between the public and private sectors, built on the expertise of each partner that best meets clearly defined public needs through the appropriate allocation of resources, risks and reward. A strong PPP allocates the tasks, obligations, and risks among the public and private partners in an optimal way. The public partners in a PPP are government entities, including ministries, departments, municipalities, or state-owned enterprises. | Canadian Council (2010) |
| 7 | The private partners can be local or international and may include businesses or investors with technical or financial expertise relevant to the project. PPPs may also include nongovernment organizations (NGOs) and/or community-based organizations (CBOs) that represent stakeholders directly affected by the project. | Carter, Kaga, & da Rosa, (2014). |
| 8 | A long-term partnering relationship between the public and private sector to deliver services. It is an approach that government has adopted to increase private sector involvement in the delivery of public services. | Singapore Ministry of Finance (SMOF) (2012) |

other infrastructure, to achieve an improved performance. Cruz & Sarmento., 2017 argued that the groundbreaking innovation PPPs create disruptive improvements, building new business models and entirely restructuring existing mobility structures. From this, it is possible the say that the P-3 arrangement plays the key role in advancing the cities to be smarter in terms of all dimensions such as, infrastructural development, people, administration apparatus/governance, economy, delivering quality services to the urban residents, financing the public projects, applying the quality urban waste management...etc.).

## 5. KEY CHALLENGES OF COLLABORATIVE GOVERNANCE IN URBAN CENTERS

According to UN (2011), more than 50 percent of the world population lives in cities and city governments face a wide range of challenges; they need to produce wealth and innovation but also health and sustainability. Urban areas, now days, are affected by multitude of challenges. Barber (2013) has argued that city government is crucial to solving global problems and he states that Mayors ruled the world. The current administrative emphasis on cities as governance centers has been doctrined by academic attention. Recently, there are wide ranges of agreements that government policies have a critical role to play in fostering smart cities and solving societal problems is not merely a question of developing good policies but much more a managerial question of organizing strong collaboration between government and other stakeholders (Torfing et al., 2012). This collaboration has been termed as smart city collaboration.

Good administration and policies may result in strong interactions at the urban level whereas a focus on smart collaboration may result in more attention to issues of collaboration than actually making things work. However, building the capacity of effective collaborative governance in this urbanized world is the key challenge facing the urban centers today. Emerson et al. (2012) argued that external system context, such as political, legal, socioeconomic and environmental factors create opportunities and constraints to collaborative governance and the existing network among organizations which might alter their decisions on forming new relationships could be created. Sometimes, those networked groups become distorted and the entire network cannot operate efficiently. The ideological differences among service providers and political interferences may form a barrier against inter-organizational collaboration. Service providers with different religious and political background, vision and mission, service targets, and boundaries may find it difficult to effectively work together and they tend to form collaboration on a superficial and short-term basis, or not form any at all (Jing, 2015). Uncontrollable and excessive urbanization is also considered as another challenge which would aggravate wicked problems in the urban centers. This, would, in turn accelerate group frustration and division in the governance arena. As a result, this group frustration and division could affect the overall performance of the city and decline the capacity of building smart urban governance using innovation technologies. The decline of PPP strategy implementation, poor urban service delivery, weak efforts of national government to strengthen collaboration and coordination, inadequacy of the existing civic and governmental institutions, weak sustainability, economic hardships, inappropriate political intervention while making collaboration and lack of stakeholders' trust in the government legitimacy could be identified as the major challenges negatively affecting urban collaborative governance in the world today.

## 6. FUTURE RESEARCH DIRECTIONS

The issues of collaborative governance are very elusive and complex to clearly put the conceptual boundary in the development agendas. There are numbers of emerging new concepts, controversial issues and challenges on this area. Thus, the results of this book chapter would provide a good insight for the future researchers who want to conduct further in-depth investigation on the areas of collaborative governance agenda. Finally, research on clear conceptualization of collaborative governance and its practical challenges, the fitness for all policy issues and clarity on the nexus of collaborative governance and development, the detail analysis on the association of collaborative governance and smart city development, the rationales of collaborative governance for building smart cities and how can DCG be applied in the smart cities, is much more required. Thus, interested researchers can do on the above-mentioned governance issues and can derive the new collaborative governance model for better understanding of the smart cities.

## CONCLUSION

The concept of collaborative governance is a new development agenda today. The author has broadly described the definitional concept of collaborative governance based on review of different literatures. The nexus between this mode of governance and development has been highlighted in this chapter. This new governance model, collectively termed as collaborative governance, has been a target in the world today than ever before. States around the world have progressively relied on collaborative governance of public, nonprofit, and business sectors to deliver publicly funded services and to bring effective service delivery. This has been emerged as a response to failures of implementation of policies and programs at the community level. It is complex and elusive to achieve development goals by single organization and thereby it is difficult to bring effective and sustainable urban development as accelerated urbanization is increasing at an alarming speed. Collaborative governance offers a vantage point to observe the widening distribution of interests and powers, and the dynamic ways of interaction and cooperation through governing practices under a unified and continuously adapting political regime. The collaborative governance model plays important roles in building smart cities. The smart city governance, smart people, smart environment and smart infrastructure of the cities can be achieved through the new governance architecture- collaborative governance and the sister model, which is termed as the PPP approach of governance. Hence, the doctrine of coordination, collaboration and partnership between and among different stakeholders (i.e., the government, business organizations or private sectors, governmental and non-governmental organizations, citizens, civil society organizations, religious organizations, community-based organizations…etc.) should be applied while designing and implementing city development policies, strategies and objectives of the countries of the world. At last, but not least, hopefully, this chapter could provide conceptual and theoretical contributions in the fields of governance and development in conjunction with their contribution to the development of smart cities, and thereby it would be an insight as well as a stone corner for the others who want to conduct further investigation on this and related thematic areas of governance.

## FUNDING AGENCY

This research received no specific grant from any funding agency in the public, commercial, or not-for-profit sectors.

## REFERENCES

Adegun, O. B. (2011). Shelter and the future African city. *The Built & Human Environment Review.*, *4*(2), 33–40.

Agranoff, R. (2006). Inside Collaborative Networks: Ten Lessons for Public Managers. *Public Administration Review*, *66*(1), 56–65. doi:10.1111/j.1540-6210.2006.00666.x

Agranoff, R., & McGuire, M. (2003). *Collaborative Public Management: New Strategies for Local Governments*. Georgetown University Press.

Alawadhi, S., Aldama-Nalda, A., Chourabi, H., Gil-Garcia, J. R., Leung, S., Mellouli, S., ... Walker, S. (2012, September). Building understanding of smart city initiatives. In *International conference on electronic government* (pp. 40-53). Springer. 10.1007/978-3-642-33489-4_4

Alonso, R. G., & Lippez-De Castro, S. (2016). Technology helps, people make: A smart city governance framework grounded in deliberative democracy. In J. R. Gil-Garcia, T. A. Pardo, & T. Nam (Eds.), *Smarter as the new Urban Agenda* (pp. 333–347). Springer International. doi:10.1007/978-3-319-17620-8_18

Aluko, O. (2010). Rule of law, planning and sustainable development in Nigeria. *Journal of Sustainable Development in Africa, 12*(7), 88–95.

Ansell, C. (2000). The networked polity: Regional development in Western Europe. *Governance: An International Journal of Policy, Administration and Institutions, 13*(2), 279–291. doi:10.1111/0952-1895.00136

Ansell, C. (2012). Collaborative governance. In The Oxford handbook of governance. Oxford University Press.

Ansell, C., & Gash, A. (2008). Collaborative Governance in Theory and Practice. *Journal of Public Administration Theory and Practice, 18*(4), 543–571. doi:10.1093/jopart/mum032

Asubonteng. (2011). *The Potential for PPP in Ethiopia*. Addis Ababa Chamber of Commerce and Sectoral Associations. Retrieved from http://www.ethiopianchamber. com/Data/Sites/1/psd-hub-publications/the-potentialfor-public-private-partnership-(ppp)-in-ethiopia.pdf

Bevir, M., & Richards, D. (2009). Decentering policy networks: A theoretical agenda. *Public Administration, 87*(1), 3–14. doi:10.1111/j.1467-9299.2008.01736.x

Bezançon, X. (2004). *2000 ans d'histoire du partenariat public-privé . Pour la réalisation des équipements et services collectifs.* Paris: Presses de l'ENPC.

Bogason, P., & Toonen, T. A. (1998). Introduction: Networks in public administration. *Public Administration, 76*(2), 205–227. doi:10.1111/1467-9299.00098

Bolívar, M. P. R., & Meijer, A. J. (2016). Smart governance: Using a literature review and empirical analysis to build a research model. *Social Science Computer Review, 34*(6), 673–692. doi:10.1177/0894439315611088

Booth, M. (2006). Public engagement and practical wisdom. In S. Paulin (Ed.), *Introduction: Communities Voices: Creating Sustainable Spaces*. University of Western Australia Press.

Boswell, J., Niemeyer, S., & Hendriks, C. M. (2013). Julia Gillard's Citizens' Assembly Proposal for Australia: A Deliberative Democratic Analysis. *Australian Journal of Political Science, 48*(2), 164–178. doi:10.1080/10361146.2013.786675

Bryson, J. M., Crosby, B. C., & Bloomberg, L. (2014). Public value governance: Moving beyond traditional public administration and the new public management. *Public Administration Review*, 74(4), 445–456. doi:10.1111/puar.12238

Bryson, J. M., Crosby, B. C., & Stone, M. M. (2006). The Design and Implementation of Cross-Sector Collaborations: Propositions from the Literature. *Public Administration Review*, 66(1), 44–55. doi:10.1111/j.1540-6210.2006.00665.x

Canadian Council for Public Private Partnerships. (2008). *Public Sector Accounting for Public Private Partnership Transactions in Canada*. Retrieved on 21ˢᵗ Jan 2013 from: https://www.pppcouncil.ca/pdf/pppfinance-072008.pdf

Carter, L., Kaga, R., & da Rosa, A. (2014). *Public-Private Partnerships: A reference guide version 2: WB*. ADB and Inter-American Development Bank.

Castelnovo, W., Misuraca, G., & Savoldelli, A. (2016). Smart cities governance: The need for a holistic approach to assessing urban participatory policy making. *Social Science Computer Review*, 34(6), 724–739. doi:10.1177/0894439315611103

Cavelty, M. D., & Sute, M. (2009). Public–Private Partnerships are no silver bullet: An expanded governance model for Critical Infrastructure Protection. *International Journal of Critical Infrastructure Protection*, 4(2), 179–187. doi:10.1016/j.ijcip.2009.08.006

Charalabidis, Y., Koussouris, S., Lampathaki, F., & Misuraca, G. (2012). ICT for governance and policy modelling: Visionary directions and research paths. In Y. Charalabidis & S. Koussouris (Eds.), *Empowering Open and Collaborative Governance* (pp. 263–282). Springer. doi:10.1007/978-3-642-27219-6_14

Chourabi, H., Nam, T., Walker, S., Gil-Garcia, J. R., Mellouli, S., Nahon, K., . . . Scholl, H. J. (2012, January). Understanding smart cities: An integrative framework. In *2012 45th Hawaii international conference on system sciences* (pp. 2289-2297). IEEE.

Chun, S. A., Luna-Reyes, L. F., & Sandoval-Almazán, R. (2012). Collaborative e-government. *Transforming Government: People. Process and Policy*, 6(1), 5–12. doi:10.1108/17506161211214868

Conti, D. D. M., Guevara, A. J. D. H., Heinrichs, H., Silva, L. F. D., Quaresma, C. C., & Beté, T. D. S. (2019). Collaborative governance towards cities sustainability transition. *Urbe. Revista Brasileira de Gestão Urbana*, 11.

Cooper, T. L., Bryer, T. A., & Meek, J. W. (2006). Citizen-Centered Collaborative Public Management. *Public Administration Review, 66*(1), 76–88. doi:10.1111/j.1540-6210.2006.00668.x

Cruz, C. O., & Sarmento, J. M. (2017). Reforming traditional PPP models to cope with the challenges of smart cities. *Competition and Regulation in Network Industries, 18*(1-2), 94–114. doi:10.1177/1783591717734794

Devas, N. (2001). Does city governance matter for the urban poor? *International Planning Studies, 6*(4), 393–408. doi:10.1080/13563470120092395

Dollery, B. (2012). *Catalyzing the renewal of local infrastructure in regional communities: The case for Local Infrastructure Australia.* Regional Australia Institute. Retrieved from: http://www.regionalaustralia.org.au/wp-content/uploads/2013/06/RAI-Renewal-of-Local-Infrastructure-in-Regional-Australia.pdf

Donahue, J. (2004). On collaborative governance. *Corporate social responsibility initiative Working Paper, 2.*

Donahue, J. D., & Zeckhauser, R. (2011). *Collaborative Governance: Private Roles for Public Goals in Turbulent Times.* Princeton University Press. doi:10.1515/9781400838103

Ellis, P., & Roberts, M. (2015). *Leveraging urbanization in South Asia: Managing spatial transformation for prosperity and livability.* The World Bank.

Emerson, K., & Nabatchi, T. (2015). *Collaborative governance regimes.* Georgetown University Press.

Emerson, K., Nabatchi, T., & Balogh, S. (2012). An integrative framework for collaborative governance. *Journal of Public Administration: Research and Theory, 22*(1), 1–29. doi:10.1093/jopart/mur011

Emerson, K., Nabatchi, T., & Balogh, S. (2012). An Integrative Framework for Collaborative Governance. *Journal of Public Administration: Research and Theory, 22*(1), 1–29. doi:10.1093/jopart/mur011

Eremia, M., Toma, L., & Sanduleac, M. (2017). The Smart City Concept in the 21st Century. *Procedia Engineering, 181*, 12–19. doi:10.1016/j.proeng.2017.02.357

Florini, A., & Pauli, M. (2018). Collaborative governance for the sustainable development goals. *Asia & the Pacific Policy Studies, 5*(3), 583–598. doi:10.1002/app5.252

Food and Agriculture Organizations (FAO). (2017). *The 2030 agenda and the sustainable development goals: the challenge for aquaculture development and management.* UN.

Forster, J. (2016). Global sports governance and corruption. *Palgrave Communications,* 2(1), 15048. doi:10.1057/palcomms.2015.48

Frederickson, H. G. (1999). The repositioning of American Public Administration. *PS, Political Science & Politics, 32*(4), 701–712. doi:10.1017/S1049096500056547

Fung, A., & Wright, E. (2001). Deepening democracy: Innovations in empowered participatory governance. *Politics & Society, 29*(1), 5–41. doi:10.1177/0032329201029001002

Gerlak, A. K., Lubell, M., & Heikkila, T. (2013). The Promise and Performance of Collaborative Governance. In S. Kamieniecki & M. E. Kraft (Eds.), *The Oxford Handbook of US Environmental Policy* (p. 413). Oxford University Press.

Gil-Garcia, J. R., Pardo, T. A., & Nam, T. (2015). What makes a city smart? Identifying core components and proposing an integrative and comprehensive conceptualization. *Information Polity, 20*(1), 61–87. doi:10.3233/IP-150354

Gollagher, M., & Hartz-Karp, J. (2013). The Role of Deliberative Collaborative Governance in Achieving Sustainable Cities. *Sustainability, 5*(6), 2343–2366. https://www.mdpi.com/2071-1050/5/6/2343. doi:10.3390u5062343

Gollagher, M., & Hartz-Karp, J. (2013). The role of deliberative collaborative governance in achieving sustainable cities. *Sustainability, 5*(6), 2343–2366. doi:10.3390u5062343

Habitat, U. N. (2013a). *Why the world needs an urban sustainable development goal?* Author.

Habitat, U. N. (2013b). *State of the world's cities 2012/2013: Prosperity of cities.* Routledge.

Healey, P. (2003). Collaborative Planning in Perspective. *Planning Theory, 2*(2), 101–123. doi:10.1177/14730952030022002

Hendriks, C. M. (2011). *The politics of public deliberation: Citizen Engagement and interest advocacy.* Palgrave Macmillan. doi:10.1057/9780230347564

Hix, S. (1998). The study of the European Union II: The 'new governance' agenda and its rival. *Journal of European Public Policy, 5*(1), 38–65. doi:10.1080/13501768880000031

Hodge, G., & Greve, C. (2011). Theorizing Public-Private Partnership Success: A Market Based Alternative to Government? *Public Management Research Conference, 1*, 1-23. Retrieved from: http://openarchive.cbs.dk/bitstream/handle/10398/8573/Greve_2011_c.pdf?sequence=1

Hood, C. (1995). The New Public Management in the 1980s: Variations on: A Theme. *Accounting, Organizations and Society, 20*(2/3), 93–109. doi:10.1016/0361-3682(93)E0001-W

Hutter, G. (2016). Collaborative governance and rare floods in urban regions–Dealing with uncertainty and surprise. *Environmental Science & Policy, 55*, 302–308. doi:10.1016/j.envsci.2015.07.028

IMF. (2005). *The IMF's Approach to Promoting Good Governance and Combating Corruption—A Guide.* Available at: www.imf.org/external/np/gov/guide/eng/index.htm

Innes, J. E., & Booher, D. E. (1999). Consensus Building and Complex Adaptive Systems: A Framework for Evaluating Collaborative Planning. *Journal of the American Planning Association, 65*(4), 412–423. doi:10.1080/01944369908976071

Iossa, E., & Martimort, D. (2015). The simple microeconomics of public-private partnerships. *Journal of Public Economic Theory, 17*(1), 4–48. doi:10.1111/jpet.12114

Islam, M. S. (2017). Governance and Development. In A. Farazmand (Ed.), *Global Encyclopedia of Public Administration, Public Policy, and Governance.* Springer., doi:10.1007/978-3-319-31816-5_1990-1

Jing, Y. (2015). Governing China. In *21st century: The Road to Collaborative Governance in China.* New York: Palgrave Macmillan.

Jomo, C. Sharma, & Platz. (2016). *Public-Private Partnerships and the 2030 Agenda for Sustainable Development: Fit for purpose?* UN Working Paper No. 148. United Nations, Department of Economic and Social Affairs.

Kooiman, J. (Ed.). (1993). *Modern governance: New government-society interactions.* Sage.

Kooiman, J., Bavinck, M., Chuenpagdee, R., Mahon, R., & Pullin, R. (2008). Interactive governance and governability: An introduction. *The Journal of Transdisciplinary Environmental Studies, 7*(1), 1–11.

KPMG International Cooperative. (2012). *A Swiss entity.* Available online: https://home.kpmg.com/us/en/home.html

Lane, J. (2000). *New public management*. Routledge.

Leach, W. D. (2006). Collaborative Public Management And Democracy: Evidence From Western Watershed Partnerships. *Public Administration Review*, *66*(s1), 100–110. doi:10.1111/j.1540-6210.2006.00670.x

Leftwich, A. (1994). Governance, the State and the Politics of Development. *Development and Change*, *25*(2), 363–386. doi:10.1111/j.1467-7660.1994.tb00519.x

Lewis, M. (2002). *Risk Management in Public-Private Partnerships*. Working Paper. School of International Business, University of South Australia.

Liu, S., Zhang, P., Wang, Z., Liu, W., & Tan, J. (2016). Measuring the sustainable urbanization potential of cities in Northeast China. *Journal of Geographical Sciences*, *26*(5), 549–567. doi:10.100711442-016-1285-0

Magnette, P. (2003). European governance and civic participation: Beyond elitist citizenship? *Political Studies*, *51*(1), 144–160. doi:10.1111/1467-9248.00417

Margerum, R. (2011). *Beyond Consensus: Improving Collaborative Planning and Management* (MA thesis). MIT Press.

McCarney, R., Halfani, M., & Rodriquez, A. (1995). Towards an Understanding of Governance: The Emergence of an idea and its implications for Urban research in Developing countries in Urban Research in the Developing World. In Perspectives on the City (pp. 91-141). Toronto: Centre for Urban and Community studies, University of Toronto.

McLaren, D., & Agyeman, J. (2015). *Sharing cities: A case for Truly smart and sustainable cities*. Massachusetts Institute of Technology.

Meijer, A. (2016). Smart city governance: A local emergent perspective. In *Smarter as the new urban agenda* (pp. 73–85). Springer. doi:10.1007/978-3-319-17620-8_4

Meijer, A., & Bolívar, M. P. R. (2016). Governing the smart city: A review of the literature on smart urban governance. *International Review of Administrative Sciences*, *82*(2), 392–408. doi:10.1177/0020852314564308

Nam, T., & Pardo, T. A. (2011, June). Conceptualizing smart city with dimensions of technology, people, and institutions. In *Proceedings of the 12th annual international digital government research conference: digital government innovation in challenging times* (pp. 282-291). 10.1145/2037556.2037602

Newig, J., Pahl-Wostl, C., & Sigel, K. (2005). The role of public participation in managing uncertainty in the implementation of the Water Framework Directive. *European Environment, 15*(6), 333–343. doi:10.1002/eet.398

Nijkamp, P., & Kourtit, K. (2013). The New Urban Europe: Global challenges and local responses in the urban century. *European Planning Studies, 21*(3), 291–315. doi:10.1080/09654313.2012.716243

Noh, A. (2012). Collaborative Public Management: Where Have We Been and Where Are We Going? *American Review of Public Administration, 42*(5), 507–522. doi:10.1177/0275074012445780

Pardo, T. A., Gil-Garcia, J. R., & Luna-Reyes, L. F. (2010). Collaborative governance and cross boundary information sharing: Envisioning a networked and it-enabled public administration. In R. O'Leary, D. M. Van Slyke, & S. Kim (Eds.), *The future of public administration around the world: The Minnow brook perspective* (pp. 129–139). Georgetown University Press.

Partnerships British Columbia. (2003). *An Introduction to Public Private Partnerships. Update June 2003*. Partnerships British Columbia.

Pateman, C. (2012). Participatory democracy revisited. *Perspectives on Politics, 10*(1), 7–19. doi:10.1017/S1537592711004877

Pereira, G. V., Parycek, P., Falco, E., & Kleinhans, R. (2018). Smart governance in the context of smart cities: A literature review. *Information Polity, 23*(2), 143–162. Advance online publication. doi:10.3233/IP-170067

Pierre, J. (1999). Models of urban governance: The institutional dimension of urban politics. *Urban Affairs Review, 34*(3), 372–396. doi:10.1177/10780879922183988

Plotnikof, M. (2015). *Challenges of Collaborative Governance: An Organizational Discourse Study of Public Managers' Struggles with Collaboration across the Daycare Area*. Academic Press.

Rhodes, R. A. W. (1997). *Understanding governance: Policy networks, governance reflexivity and accountability*. Open University Press.

Roehrich, J. K., Lewis, M. A., & George, G. (2014). Are Public-Private Partnerships a Healthy Option? A systematic Literature Review. *Social Science & Medicine, 113*, 110–119. doi:10.1016/j.socscimed.2014.03.037 PMID:24861412

Rouhani, O. M., Geddes, R. R., Gao, H. O., & Bel, G. (2016). Social welfare analysis of investment public–private partnership approaches for transportation projects. *Transportation Research Part A, Policy and Practice*, 88, 86–103. doi:10.1016/j. tra.2015.11.003

Roumboutsos, A. (2015). Public private partnerships in transport infrastructure. *International Review (Steubenville, Ohio)*.

Satterthwaite, D. (2007). *The transition to a predominantly urban world and its underpinnings* (No. 4). Academic Press.

Savas, E. S. (1982). *Privatizing the Public Sector: How to Shrink Government*. Chatham House Publishers.

Scholl, H. J., & Scholl, M. C. (2014). Smart governance: A roadmap for research and practice. *Conference 2014 Proceedings*. Available at: https://www.ideals.illinois. edu/bitstream/handle/2142/47408/060_ready.pdf?sequence=2

Scott, T. (2015). Does collaboration make any difference? Linking collaborative governance to environmental outcomes. *Journal of Policy Analysis and Management*, *34*(3), 537–566. doi:10.1002/pam.21836

Selin, S., & Chevez, D. (1995). Developing A Collaborative Model for Environmental Planning and Management. *Environmental Management*, *19*(2), 189–195. doi:10.1007/BF02471990

Silvia, C. (2011). Collaborative Governance Concepts for Successful Network Leadership. *State & Local Government Review*, *43*(1), 66–71. doi:10.1177/0160323X11400211

SMOF. (2012). Public Private Partnership Handbook, Version 2. Singapore: SMOF.

Tang, S. Y., & Mazmanian, D. A. (2010). *Understanding Collaborative Governance from the Structural Choice-Politics*. IAD, and Transaction Cost Perspectives.

Testoni, C., & Boeri, A. (2015). Smart Governance: Urban regeneration and integration policies in Europe. Turin and Malmö case studies. *International Journal of Scientific and Engineering Research*, *6*(3), 527–533.

Torfing, J. B., Peters, G., Pierre, J., & Sorensen, E. (2012). *Interactive Governance: Advancing the Paradigm*. Oxford University Press. doi:10.1093/acprof:o so/9780199596751.001.0001

Ulibarri, N. (2019). Collaborative governance: A tool to manage scientific, administrative, and strategic uncertainties in environmental management? *Ecology and Society, 24*(2), 15. doi:10.5751/ES-10962-240215

UN. (2012). World urbanization prospects: the 2011 Revision. New York, NY: UN.

UN. (2015). *Critical Milestones towards a coherent, efficient and inclusive follow up and review of the 2030 Development Agenda for SDGs.* United Nations.

UN. (2015). *Transforming our world: the 2030 Agenda for Sustainable Development.* Accessed from: https://sustainabledevelopment.un.org/post2015/transformingourworld

UN. (2017). *The new urban agenda.* Retrieved from: https://habitat3.org/wp-content/uploads/NUA-English.pdf

UN-ESCAP. (2011). *A Guidebook on Public-Private Partnership in Infrastructure.* Author.

UN-Habitat. (2004). *Urban Governance Index: Conceptual Foundation and Field Test Report.* United Nations Habitat.

UN-Habitat. (2012). *Enhancing urban safety and security: Global report on human settlements 2007.* Routledge.

UN-Habitat. (2013). *Water and sanitation in the world's cities: Local action for global goals.* Routledge.

UNDP. (1997). *Governance for Sustainable Human Development.* United Nations Development Program.

UNDP. (2015). *Prospects of Public- private Partnership (PPP) in Ethiopia.* Development brief, NO. 1/2015. UNDP.

United Nations. (2011). *World urbanization prospects: The 2011 revision.* Available at: https://www.un.org/en/development/desa/publications/world-urbanization-prospects-the-2011-revision.html

United Nations Human Settlements Programme. (2010). *The State of African Cities 2010: Governance, Inequality and Urban Land Markets.* UN-Habitat.

Urio, P. (2010). *Public - Private Partnerships: Success and Failure Factors for in Transition Countries.* University Press of America.

Van Buuren, A., Edelenbos, J., & Klijn, E. H. (2007). Interactive governance in the Netherlands: The case of the Scheldt Estuary. In *Democratic network governance in Europe*. Palgrave Macmillan. doi:10.1057/9780230596283_8

Weber, M. (2015). *The Role of Good Governance in Sustainable Development.* Accessed from https://www.wri.org/blog/2015/02/qa-mark-robinson-role-good-governance-sustainable-development

Weiss, T. (2000). Governance, Good Governance and Global Governance: Conceptual and Actual Challenges. *Third World Quarterly*, *21*(5), 795–814. doi:10.1080/713701075

Weymouth, R. & Hartz-Karp, J. (2015). Deliberative collaborative governance as a democratic reform to resolve wicked problems and improve trust. *Journal of Economic and Social Policy*, *17*(1), 4.

World Bank. (2016). *International Bank for Reconstruction and Development (IBRD) & International Development Association (IDA).* Retrieved from: https://blogs.worldbank.org/sustainablecities/category/regions/south-asia

World Bank Institute. (2012). *Public-Private Partnerships - Reference Guide Version 1.0.* WB.

World Commission on Environment and Development (WCED). (1987). *Our Common Future*. Oxford University Press.

Xu, L. M. C. M. L., & Afsarmanesh, H. (2012). *Collaborative networks in the internet of services.* Available at: https://scholar.google.com/scholar?hl=en&as_sdt=0%2C5&q=Collaborative+Networks+in+the+Internet+of+Services&btnG=

Yohanes, H. (2017). Assessment of Challenges and Prospects of Good Governance in Eastern Zone of Tigray: The case of Adigrat City Administration. *Journal of Citizenship and Morality*, *1*(1), 83–99.

Zadek, S. (2006). *The logic of collaborative governance.* Harvard Kennedy School of Government Working Paper, No. 14.

## KEY TERMS AND DEFINITIONS

**Collaboration:** A coordination and working jointly with other stakeholders for the purpose of the common good.

**Collaborative Governance:** It is a new form of governance which deals with a governing arrangement of collective decision making between and among different stakeholders.

**Development:** It is a continual process of change in terms of both qualitative and quantitative aspects of human life.

**Goals:** They are observable and achievable end results of development which can be successful at the termination period.

**Governance:** A process, mechanism, and technique in which collective decision making has been made for the benefits of the public at large (for the public importance).

**Policy:** A general guideline which provides clear direction to formulate specific programs.

**Stakeholders:** They are active participants or actors in the governing arrangement.

Chapter 2

# E-Scooter Systems:
## Problems, Potentials, and Planning Policies in Turkey

**Betül Ertoy Sariişik**

(iD) https://orcid.org/0000-0002-3320-8575
*Gazi University, Turkey*

**Ozge Yalciner Ercoskun**
*Gazi University, Turkey*

## ABSTRACT

*Transportation planning, as one of the essential parts of city planning, has the potential to solve many problems on a global scale. These problems can be listed as traffic congestion, air pollution, fossil-fuel consumption, accessibility problems, global warming, climate change, and psychological problems affecting human lives. In recent years, transportation planning studies have come to the fore within the concept of sustainable urban mobility. The focus of this research is e-scooter systems, one of the micromobility options within the scope of urban mobility. The study explores how the availability of this micro transport mode can affect the time, cost, and ease of travels. In order to get information about the applications in Turkey, provider representatives were interviewed, and mobile applications and expert opinions were consulted.*

DOI: 10.4018/978-1-7998-5326-8.ch002

## INTRODUCTION

Due to the increase in population, the demand for basic public services such as housing, employment, health, education, and food is increasing and demographic changes being experienced. There is an increasing social expectation for the economic, fair, and efficient use of resources. With the information and communication technologies becoming a part of daily life, the actions of change and transformation have taken a new dimension with the spatial and social movements that started in the cities with globalization. Developments in information and communication technologies bring to the agenda the concept of "smart cities", which is the scene of a versatile and holistic change in a way that affects economic life, social life, architecture, political life, and administrative structure (Köseoğlu and Demirci 2018). The concept of smart mobility, one of the smart city components, includes an accessible, sustainable transportation system that is integrated with information and communication technologies. In this context, this study focuses on a micromobility option in which "sustainability, accessibility and technological" features come to the fore in transportation systems.

The demand for environmentally friendly transportation vehicles started to increase after the environmental effects of standard transportation vehicles were revealed. This study investigates electric scooter (e-scooter) systems that have started to find their place in urban transportation in the last few years as an environmentally friendly means of transportation. Shared e-scooter systems, which were first launched in the USA in 2017, later started to be widely used in Europe (Gössling, 2020). This new method of transportation has different problems and potentials compared to other transportation vehicles such as mechanical requirements and user demands.

In this study, it is aimed to provide an overview of the potential benefits and problems using the information in literature, interviews with the users and regulatory parties of e-scooter systems, and the information obtained through the applications of e-scooter systems.

In Turkey, the e-scooter is a tool that has yet to find a place in legal sources such as transportation plans and transportation guides. However, in some cities such as Istanbul and Ankara, it has started to be used in pilot areas or city centers through e-scooter providers. Although this process is considered as an advantage by both e-scooter manufacturer-provider companies and user groups, it cannot be integrated into the planning as there is no legal regulation put into effect by the authorities. It was deemed important to describe the e-scooter systems and regulatory tools used in Turkey, through this study. The study provides to the literature and is limited to contacted companies and settlements using e-scooter systems with smartphone applications. Transportation is one of the basic needs of the people's daily lives. With the widespread use of motor vehicles, transportation plans in cities have been prepared on the basis of vehicle mobility. After they experienced problems such as excessive growth of road infrastructure, air-noise pollution, and widespread diseases. the developed countries that prefer vehicle mobility have shown a number of trends in their urban mobility patterns. (Kostrzewska and Macikowski, 2017). First, the Scandinavian countries, then the Netherlands and Germany, pioneered a few models such as bicycling cities, walkable cities, cities for people. Cities that are undergoing a technology-based paradigm shift in transportation have been experimenting with the use of e-scooters in recent years and they have been adopted and are being used in many countries. These light vehicles, which provide advantages in settlements where public transportation systems do not allow door-to-door access, also offer an environmentally friendly transportation system as they have electrically rechargeable engines. E-scooter systems, which are widely used in certain countries with environmentally-friendly vehicle policies such as the U.S., Germany, and Canada, have some similarities and differences between them regarding their implementation arrangements. This study examines the e-scooter regulations of some of these cities.

The transportation plans implemented in Turkey are based on vehicle mobility, but in recent years walkable city centers, bicycle corridors, and e-scooters have been brought to the agenda. The working principles and conditions of use of e-scooter systems, which have just started to be used in Turkey and serve through private companies, are analyzed within the scope of the study.

The aim was to do research on the e-scooter systems in world cities and in Turkey in terms of implementation regulations, to analyze their areas of usage and design principles. The possible benefits and problems of using e-scooters are clarified using the literature research approach, and are also supported by the opinions and recommendations of some e-scooter companies in Turkey. The spatial problems of e-scooter transportation in the cities of Turkey, where transportation mobility is limited on a micro-scale, are examined by means of meeting with e-scooter providers and regulatory companies and e-scooter users, and it is questioned whether different companies have different implementations. It is aimed to provide solutions to the problems of the systems used in Turkey. For this reason, the features of companies that offer multiple alternatives to their users in cities were opened up for discussion. Research questions for which answers were sought in the literature review and the fieldwork are as follows:

- What are the problems of e-scooter systems in urban areas?
- What are the environmental benefits of the e-scooter systems?
- What are the priorities in city planning policies for this mode of transportation?

The second part of the research includes a literature review on the usage of e-scooters and regulations. The literature review consists of the examination of the studies on the use of e-scooters around the world. Studies by different researchers provide a wide perspective on e-scooter systems with different applications. In the field study discussed in the third part of the research, questions directed to e-scooter companies and e-scooter users and their answers are discussed. In this section, the routes determined by different e-scooter companies operating in Turkey, e-scooter utilization practices, spatial problems, and security measures are presented in light of personal interviews. The fourth part of the study includes findings of the literature review and fieldwork. In the conclusion section, suggestions are made for the current situation and the future, after which recommendations are made to researchers who would like to conduct studies on e-scooters.

## BACKGROUND: E-SCOOTER USE AND EXAMPLES OF REGULATIONS

While cities around the world are trying to alleviate problems associated with traffic congestion, air pollution, and traffic injuries, city planners are testing walking, cycling, and public transport systems, and working on less space-intensive and less polluting mobility options (Gössling, 2020).

In recent years, in which sustainable living practices have gained attention, environmental and social threats of transportation systems are being discussed. Because walking, using bicycle systems, or using public transportation requires less transportation infrastructure and causes less environmental pollution, they become the desired mobility types in cities. Urban systems, aiming at sustainability especially in urban transportation, conduct studies on transportation master plans and sustainable urban mobility plans related to these. The concept of shared mobility, which is included in sustainable urban mobility, was primarily included in transportation systems with vehicle sharing and e-bike systems. The e-scooter system, which has been included in the concept of shared mobility in recent years, has come to the fore as individual and dockless mobility. The dockless mobility mentioned in the study is defined as the mobility enabled by technology such as unlocking a device, making reservations through the application and paying for its use and it generally refers to e-scooters and bicycles (Guo et al., 2019).

The e-scooter sharing service is a system the uses a service-specific mobile application. The process of renting starts when a user accesses the map of available scooters, goes up to a scooter, scans the quick response (QR) code on the vehicle, and unlock it (Mc Kenzie, 2019). Travel is charged from a credit card added to the mobile application. The cost of using a scooter in most US cities is $ 1 to unlock and $ 0.15 per minute in 2019 (Mc Kenzie, 2019).

## ISSUES, CONTROVERSIES, PROBLEMS

Cities need innovative approaches in order to sustain social welfare and meet their needs in the face of globalization. New technologies and approaches bring along complexity and a rapid change process. While analyzing, holistic approaches and systematic progress are needed. Stakeholder cooperation and participation processes are viewed as an aid in this analysis. The smart city approach is included in the literature as the general name of the analysis in the processes of collaboration, participation, and evaluation of new approaches and new technologies. What are aimed with smart cities are as follows (Ecobuild website, 2020):

- To turn the expectations and problems in cities into opportunities in all of its systems
- To be able to handle physical, social, and digital planning together
- To systematically identify and address emerging challenges
- To provide integrated services by providing interaction between organizations in the city and revealing the potential for innovation.

Smart cities are categorized under six main titles as "Smart People, Smart Living, Smart Environment, Smart Mobility, Smart Government, and Smart Economy" (Ateş and Önder, 2019). The smart mobility concept refers to the integration of transportation systems with information and communication technologies. Local accessibility, international accessibility, information and communication infrastructure, and sustainable transportation systems are included in the literature as smart mobility components.

The concept of smart cities points to cities integrated with a knowledge-based economy, which uses the development in science, industry, and trade to research new technologies (Yalçıner Ercoşkun, 2016). The concept is also discussed in the use of modern technology in everyday urban life. This includes not only information and communication technologies but also modern transport technologies as "smart" systems that improve city traffic and the movement of city dwellers (Giffinger et al., 2018). E-scooters enable the use of shared vehicles in cities and this offers a new transportation practice for the citizens. The concept of smart mobility, one of the smart city components, offers the opportunity to implement e-scooter systems as a sustainable and accessible choice.

Urban mobility, an ecological and physical activity, plays an increasingly important role in the process of creating a healthy city, and the possibility of combining different forms of mobility with public transport is one of the methods (Kostrzewska and Macikowski, 2017). The developed countries are experiencing the consequences of providing technical infrastructure for cars and planning cities based on road transportation as overgrown road infrastructure, polluted air from spatially fragmented cities, noise, and widespread diseases. This proves that mistakes were made while solving the problems. (Kostrzewska and Macikowski, 2017). Nowadays transport planners are confronted with increasing traffic volumes. It is stated that the drivers of individual motorized transportation vehicles spend a significant and increasing amount of travel time during rush hours. The rapid movement of shared mobility alternatives in congested lanes provides cheap, comfortable, and flexible alternatives. (Gössling, 2020). Unlike traditional planning approaches, sustainable urban mobility plans that allow the participation of stakeholders are seen as a suitable implementation tool for shared mobility construct. Due to their positive environmental characteristics, e-scooters can help reshape existing mobility and solve problems arising in the urban environment (Hardt and Bogenberger, 2018).

Micromobility, a concept that has yet to find a place in transportation plans in Turkey, can alleviate some of the problems faced by large cities because they occupy less space in transportation spaces and can pave the way for more sustainable urban transport because they have a lower carbon footprint (Eccarius and Lu, 2020). Shared micromobility also has the potential to free up public space relative to the use of private micromobility vehicles. E-scooter systems, which have come to fore in recent years, are among the micromobility options. Although there have been studies on solving the problems for this system, which has encountered many problems since its first use, there have been attempts to eliminate the e-scooter system. Carrignon (2019) reports that after the 1920s, when there was no transportation infrastructure, the road network developed, the network was gradually adapted to the car, and many opposing views were encountered in response to increased automobile traffic, speed, and accidents. Stating that the emergence and standardization of the automobile took 30 years, Carrignon (2019) remarks that once the car was chosen as the mode of transport to be introduced and developed, it influenced and changed road transport infrastructures, laws, and jurisdictions of police and civil servants, to meet its needs. The system, which has been used in the world for a few years, needs to reach maturity in order to be adopted and used by the society with minimal problems.

Smith and Schwieterman (2018), who researched how to integrate e-scooter sharing into the rapidly developing transportation system, stated that private cars and private bicycles are the fastest modes according to statistical studies and adding e-scooters as a transportation option will fill the gap between cycling, walking, and public transport and this can create savings in travel time by combining modes on one-way journeys. Compared to rides based on e-scooters only, e-scooters used as a crossing show better performance in terms of time savings. Urban planner Porter Stevens stated that e-scooters are considered as promising urban planning tools and that if appropriate regulation can be found, they can be a part of urban transportation (Rubin, 2019). The researcher also notes that e-scooters have the potential to get people out of their personal vehicles, but this is not easy since most streets are designed for cars.

Beyond commuting to the city center, the use of e-scooters for short-average distances is seen as a solution to a fundamental problem for city planners: the last mile problem (Rubin 2019). The last mile refers to the distance from a transportation hub such as a bus stop to the final destination. Riggs and Kawashima (2020) listed following as potential benefits of e-scooters: They are a potential solution to the first and last mile problem, as they can help individuals connect with other transport options; Greenhouse gas emissions will be reduced; Very little parking space will be needed as their physical footprint is small. Stating that America is in the midst of the micro-mobility revolution, McKenzie (2019) mentions that privately-owned scooter-sharing companies, presented as a solution to the last mile problem, are taking over cities very quickly and that municipalities are struggling to assess the impacts on existing services, determine the legality and analyze the safety of the citizens.

Lime, an e-scooter provider, reported that 30% of their riders used e-scooters replacing vehicles on their most recent ride and that micromobility solutions have a positive effect on reducing congestion (Figure 1).

*Figure 1. The reason for using an e-scooter-Lime company (Lime website)*

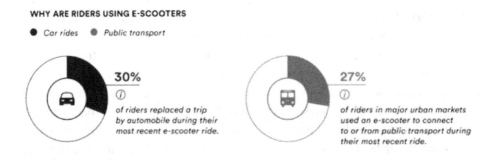

**WHY ARE RIDERS USING E-SCOOTERS**

● Car rides    ● Public transport

**30%**
ⓘ
*of riders replaced a trip by automobile during their most recent e-scooter ride.*

**27%**
ⓘ
*of riders in major urban markets used an e-scooter to connect to or from public transport during their most recent ride.*

E-bike and e-scooter systems (PMDs), defined as motorized personal mobility devices, are viewed as promising for cities seeking equality of citizens, a compact city design that can ensure the elimination of privileges for vehicle users, ecological individual public transport, and democratization in urban lifestyle (Kostrzewska and Macikowski, 2017). Rubin (2019) defines e-scooters, which can be an alternative to walking, as follows: "When you're new to an area, you really get to take in the sights at your own pace."

Smith and Schwieterman (2018) state that the benefits of shared e-scooters consist of 3 items:

- Dockless e-scooters fill a void caused by the limited transit coverage available for intra-neighborhood trips.
- E-scooter systems tend to reduce the amount of time needed to access a vehicle. The potentially broad coverage of e-scooters means that travelers can often access a scooter more quickly than built-in stops.
- E-scooter users do not encounter a last-mile problem. They can park their vehicles directly at their destination.

The main concerns about micromobility vehicles and e-scooters are safety and whether cities' current infrastructures will support the flow of these vehicles. Frequently asked questions are "How can we prevent e-scooters from being parked on an unwanted spot?" and "How can we organize our bike lanes to keep e-scooter riders and cyclists safe, while at the same time maintaining sufficient pavement space for pedestrians?" (Ajao, 2019).

Kostrzewska and Macikowski (2017) define the transportation system where public transportation and e-scooters are used together as hybrid mobility and explain possible problems as incompatibility of cities and buildings with this means of transportation and charging problems/device malfunctions. They state that it is possible to eliminate these problems, but plans need to be improved and long-term adaptation processes are needed.

Moreau et al. (2020) state their e-scooter concerns as parking on the pavement, the number of accidents and injuries, short-lived engines, and problems with charging.

Many cities are trying to clarify where to drive e-scooters. For example, for Saint Paul, some criteria have been determined such as not using the pavement other than parking the scooters, collecting the vehicles every night except the user lanes, and no parking on the pedestrian crossings (Guo et al., 2019).

There is a law on using micromobility services in Austin regarding the solution of these problems. The right of way rule is applied to move safely (Figure 2).

There is a design guide for e-scooter riding in Austin. The regulations and warnings in Figure 2 and Figure 3 provide guidance for drivers and pedestrians.

Along with warnings such as it is necessary to yield to people on foot, people under the age of 18 should not use e-scooters, and drivers should wear helmets for safety, it is also stated that people who are walking, biking, and in a wheelchair should be given priority. A priority rule has been created for the use of pedestrian roads and sidewalks, and compliance is compulsory for safety and order. Also, parking areas have been determined on the sidewalks parallel to the roads, and e-scooters are expected to be parked in these areas (Figure 3).

*Figure 2. The City of Austin e-scooter laws (Austin government website)*

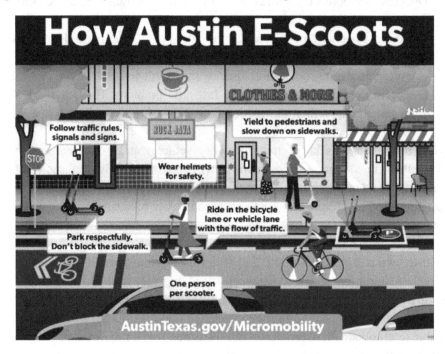

*Figure 3. The City of Austin e-scooter laws and regulations-2 (Austin government website)*

In the Austin e-scooter system, where the service areas of the e-scooter providers are designated (Figure 4, Figure 5), a planned progress is targeted by determining how many scooters will be available in an area and which companies will provide the services.

*Figure 4. E-scooter company Lime's areas of operation in Austin (Austin government website)*

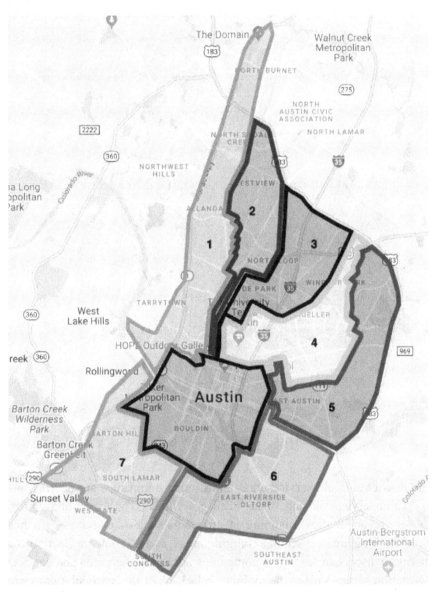

*Figure 5. scooter company Spin's areas of operation in Austin (Austin government website)*

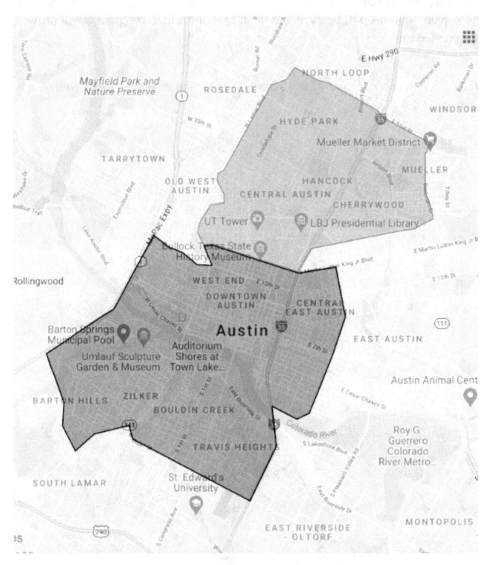

The distribution and service areas of different companies are detailed on the transportation services webpage of the Austin government. These maps and regulations of the service areas allow planning in processes such as e-scooter distribution, e-scooter parking areas, e-scooter charging areas, and e-scooter collection routes. Furthermore, users can see which companies operate in their area and can request transportation services using the mobile application of that particular company.

The necessity of making infrastructure arrangements in transportation is mentioned in many studies. In order for the road authorities to start the infrastructure regulation process for a vehicle technology, it must reach maturity (Carrignon 2019). When the use of electric scooters became widespread in France in recent years, many problems have been encountered due to lack of a legal basis, but the decision regulating the rules of the newly defined "motorized personal transport vehicle" was officially approved and included in the Code de la Route (The Highway Code) in October 2019. (The Local France website). According to this decision (Compagnon, 2019) (Leva website, 2019), restrictions are listed as follows:

- Maximum speed is restricted at 20-25 km/h. Non-compliance will result in a fine of 1500 Euros.
- Drivers should be 12 years old and over.
- E-scooters are for personal use only. Non-compliance will result in a fine of 35 Euros.
- Using headphones is prohibited.
- Bicycle paths with a maximum authorized speed of 50 km/h will be used for driving.
- Riding on sidewalks is prohibited. Non-compliance will result in a fine of 135 Euros.
- Parking on sidewalks is prohibited, however, they can be used for parking if the pedestrians are not affected.
- Use of helmets is encouraged but not mandatory.
- Drivers should wear reflective clothing at night and, if the visibility is poor, during the day.
- Owners of e-scooters must take out insurance for vehicles and drivers.

In a study, indicating that the reason for many regulatory challenges is the decision of a scooter company to start a fleet in a new city (Kennedy, 2019), it is stated that in San Francisco, all e-scooters were temporarily banned due to a company launching fleets of e-scooters without consulting the city authorities. Later on, two companies were given permission to use a certain number of e-scooters.

The study also states that this paved the way for the behavior of asking city officials for their acceptance rather than asking them for permission.

Lime, one of the e-scooter providers, is used in many countries around the world. Driving and parking arrangements accessible via the application inform and guide the users. The e-scooter locations obtained from Lime company and the guiding arrangements are shown on the map below. Lime company is a shared mobility provider that is frequently located in countries such as European countries, the UK, and the US, but not in Turkey.

In order to use an e-scooter, the application is downloaded from mobile devices and then the locations of the existing e-scooter devices can be accessed. In order for the e-scooter to be unlocked for the user, the credit card that will be used to pay for the service must be added to the application and then the QR code on the e-scooter must be scanned using the application.

The application, which shows the locations of e-scooters using its logo, reports the areas where driving and parking are prohibited as red-shaded areas (Figure 6). The application also provides convenience for the driver by reporting the areas where the speed limit varies, charging stations, and parking areas.

*Figure 6. Lime locations around Turkey (Lime website) (Date of access: 29.04.2020)*

The data obtained via Lime's mobile application presents information about the locations of e-scooters, areas where riding is permitted, areas where riding prohibited, parking zones, and no-parking zones (Figure 7).

The app provides information such as the charge status of the e-scooter, the distance that can be covered with the remaining charge, the distance of the scooter to the user's current location, and the fixed rate to unlock a vehicle (Figure 8). The ride is ended by re-scanning the QR code on the vehicle after parking and the fee is collected from the added credit card over the covered distance (Figure 9).

*Figure 7. Display of Lime's no-parking zones and permitted zones for London (Lime website) (Date of access: 29.04.2020)*

*Figure 8. Lime's locations and restricted zones for Lisbon (Lime website) (Date of access: 29.04.2020)*

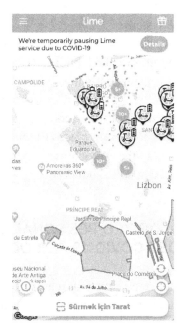

*Figure 9. Lisbon e-scooter park areas (Lime website) (Date of access: 29.04.2020)*

According to the literature review, charging e-scooters is a major issue. Provider companies trying different ways to solve this problem are developing park-charge-use systems such as parking-spot charging and user-charging systems, instead of the collect-charge-distribute system.

The Lime company pays citizens to recharge e-scooters on their private property through a crowdsourcing program called Juicing (Lime website). According to Lime data, an e-scooter can only run continuously for 2 hours. With a fully-charged e-scooter, 30 miles can be traveled at a speed of approximately 15 mph. In the Juice program, participants are asked to collect e-scooters that have low batteries at the end of the day and leave them to certain places the next morning. It is seen that there are works in progress about the e-scooter battery change and charging points and alternatives are being developed to address this problem.

## E-SCOOTERS AS MOTORIZED PERSONAL TRANSPORT VEHICLES IN THE POST-COVID-19 PERIOD

COVID-19 is widely-known to cause situations that create devastating global effects. When daily life activities that are temporarily suspended start to continue from where they left off, transportation is the basic requirement for people to do their daily shopping or to carry out activities such as vacation, work, and education. In various settings, post-COVID-19 transportation methods and the necessity of integrating micromobility options into daily transportation needs are being discussed.

Stating that micromobility is an effective tool for short-distance travels in the post-COVID-19 period, Dhanoa (2020) describes micromobility options as a way of transportation with which social distance is maintained while driving, as an alternative to boarding crowded transportation systems, and a way to reduce the load on public transportation vehicles. He states that micromobility vehicles are exposed to natural disinfection in the open air. Because of these benefits, Dhanoa (2020) argues that many transport markets around the world are transforming into micromobility and that micromobility is an effective tool to be included in the planning of the gradual transition to normalcy.

According to the shared data, there is a 67% increase in New York, 105% in Chicago, 200% in the use of medium distance micromobility in China, and 300% in Wuhan. It was revealed that temporary cycling lanes have been created overnight in order to maintain social distance in Berlin, Bogota, Cleveland, Denver, Minneapolis, Mexico City, New York, Portland, and some other areas.

In addition to this debate, because of the impact of the economic and social life recession caused by Covid-19 on the economy of micromobility options, many companies have withdrawn or went to restrictions in the market (Hawkins, 2020).

Hawkins, (2020) reported that Lime will suspend service in many countries, Bird has decided to stop operators in all European markets, and Spin had to suspend service in some cities. Nevertheless, Spin stated that they have been asked to increase the number of e-scooters by some cities to help fill the transportation gaps after the city bus system was closed. It is also included in the study of Hawkins (2020) that the production of components of some automotive, bicycle, and scooter parts of Lyft company is delayed due to the pandemic in China.

After the World Health Organization (WHO) declared COVID-19 a global pandemic on March 11, 2020, most of the world is now following curfew restrictions to prevent the spread of the virus. It is thought that this will cause a sharp decline in transportation demand at the regional and continental level, and the epidemic will have long-term effects on individual behavior, lifestyle, working, consuming, and traveling patterns (Ibold et al.,2020). It is reported that the serious economic effects of the epidemic are felt in the public transportation and shared mobility sectors and the providers are dealing with economic losses arising from decreasing demand (Ibold et al., 2020).

COVID-19 had a significant impact on people's mobility behavior. Shared micromobility vehicles are among the healthy living practices as an active transportation model for the periods when people spend more time at home. Denmark recommended public transport users to walk or use a bicycle-like vehicle if possible after COVID-19 (Ibold et al., 2020). Some companies have taken precautions to be suitable for post-COVID-19 use and inform users via applications. Globally, cities and countries are currently taking numerous measures in the field of transportation to stop the further spread of COVID-19. For example, Tier, an e-scooter company, disinfects e-scooters after each battery change and charge (Ibold et al., 2020).

Although e-scooter systems, which were launched before the COVID-19 pandemic, have problems and are interrupted due to the economic effects of the global epidemic, they are among the transportation options as a type of micromobility that is tried to be developed and made suitable for the use of the post-pandemic society.

## RESEARCH ON E-SCOOTER SYSTEMS IN TURKEY

The fieldwork of the research is based on interviews conducted with officials of e-scooter providers Hey Scooter (Bursa), Hop Scooter (Ankara), and Palm Scooter (İstanbul), that are operating in Turkey. The research is also supported by personal interviews conducted with authorized people operating in the planning sector. The personal experiences shared by several drivers who used e-scooters in the city of Ankara were included in the research in order to benefit the study. Questions asked to e-scooter officials are limited to spatial arrangements, rules deemed to be followed, and prohibitions.

## THE EXISTING ARRANGEMENTS FOR E-SCOOTER SYSTEMS IN TURKEY

### Palm Scooter-İstanbul

In the first interview with the Palm scooter official, it was learned that the vehicles belonging to the company were used in Istanbul Technical University (ITU) campuses, Özyeğin University, and Mersin coastline. Stating that campuses were preferred as the starting areas, the company official stated that users could take the vehicle from anywhere on the campus and leave it wherever they want. The official stated that they left more vehicles on the routes with high student density and this provided convenience to students. The official informed us that e-scooter maintenance was carried out every day, the company had a live support line for technical malfunctions, users could not recharge the vehicles, and that the vehicles with discharged batteries were collected with by the company employees and recharged in the warehouse.

Remarking that e-scooters use the bicycle route since there is one available in ITU, the official stated that they recommended the use of shared roads on the far right lane in places without bicycle lanes. The company official stated that they determined the routes, rules, and prohibitions on the campus. He also stated that there were no traffic or warning signs in place since there is no legislative mechanism available. The official also stated that when the application was launched, a route map determined by the company was created, the users were directed accordingly, and wearing a helmet was not mandatory but the maximum speed of the vehicles was limited at 18-20 km/h. We were informed that their biggest problem was the lack of dedicated routes and local authorities were needed to solve this problem.

The starting fee of a Palm scooter is 2 TL and later 0.35 TL per minute in 2019 (Papuççiyan, 2019) (Figure 10).

*Figure 10. Palm e-scooter locations display (Palm website) (Date of access: 29.04.2020)*

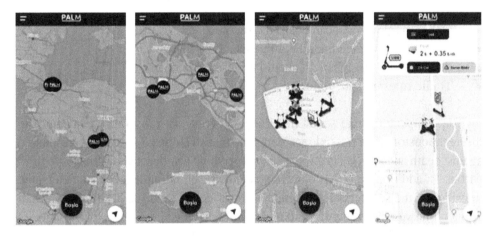

## Hop Scooter-Ankara

In the second interview that was conducted with the Ankara Bilkent Hop Scooter company, the official stated that e-scooter arrangements were made within the scope of Bilkent Cyberpark, they were currently used only on the Bilkent campus, and that there was no legal regulation in Turkey.

Hop Scooter company official stated that the scooters should be parked on the roads and sidewalks in a way that does not prevent pedestrian and vehicle traffic within the campus, they can impose penalties according to the contract for improperly parked scooters that disturb the environment, and that it is mandatory to take a photo and upload it on the application after each rental to end the ride. Furthermore, under the contract, users pay a fee for e-scooters that were damaged while rented. In the event of intentional damage to property or theft, the responsible are tried to be found working with the police force using the street-facing cameras that many businesses have.

Stating that e-scooters have to be physically locked and this is mostly done in order not to create a mess in urban areas, the official said that the e-scooters have integrated locks on them to prevent them from fall to the ground and get damaged as a result of contact by passers-by.

It is forbidden to use scooters on the sidewalks, and it is deemed appropriate to travel on the bicycle route with a maximum of two scooters side by side. Where bicycle routes are not available, riders should travel in the far-right lane of the vehicle roads. The company representative states the following as mandatory for driver safety:

- Wear a helmet (recommendation),
- Use the bicycle route, if there is no bicycle route, use the right lane of the road,
- Only a single person can board the scooter,
- Do not drive while under the influence,
- People under the age of 18 should not use the scooters,
- Traffic rules must be followed.

The company official stated that they cooperate with insurance companies to insure the customer for possible accidents and that all Hop Scooter rentals are insured against death and injuries in a way to cover personal accidents and damages to third parties. In addition, in order to prevent accidents, branding labels on scooters and the sides of the scooters are designed with reflectors, and the headlights and tail lights of the vehicle are lit day and night while driving.

The starting fee of a Hop scooter is 3 TL and later 0.50 TL per minute in 2019 (Papuççiyan, 2019) (Fig. 14).

## Hey Scooter-Bursa

In the interview, representative of the distributor company for the scooter with the brand name Serim stated that they will be on the field soon with the Hey scooter application and shared information about the pre-field e-scooter activities.

Stating that after the decision to start on the e-scooter project, they started to work by doing business, process, demand, and field analyses using the examples from different parts of the world with stakeholders, the representative pointed out that the e-scooter systems widely used the "pick up from where you are in a certain region and drop it wherever you want" model. He reported that this model creates freedom, but makes the property vulnerable to vandalism, which increases operating costs, threatens pedestrian safety, and causes visual pollution as it allows scooters of many brands to be parked on the street.

*Figure 11. Hop Scooter (Hop Scooter website)*

Stating that the biggest problem in this business model is collecting and re-charging the e-scooters that have run out of charge at a specific place, the provider company explained that every company doing this business follows a policy of charging in this way, but there are also companies that follow a policy of parking in charging stations. For example, charging stations placed at subway exits provide convenience for parking and charging, but this system limits the freedom provided by e-scooters and increases the initial construction cost.

The company official explained that they have developed a hybrid model and that they are working on solar charging stations within the scope of their projects. In this hybrid system, the scooters can be picked up from a charging station and left at a charging station or anywhere the user want.

This newly emerging transportation culture is accepted very quickly because it is considered fun and provides freedom of transportation, however, the lack of or insufficient bicycle routes in Turkey is seen as a disadvantage. Stating that municipalities do not have legal regulations or standards, the company representative stated that e-scooter drivers and their suppliers have problems due to this and estimated

*Figure 12. Hey Scooter (Hey Scooter website)*

that the regulations of the elements such as security will be made subsequently in Turkey as was the case in the world (Figure 15).

At an academic meeting consisting of urban planners, architects, and civil engineers, the opinions of the participants regarding the use of e-scooters and arrangement suggestions were consulted. (Transportation Guide Workshop of the Association of Municipalities of Turkey on April 24, 2020)

The opinions and suggestions reported on the subject are as follows: E-scooters have no legal regulations and therefore there are usage patterns that will endanger safety; Although scooters have an aspect that is liberating transportation, they exhibit uncontrolled development; Their lack of designated routes is concerning; They are easy and fun for personal use and access, but e-scooters cannot be found in close proximities; Their fees are less economic compared to another micromobility vehicle, bicycle; If developed in a planned and controlled manner, they can positively change many aspects in transportation.

## FINDINGS AND PLANNING RECOMMENDATIONS FROM TURKEY

After the interviews, it was understood that e-scooters were widely used in Istanbul and Ankara, in Turkey. Some companies were observed to distribute e-scooters primarily on university campuses as pilot regions. It also was observed that some companies left e-scooters on the main arteries and at subway stations in the city.

This situation is related to the budget of the companies, the number of employees they have, and the rider profile they want to reach as an e-scooter provider. The most widely used e-scooters in Turkey belong to the company named Martı, and no interview could be made with the officials of this company.

Palm and Hop primarily preferred campuses for their scooters. It was stated that the reason for this is to start a habit of using e-scooters, which are a new transportation option for consumers, and to be able to identify the problems that may arise. Both companies stated that it was they who made the regulations within campuses. It was mentioned that there were existing bicycle paths and that it was allowed for the e-scooters to be used on these routes. It was also stated that wearing a helmet was not mandatory, yet information obtained from the literature suggests that the injuries were mainly due to not wearing a helmet. Since there are no parts on e-scooters to put helmets on, it is recommended to provide helmets in designated parking areas. It can be stated that the use of e-scooters within campuses is advantageous in terms of routes and parking. However, the need for a motor vehicle for the distribution and collecting operations, as a result of the policy of "pick-up and drop-off wherever you want" is viewed as a weakness of this system. Regarding the subject, Hey reported that they were planning to change the batteries on location and that they were also developing options such as picking up from charging stations and leaving wherever you want or back to the charging station. In addition to providing micromobility and freedom in transportation, it is also important that e-scooters are environmentally friendly. Different applications of different companies create competition and offer options to drivers.

Interviewed companies have stated that e-scooters can be used on the bicycle paths, and if not available, on the far right of the vehicle roads where the maximum vehicle speed is 50 km/h. There is not yet a map application for Turkey on which the roads where e-scooters can be used can be viewed. There maps in the applications of companies, of the driving zones, restricted zones, and parking areas, that can only be viewed when the travel starts. Although there are no legal regulations and no defined routes, e-scooters are being used and are attracting attention. This micromobility vehicle is becoming widespread in the country and it is predicted that it will be regulated by law as soon as possible.

The international examples examined within the scope of the study and the e-scooter applications in Turkey suggest that it is important to run pilot studies in restricted areas. Shared micromobility tools are a paradigm shift in transportation. Therefore, the relationship between social acceptance and applicability is very important. This also makes it easy to get feedback in a short period of time. The use of e-scooters by students, a group that will increase interaction in society, is an important advantage for companies. Via smartphones, which are important technological innovations in smart cities, users reserve E-scooters, pay for them, and use the navigation services determined by the company while driving. E-scooters are definitely interesting for the part of the society who can use information and communication technologies comfortably, who are open to innovation and are interested in technological developments.

Although there are no legal regulations regarding the practices in Turkey yet, there are rules and prohibitions determined jointly by companies. These include not exceeding a speed of 18 km/h, riding one person at a time, driving on a designated route, not parking on pedestrian crossings and sidewalks, locking the e-scooter after the ride is over, taking a photo and uploading it to the application, and using if over the age of 18. It is estimated that this framework will be taken into account when legal regulations are established. Furthermore, it is anticipated that the regulations will include route definitions and criminal charges.

## SOLUTIONS AND RECOMMENDATIONS

### Legislation Regarding E-Scooter Systems in Turkey

In Turkey, the definition of e-scooter is not included in the Highway Traffic Law No. 2918. However, since the bicycle description includes features of e-scooter, the laws applicable to bicycles are deemed valid for e-scooters. The definition of a bicycle specified in the Highway Traffic Law is as follows (KGM website):

Bicycle: (Amendment: 12/7/2013-6495/13 art.) Non-motorized vehicles that move by turning the wheel with a pedal or hand with the muscle power of the person on it. Electric bicycles, whose maximum continuous rated power does not exceed 0.25 KW, whose power decreases as they accelerate, and whose power is completely cut off after reaching a maximum speed of 25 km/h or immediately after interruption of pedaling also fall into this category. (Amendment: 12/7/2013-6495/13 art.)

Rules regarding bicycle, motorized bicycle and motorcycle riders specified in the Highway Traffic Law (KGM website):

Article 37 - Although it is not compulsory to obtain a driver's license, it is imperative that those using bicycles are over the age of 11 and those using non-motorized vehicles and animal riders are 13 years old and are physically and mentally healthy.

Article 66 - The following rules apply to bicycle, motorbike, and motorcycle riders.

*If there is a separate bike path available, it is forbidden to ride bicycles and motorized bicycles on the carriageway, to ride bicycles, motorized bicycles, and motorcycles on roads that are reserved for pedestrians, and to ride more than two of these side by side in a lane of the carriageway.*

*It is obligatory for drivers to ride their bicycles with at least one hand, motorized bicycles with both hands, except when signaling for maneuver, and motorcyclists to ride their vehicles with both hands and comply with the safety requirements specified in the regulation.*

*It is forbidden for the riders of bicycles, motorized bicycles, and motorcycles without a sidecar to carry other people unless there is an adequate seat behind the rider and to carry loads more than the limit specified in the regulation. No more than one person can be transported with bicycles, motorized bicycles, and motorcycles without a sidecar, using separate seats behind the driver. (Amendment: 21/5 / 1997-4262 / 4 art.) Drivers who do not comply with the provisions of this article will be fined 3,600,000 liras.*

The necessity of riding the e-scooter with a single user, with both hands, and with the condition of being over the age of 18 are the common conditions of use obtained as a result of interviews. While the e-scooter, which is not included in the Highway Traffic Law, is compatible with the laws regarding bicycles in some conditions, it coincides with motorized bicycles in some others.

With the Metropolitan Municipality Law No. 5216, transportation services within the borders of the metropolitan municipality were transferred to the metropolitan municipalities and, within their borders, the duties of the provincial traffic commissions were transferred to the Transportation Coordination Center (UKOME) (TBB website).

As a UKOME decision regarding e-scooters, only the decision provided by the Izmir Metropolitan Municipality Head of Transport Department was obtained.

The issue of determining the criteria for the use of e-scooters within the boundaries of the Izmir Metropolitan Municipality was discussed at the UKOME General Assembly Meeting on 28.08.2019, and with the Decision No. 2019/400, an example of which is attached, it was decided that: "Within the borders of Izmir Metropolitan Municipality:

Scooters should have a maximum motor power of 0.25 KW and a maximum of 25 km per hour speed as specified in the Highway Traffic Law.

They should be used on bicycle routes and in the right lane of the roads without bicycle routes and where the speed limit is below 50 km/h.

They should have headlights and tail lights.

It was decided that e-scooter users:

Should not travel without a helmet and joint protective equipment,

Should comply with all the rules in the Highway Traffic Law,

Should leave their e-scooters properly in areas that will not interfere with pedestrian crossings or traffic patterns after use,

Who act against the above-mentioned criteria will be charged within the scope of the Highway Traffic Law No. 2918 and the Regulation of Izmir Metropolitan Municipal Police Department on Municipal Orders and Prohibitions.

The chairman of the Istanbul Metropolitan Municipality Department of Transportation stated that there are ongoing studies for the companies to provide the necessary services. The chairman reported that it will be mandatory to provide training to users via mobile/web applications and that companies can take part in the market with at least one thousand scooters and six quality management system certificates (Haberler Website). According to the Haberler website (2020), the maximum e-scooter starting fee will be determined as two full-fares of electronic tickets and the minimum will be determined as a half-fare. Thus, it is aimed to create a market where companies can survive in a competitive environment. Furthermore, it is reported that there will be sanctions in place for both the companies and the users and that's why e-scooters must have an identification number/traffic plate visible from all sides.

Prof. Mustafa Ilıcalı, Head of the Public Transportation Science Board within the Governorship of Istanbul, had an interview with a newspaper on e-scooters and stated that they have positive contributions to transportation and that it is an environmentalist practice (Sözcü, 2020). Stating that it is risky for scooters to hit the traffic before the regulation work is completed, Ilıcalı emphasized the necessity to make arrangements in the Grand National Assembly of Turkey and the importance of making new-tech vehicles and road arrangements compatible with new technology vehicles.

The founder of Martı, an e-scooter provider operating in Istanbul and many other cities, stated that he met e-scooters during a business trip in Los Angeles and reported that they have been on the field since September 2018 (Sözcü, 2020). Martı company representative stated the purpose of providing e-scooters as providing comfort at points where there is congestion in transportation. Stating that demand is measured regularly, Martı company representative said that people demand more because it is a tool through which social distance can be maintained during the pandemic period.

There is no legal basis that defines e-scooter systems and has recommendations for regulation in Turkey. Although the Highway Traffic Law has included some definitions for motor vehicles and bicycles, there are no regulations for light vehicles (bicycles, e-scooters, etc.) participating in urban traffic. However, shared vehicle companies, which are popular in some cities in line with user demands, apply to the Transportation Coordination Center through local administrations in order to ensure the safety of users and to find a place in urban traffic. The resulting decisions provide an agreement between the company and the user. The decisions taken by İzmir Metropolitan Municipality for e-scooter providers and users create trust by providing a legal basis for the new transportation model. The legal basis is considered to be of importance for the efficiency and continuity of using e-scooters in the social order.

# CONCLUSION AND FUTURE RESEARCH DIRECTIONS

Participation and people-oriented planning approaches are important features of the smart city concept. E-scooter systems are a mobility option in the people-oriented planning approach, as a result of the integration of information and communication technologies and technological innovations. Environmental practices, which are also necessary for the smart environment, create the need for sustainable transportation vehicles. E-scooters are thought to be included in the transportation policies of smart cities as a shared and environmentally friendly vehicle option.

The concept of the smart city includes an approach that involves modern urban production factors where awareness of environmental problems is developed and the participation of citizens and stakeholders is essential. Sustainable urban mobility plans (SUMP) overlap with the smart city concept in this context. Shared micromobility vehicles are not only products of modern technology but also an innovative mode of transportation. With this planning approach, it was understood that the biggest problem in Turkey and in the examples examined were the routes and the parking areas. Legal regulations are considered to be necessary and the supervision of local authorities is deemed important in this regard. It will also be an important step to produce micromobility maps and to present the routes to the drivers via smartphones. Since e-scooters parked on pedestrian walks in the city impair accessibility and create disorganization in urban areas, priority parking areas should be determined and drivers should be guided on maps. In light of the information obtained from the literature and the field study, the intense interest in shared e-scooters shows that they can be integrated into transportation systems after necessary planning arrangements.

E-scooters are motorized transport systems that are now being used in Turkey. Although companies and users have stated that they have yet to reach full compliance, it is anticipated that harmony will be ensured in the process in Turkey as it was achieved in the world. However, the lack of regulatory policies developed by local authorities shows down this process. Although the use of e-scooters carried out with UKOME decisions provides some basis for companies, there are gaps such as determining the areas of use and the design of these areas. The lack of legal regulations is liberalizing the providers in traffic areas but cornering them on the economic front. While e-scooter providers are allowing rides in the regions they designated, their economic expenses are high as they do not receive financial support.

The process of distributing, using, collecting, and charging e-scooters is an important process. Ensuring this cycle and integrating this type of micro-transportation into transportation systems will provide encouragement and ease of use. In the meetings with company officials, it was reported that e-scooter systems could move forward with the contribution and support of local authorities. In addition, the routes, which are not legally based, which do not have any definition in urban transportation, and are determined by the companies themselves pose a big problem. The route and parking-area needs that can meet the expectations of users and providers for safe driving can only arise in line with local authorities and the design principles to be regulated.

Findings signaling an increase in the demand for personal mobility devices indicate that there may be a paradigm change in transportation in the post-COVID-19 period. In the new normal period in which life practices are changing, it is predicted that the demand for transportation options will increase. It is anticipated that the demand for personal vehicles and frequently disinfected vehicles will increase and this situation may lead to radical changes in transportation and new transportation decisions will be produced in line with sustainable urban mobility plans.

In this study, answers to research questions concerning e-scooter systems were sought.

E-scooter problems in the urban area were addressed through literature research and fieldwork. Problems such as the absence or insufficiency of regulatory proposals for e-scooter systems in the urban areas, charging methods, parking and route problems, and scooters' occupation of pedestrian areas were included in the study. While the problems in the literature include e-scooter systems that are used as mobility without parking spaces, the urban area problems in Turkey mostly stem from insufficient legal regulations or lack thereof. Definitions of e-scooters and micromobility are not included in the of the Highways Traffic Act in Turkey. This legal loophole contains mistrust and threat to the e-scooter systems marketed in Turkey. Because the necessary legal restrictions are not in place, loss of life may occur after improper use. Providers express the need for legal regulation in this regard.

The environmental benefits of the e-scooter systems were examined in a literature review. This vehicle, which operates with an electric motor without the use of fossil fuels and allows low speeds, falls under the classification of environmental vehicles. It also has a low carbon footprint and takes up less space in transportation. These are the vehicles that encourage public transportation by filling the gap between public transportation vehicles or enable people to reach their destinations by using e-scooters after public transportation and provide environmentally friendly access in short distances. In this study, the environmental benefits were not revealed for Turkey, and the users in the pilot areas stated that they found this type of transportation fun. E-scooters are good touring tools, especially in touristic areas, as they allow to enjoy your surrounding while traveling at a slightly faster speed than walking speed but slower than the car.

City planning policies in the use of e-scooters were both examined in the literature and asked the company officials interviewed. In countries where the e-scooter system is widespread, the routes for light vehicles such as bicycles and e-scooters have been defined and included in the highway laws. In addition, it was observed that driving rules and parking areas were established on the routes for the safety of e-scooter riders and for them not to disturb pedestrians and cyclists. While in some settlements the e-scooters used in short distances were scattered without parking spaces, in others, systems were planned in a way that they were regularly locked to a public space. In Turkey, each company determines its own policy, but these policies show similarities. For example, while dockless e-scooters are not recommended in Turkey, they are expected to be fixed to charging spots or a public area. In Turkey, e-scooters are suggested to be used on bicycle routes and it is stated that they can be used in the far right lane of the roads in compliance with the set speed limit and rules only if a bicycle route is not available. The routes specified in mobile applications are being used and users are required to pay attention to the areas with parking and driving prohibitions. The last mile problem, one of the problems within public transportation, is defined as a weakness for accessibility. Micromobility options are offered as transportation planning recommendations at points where public transportation does not provide house-to-house transportation services. Micromobility options are a good alternative to reduce the use of private cars or commercial taxis for short distances in the central business districts or teaching areas.

As a result of the e-scooter research, e-scooters are observed to be integrated into transportation practices without any problems in many countries. This transportation action requires a process and the support of administrators and regulators is critical. Regulatory rules should be determined and tiered by applying in pilot areas. Options regarding the charging problem should be evaluated and arrangements should be made according to the feedback of the providers and users. Security-related penal sanctions should be brought on the agenda. Micromobility and shared mobility types are a paradigm shift in transportation. Social acceptance is the most important process for this.

In order to understand micro-mobility services in technology-related paradigm changes in transportation, it is necessary to do research on the demographic and socio-economic status of the users. Since these studies have not been carried out yet, no comments can be made on e-scooter users. Therefore, it is recommended to focus on micro-mobility users in future studies.

There have been discussions that e-scooters are not an environmentally-friendly means of transportation in connection with their design and usage. Therefore, for future studies, it is recommended to prepare a design guide on the use of e-scooters as an environmentally friendly means of transportation. In settlements where e-scooter providers are located, e-scooter maps should be created and driving rules and routes that can meet the needs of e-scooter users should be determined. This is considered to be beneficial in terms of helping the public understand the micro-mobility services and making these services socially acceptable. Moreover, updating e-scooter mobile applications in line with user research to be conducted is another issue that should be addressed in future studies.

COVID-19 has caused transportation systems worldwide to halt for a long period. The effects of interruption in transportation on the environment are being discussed and transportation practices are being reshaped for the post-COVID-19 period. In the words of Rahm Emanuel: "You never let a serious crisis go to waste. And what I mean by that it is an opportunity to do things you think you could not do before". With this perspective, it may be possible to rearrange transportation practices in accordance with sustainable urban mobility and to incorporate personal mobility vehicles into daily life. The excessive growth of road infrastructure and the increasing number of vehicles in the world brings with it environmental problems. Transportation is an activity that is necessarily included in the daily lives of people and demand is increasing each day. One of the solutions for countries experiencing the dramatic consequences of this situation is e-scooters. With the emergence of health and human quality of life topics after COVID-19, it is thought that changes in transportation systems will be opted for.

## REFERENCES

Ajao, A. (2019). *Electric scooters and micro-mobility: Here's everything you need to know.* https://www.forbes.com/sites/adeyemiajao/2019/02/01/everything-you-want-to-know-about-scooters-and-micro-mobility/#4e7112cc5de6

Aksoy, A. (2019). *Martı e-scooter experience review.* https://medium.com/@ardaksoy/vaka-analizi-mart%C4%B1-elektrikli-scooter-kiralama-deneyimi-i%CC%87ncelemesi-kullan%C4%B1c%C4%B1-g%C3%B6z%C3%BCnden-2-f16961053530

Arndt, W. H., Drews, F., Hertel, M., Langer, V. & Wiedenhöft, E. (2019). *Integration of shared mobility approaches in Sustainable Urban Mobility Planning.* German Institute of Urban Affairs (Difu).

Ateş, M., & Önder, D. E. (2019). The Concept of 'Smart City' and Criticism within the Context of its Transforming Meaning. *Megaron, 14*(1). https://austintexas.gov/department/shared-mobility-services

Carrignon, D. (2019). *Connected and autonomous vehicles, electric scooters and their implications for road network design* [Conference presentation]. European Transport Conference, Dublin, Ireland.

Compagnon, S. (2019). *Les trottinettes électriques entrent dans le Code de la route.* https://www.leparisien.fr/amp/societe/les-trottinettes-entrent-dans-le-code-de-la-route-24-10-2019-8179773.php?__twitter_impression=true

Dhanoa, J. (2020). *Will e-scooters form vital part of travel post Covid-19 restrictions in the region?* https://gulfbusiness.com/will-e-scooters-form-vital-part-of-travel-post-covid-19-restrictions-in-the-region/

Eccarius, T., & Lu, C. C. (2020). Adoption intentions for micro-mobility–Insights from electric scooter sharing in Taiwan. *Transportation Research Part D, Transport and Environment, 84*, 102327. doi:10.1016/j.trd.2020.102327

Ecobuild website. (n.d.). *Smart city definition and applications in our country.*_https://www.ecobuild.com.tr/post/ak%C4%B1ll%C4%B1-%C5%9Fehir-tan%C4%B1m%C4%B1-ve-%C3%BClkemizdeki-uygulamalar#:~:text=D%C3%BCnyada%20ge%C3%A7erli%20ak%C4%B1ll%C4%B1%20%C5%9Fehircilik%20tan%C4%B1mlar%C4%B1,%C3%87evre%2C%20Finans%20ve%20Ekonomi%20%C5%9Feklindedir

Giffinger, R., Fertner, C., Kramar, H., Kalasek, R., Pichler-Milanovic, N., & Meijers, E. (2018). *Smart cities–Ranking of European medium-sized cities.* Centre of Regional Science.

Gössling, S. (2020). Integrating e-scooters in urban transportation: Problems, policies, and the prospect of system change. *Transportation Research Part D, Transport and Environment, 79*, 102230. doi:10.1016/j.trd.2020.102230

Guo, J., Lynch, L., & Isaac Mitchell, I. (2019). *Shared mobility in the city of Saint Paul.* The University of Minnesota.

Haberler Website. (n.d.). *The Istanbul Metropolitan Municipality e-scooter rules.* https://www.haberler.com/ibb-harekete-gecti-elektrikli-scooter-larda-13476754-haberi/

Hardt, C., & Bogenberger, K. (2019). Usage of e-scooters in urban environments. *Transportation Research Procedia, 37*, 155–162. doi:10.1016/j.trpro.2018.12.178

Hawkins, A. J. (2020). *Electric scooter-sharing grinds to a halt in response to the COVID-19 pandemic.* https://www.theverge.com/2020/3/20/21188119/electric-scooter-coronavirus-bird-lime-spin-suspend-bikes

Hop website. (n.d.). https://hoplagit.com/

Ibold, S., Medimorec, N., Wagner, A., & Peruzzo, J. (2020). *The COVID-19 outbreak and implications to sustainable urban mobility – some observations.* https://www. transformative-mobility.org/news/the-covid-19-outbreak-and-implications-to-public-transport-some-observations

Kennedy, A. (2019). *How can cities get a handle on electric scooters?* https://dirt. asla.org/2019/01/16/how-can-cities-get-a-handle-on-electric-scooters/

KGM website. (n.d.). https://www.kgm.gov.tr/sayfalar/kgm/sitetr/trafik/ kanunyonetmelikler.aspx

Kostrzewska, M., & Macikowski, B. (2017). Towards hybrid urban mobility: Kick scooter as a means of individual transport in the city. *IOP Conference Series. Materials Science and Engineering, 245,* 052073. doi:10.1088/1757-899X/245/5/052073

Leva website. (n.d.). *New French e-scooter rules.* https://leva-eu.com/2019/10/31/ new-french-e-scooter-rules/

Lime website. (n.d.). https://www.li.me/tr/

McKenzie, G. (2019). Spatiotemporal comparative analysis of scooter-share and bike-share usage patterns in Washington, DC. *Journal of Transport Geography, 78,* 19–28. doi:10.1016/j.jtrangeo.2019.05.007

Moreau, H., de Jamblinne de Meux, L., Zeller, V., D'Ans, P., Ruwet, C., & Achten, W. M. (2020). Dockless e-scooter: A green solution for mobility? Comparative case study between dockless e-scooters, displaced transport, and personal e-scooters. *Sustainability, 12*(5), 1803. doi:10.3390u12051803

Palm website. (n.d.). *Palm e-scooter.* https://letspalm.com/

Papuççiyan, A. (2019). *E-scooter sharing at the university: Palm.* https://webrazzi. com/2019/07/22/universitelerde-hizmet-veren-elektrikli-scooter-paylasim-girisimi-palm/

Papuççiyan, A. (2019). *E-scooter sharing in Ankara: HOP!* https://webrazzi. com/2019/12/13/ankara-merkezli-elektrikli-scooter-paylasim-girisimi-hop/

Riggs, W., & Kawashima, M. (2020). *Exploring Best Practice for Municipal E-Scooter Policy in the United States* [Conference presentation]. 99th Annual Meeting of the Transportation Research Board, Washington, DC.

Rubin, E. (2019). *Not just for fun: The role of e-scooters in urban planning.* https://www.leoweekly.com/2019/12/not-just-for-fun-the-role-of-e-scooters-in-urban-planning/

Serim website. (n.d.). *Serim e-scooter.* http://www.serim.com.tr/Urunlerimiz/Elektrikli-Scooter-Paylasim-Platformu-3-3075

Smith, C. S., & Schwieterman, J. P. (2018). *E-scooter scenarios: evaluating the potential mobility benefits of shared dockless scooters in Chicago.* Chaddick Institute For Metropolitan Development At Depaul University.

Sözcü Website. *Legal regulations about e-scooters.* https://www.sozcu.com.tr/2020/ekonomi/elektrikli-scooterlar-icin-yasal-duzenleme-cagrisi-5929626/

TBB website. (n.d.). https://www.tbb.gov.tr/

The Local France website. (2019). *Speed limits and no sharing: These are the new laws on electric scooters in France.* https://www.thelocal.fr/20191025/speed-limits-and-no-sharing-these-are-the-new-laws-on-electric-scooters-in-france

Yalçıner Ercoşkun, Ö. (2016). Ultimate ICT Network in Turkey For Smart Cities. *Planlama Dergisi*, *26*(2), 130–146.

## KEY TERMS AND DEFINITIONS

**Dockless E-Scooter:** E-scooters that do not have designated parking spaces, that can be taken from any desired location and parked at any desired location.

**E-Scooter Providers:** Companies that distribute vehicle fleets around the city and allow individuals to access and pay for these vehicles using an application.

**Hybrid System Charging:** Picking e-scooters up from charging stations and dropping them off at charging stations or at any desired location.

**Light Vehicles:** Vehicles such as bicycles and e-scooters that have a certain speed and can be transported using manpower.

**Micromobility:** Motorized or non-motorized access mobility that is portable and can be used to travel short distances.

**Permitted Zones:** Allocated transportation areas designed for light vehicles in vehicular traffic.

Chapter 3

# Learning Cities as Smart Cities:
## Connecting Lifelong Learning and Technology

**Leodis Scott**
iD https://orcid.org/0000-0001-7749-7455
*DePaul University, USA & Teachers College, Columbia University, USA*

## ABSTRACT

*The purpose of this chapter is to explore the connections between technology and lifelong learning and the respective initiatives of smart cities and learning cities. The Pew Research Center reports that place-based learning remains vital for pursuing knowledge especially from digital technology. This means that although learning occurs in traditional places (home, work, or community), the use of technology further enhances learner engagement across the entire society. As such, learning cities is a placed-based initiative for implementing education and lifelong learning. Smart cities, similarly, expand the implementation of education and lifelong learning, but through a broader medium of digital technology and the internet. The important connection between lifelong learning (as learning cities) and technology (as smart cities) is the aim for providing access to every individual in society. This chapter offers an analysis of two concepts representing these two cities' initiatives.*

## INTRODUCTION

This chapter considers the socio-technical impact of smart cities from the alternate direction of lifelong learning, its potential connection to technology. In this consideration, this chapter introduces another description of the city, called "learning

DOI: 10.4018/978-1-7998-5326-8.ch003

cities," and its possible future impact upon smart cities. The Pew Research Center (2016) reports that placed-based learning remains vital for pursuing knowledge especially from digital technology. This means that although learning occurs in traditional places (home, work, or community), the use of technology further enhances learner engagement to the entire society. As such, learning cities is a placed-based initiative for implementing education and lifelong learning (Scott, 2015). Smart cities, similarly, expand the implementation of education and lifelong learning, but through a broader medium of digital technology and the Internet. The important connection between lifelong learning (as learning cities) and technology (as smart cities) is the aim for providing access to every individual in society. The role of cities or metropolitan areas is equally vital for providing lifelong learning and technology to their communities.

According to the Pew Research Center (PRC), lifelong learning can be either for personal or professional purposes. Majority of people (82% of respondents) have done some personal learning with a smartphone and home broadband connection (PRC, 2016). However, professional learning varies between groups such as educational level, household income, technology assets (smartphones, broadband connection), race-and-ethnicity, and type of job (government versus small business).

In fact, the focus on cities involves governance that can alleviate many disparities between education, income, and technology. Also, cities have the potential to transform work, leisure, and communities thus becoming sustainable and prosperous (Dirks & Keeling, 2009; Florida, 2012). Chourabi et al. (2012) view the importance of "people and communities" regarding smart cities with such factors as education, communication, participation, and accessibility with quality of life. Likewise, Scott (2015) explain learning cities as the "citizenship of learning" where everyone participates in its education and learning. Given the dominance of smart cities' discussion that features technology, infrastructure, and economic development, this chapter contends that any socio-technical discussion of smart cities, must not bypass the social dynamics of education and learning by the people and communities. The following sections will introduce a new audience to learning cities, its direct connection to learning cities, and its potential partnership with smart cities.

## INTRODUCTION OF LEARNING CITIES

Learning cities represent one of the emerging topics in adult continuing education that contributes to changing boundaries in the field (Ross-Gordon, Rose, & Kasworm, 2017). The learning cities topic develops from historical interests in creating a learning society to more contemporary ambitions toward lifelong learning for all (Cobb, 2013; Facer & Buchczyk, 2019; UNESCO, 2016; Valdes-Cotera, Wang, &

Lunardon, 2018). Over several decades, lifelong learning has supplanted other concepts such as community, recurrent, and lifelong education (Jarvis, 2004; Martin, 1987; Yorks & Scott, 2014). Hence, there are many interpretations of lifelong learning, due to its wide-ranging goals in the adult continuing education field. The concept of lifelong learning ranges from personal to professional purposes (Pew Research Center, 2016); economistic to humanistic perspectives (Regmi, 2017); neo-liberalism to social democratic political ideologies (Fuller, 2018; Lee & Jan, 2017); and from other viewpoints regarding lifelong or "life-wide" learning within formal, informal, and nonformal settings including technology and digital environments (Borkowska, & Osborne, 2018; Boshier, 2005; Marsick et al. 2016).

The topic of learning cities provides a practical platform for considering the appropriate application and expression of lifelong learning (and many other concepts). The idea of learning cities and its diplomatic establishments around the world have occurred mostly in developed countries in Europe and Asia (Choi & Yang, 2012; Kearns, 2012; Li, Hao, & Nanchen, 2013: Longworth, 1999; Osborne, Kearns, & Yang, 2013). However, the vision and viability of learning cities span around the globe in Africa, Australia, and South America for developed and undeveloped countries (Biao, 2013; Walters, 2005; Wang & Kintrea, 2019). Unfortunately, the formal establishment of learning cities (by international recognition) have not yet taken place in the United States (U.S.), despite North American advances in Canada and Mexico. There are multiple explanations for the absence of learning cities in the U.S. mostly involving political and ideological reasons and its tenuous relationship with major international organizations in global education and lifelong learning policy.

Post-2000 period, there are four major international organizations in the "arena of lifelong learning policy discourse" (Lee & Jan, 2017; p. 375): 1) UNESCO (the United Nations Educational, Scientific, and Cultural Organization); 2) OECD (the Organization for Economic Cooperation and Development); 3) EU (European Union); and 4) the World Bank. These international organizations are key players in the field of global educational development that includes lifelong learning (and policies) as a core part of discourse (Lee & Jan, 2017). Their contributions to lifelong learning, lifelong education, and learning cities are numerous from seminal reports (Faure Report, 1972 and Delors Report, 1996) to contemporary international databases, directories, surveys, policy documents, case studies, and other reports (e.g., *Memorandum of Lifelong Learning*, 2000; *Promoting Adult Learning*, 2005; *Learning For All*, 2011; *EPALE-Electronic Platform for Adult Education in Europe*, 2015) (Lee & Jan, 2017).

The emergence of learning cities within the discourse of lifelong learning explain how many legislators, policymakers, even educators have condensed the topic of learning cities as only an economics-based implementation of lifelong learning policy (e.g., human capital) (U.S. Dept of Health, Education, and Welfare, 1978).

However, Nichols and Dobson (2018) have considered learning cities as "placed pedagogies" with multiple explorations into the places and spaces where learning happens. Others have considered environmental awareness and sustainability (Kearns, 2012; Pavlova, 2018; Wang & Kintrea, 2019). Also Scott (2015) has regarded learning cities for adult learners in the United States that comprehensively include not only policies and programs (including pedagogies), but also partnerships and pursuits including art, public health, music, sports, and other creative applications/expressions of education and learning.

Unfortunately, viewing the topic of learning cities only through economics and policies further explain argumentative political, ideological, and economical debates about the actual purposes of lifelong learning. These critics point to how lifelong learning has not carried on the important purposes of other concepts, especially the concept of lifelong education (Boshier, 2005; Wain, 2000) relating to global educational reform and geo-social policy. Since the learning cities topic has been tied to lifelong learning, further critiques worth noting involve whether learning cities is the "real deal or fake news" (Boshier, 2018). Since the learning cities topic has reasonably been described regarding policies of lifelong learning, there are other underlying concepts and conditions by which the learning cities must also be considered. For these reasons, a broader view such as learning cities-for-all invites a more comprehensive discussion about multiple purposes of learning cities including lifelong learning at both individual and system levels.

## LEARNING CITIES-FOR-ALL (INCLUDING SMART CITIES)

Learning cities-for-all is a conceptual model that takes on many of the previous ideas of learning cities but re-purposes them into a broader view that acknowledges the dominant role of lifelong learning in conjunction with other adult-educational concepts. The challenges for the adult continuing education field is its struggle to sort through the distinctive characteristics of other concepts that have been supplanted, replaced, or even unseated by lifelong learning. Also, the field's often wide acceptance of lifelong learning has allowed this concept to expand unexamined, unmeasured, and still underutilized. This chapter takes on the challenge of lifelong learning through a learning cities-for-all conceptual model that places adult-educational concepts into more accurate description. When lifelong learning is assessed more thoroughly related to learning cities, then the concept of lifelong learning can be advanced in appropriate context and condition. As such, this article advances broader philosophical, theoretical, and conceptual connections of learning cities beyond simply lifelong learning.

One of the other challenges and concerns of the field involves clarifying concepts for scholars, researchers, and practitioners such as lifelong learning and many others. Thus, this model will provide distinctions between adult-educational concepts namely experiential education, lifelong education, experiential learning, as well as lifelong learning. One immediate step in clarifying these concepts is to distinguish them by the domains of education and learning (Thomas, 1991) and the qualities of experiential and lifelong. The learning cities-for-all model invites students, community members, workers, and adult learners to continually participate in the real-world development of learning cities around the world.

This learning-cities-for-all learnership (LCLL) model and its components describe the underlying process of decisions for all learners, especially adults. Thus, there are three essential purposes of the LCLL model; for conceivably this model:

1.  Clarifies adult-educational concepts between experiential education, lifelong education, experiential learning, and lifelong learning;
2.  Attributes specific roles and responsibilities between cities and citizens; and
3.  Offers a practical plan for implementing policy, programs, partnerships, and other distinctive pursuits.

This model is a simplified version of the actual underlying parts being suggested. This means that it identifies several important aspects about how adults, within their environment, make decisions about education and learning. Yet this model does not capture all the dimensions or distinctions of learning cities; especially without becoming more complex or even more confusing.

Table 1: Learning Cities-for-All Learnership (LCLL) Model Components proposes multiple concepts important to understanding the learning cities-for-all model introduced (Scott, 2015) and further advanced in this article, including learner-leadership (or learnership) that connects education-learning with leadership-citizenship. While this table is a snapshot of conceptual distinctions, it decisively serves as a guide about learning cities for adult continuing education researchers, scholars, and practitioners.

Table 1 illustrates how lifelong learning is connected to a complex framework of other concepts and categories. Also, it explains the alignments of lifelong learning and the reasons for its criticisms and concerns.

For example, this table has been organized based upon four essential distinctions, from ultimate ideals to practical implementations. Such that if we assume each distinction is vertically aligned, then we can immediately see how historical and contemporary concepts have been misaligned and miscategorized (for example, differences between the main purposes of lifelong learning and lifelong education).

*Table 1. Learning Cities-for-All Learnership (LCLL) Model Components*

| Ultimate Ideals | Knowledge | Wealth | Unity | Freedom |
|---|---|---|---|---|
| *Adult Educational Concepts* | Experiential Education | Lifelong Education | Experiential Learning | Lifelong Learning |
| *Bolman & Deal (1984/ 2016) Organizational Frames* | Structural | Political | Human Resources | Symbolic |
| *Weil & McGill (1989) Villages (Ordinal)* | Experience as Educational Outcome (I) | Experience as Social Change & Action (III) | Experience as Interpersonal and Personal (IV) | Experience as Learner-Centered & Controlled (II) |
| *Delors Report (1996) Four Pillars* | Learning to Know | Learning to Do | Learning to Live Together | Learning to Be |
| *Usher, Bryant, & Johnston (1997) Social Practices* | Vocational | Critical | Confessional | Lifestyle |
| *Senge (1990/2006) Core Disciplines for Systems Thinking* | Mental Model | Team Learning | Shared Vision | Personal Mastery |
| *Scott (2015) Learning Cities-for-All Aspects* | Academic | Economic | Politic | Iconic |
| *Citizen Roles & Responsibilities* | Learner as Student | Learner as Worker | Learner as Member | Learner as Leader |
| *City Roles & Responsibilities* | City as Institution | City as Workplace | City as Community | City as Learning |
| *Practical Implementations* | Programs/ Projects | Policies/ Provisions | Partnerships/ Pacts | Pursuits/ Pioneers |

For simplicity, this table has been further organized into three sections: First, this table begins by stating ultimate ideals in society (knowledge, wealth, unity, and freedom) by aligning them to distinctive adult-educational concepts (experiential education, lifelong education, experiential learning, and lifelong learning). Second, this table further aligns noteworthy scholarly contributions and their respective concepts across distinctive characteristics (Bolman & Deal, 1984/ 2016; Delors Report, 1996; Senge, 1990/2006; Usher, Bryant, & Johnston, 1997; Weil & McGill, 1989).

Third, this table advances the aspects of learning cities-for-all (Scott, 2015) by attributing specific roles, responsibilities, and practical implementations between cities and citizens. Also, this overall LCLL model represents distinctions among learners (at an individual and collective level) and cities (at a singular and systems level) that promotes learner-leadership, stated as learnership (Tight, 2001).

Given some of the divisive debates surrounding citizenship, learning cities as a phrase, instead promotes an all-inclusive, "citizenship of learning," *civitas cognitionis* (Scott, 2015) that views all learners as citizens of learning without exclusion. Despite the current local climate about foreigners, undocumented immigrants, workers, students, or more divisive language such as illegal aliens, this citizenship of learning and the practice of learnership can belong to everyone by viewing all adults as learner-leaders. Likewise, Tight (2001) views learnership as a social adult role just as other roles such as student, worker, or parent. Learnership, in the context of the learning cities-for-all model, includes social roles such as student, worker, member, or leader, but also through the function of lifelong learning, encompasses broader pursuits of scholarship, entrepreneurship, citizenship, and leadership. Lastly, this model applies an analytic approach to adult-educational concepts including learnership for the purposes of concept clarity and understanding of lifelong learning and learning cities (Eckert, et al. 2012; Elias & Merriam, 2007).

## Section 1: Ultimate Ideals and Adult Educational Concepts

Many thinkers have associated learning cities (regions or communities) with the broader vision of a learning society (Merriam et al., 2007). In fact, one of the appeals toward the learning cities concept is due to how it grounds the historically idealistic learning society concept to geographic locations (Ross-Gordon, et al, 2017). While there is a benefit to moving the learning society vision toward more practical actions, this should not remove the utopian ideals from complete view. So, the model components still reflect ultimate ideals such as knowledge, wealth, unity, and freedom. These ideals are even wider than benefits of learning cities than individual empowerment/social cohesion, sustainable/economic development, and cultural prosperity (UNESCO, 2016; Valdes-Cotera et al. 2018).

Although learning cities may set-in-motion the utopian view of the learning society, it further promotes ideals that are common in many societies. The model further aligns these ideals to four distinctive adult educational concepts including lifelong learning. To make such an alignment, at first sight, may appear overreaching, but the remaining sections will help to provide context and content toward these concepts and ideals. But for now, experiential education is aligned to the ideal of knowledge; lifelong education to wealth; experiential learning to unity; and lifelong learning to freedom.

## Section 2: Noteworthy Scholarly Contributions

The model incorporates many scholarly contributions and research relevant to adult continuing education (Scott, 2012). More specific, it features five significant references to help explain both the interests of both the society and the self (Bolman & Deal, 1984/ 2016; Delors Report, 1996; Senge, 1990/2006; Usher, Bryant, & Johnston, 1997; Weil & McGill, 1989). The interplay and engagement between society-and-self is at the core of the learning cities-for-all learnership model (Scott, 2015). Adult continuing education is an interdisciplinary field. These five references and their contributions to the model include disciplines such as higher education, leadership theory, philosophy, economics, sociology, systems theory, political science, public policy, anthropology, and organizational development.

**Bolman & Deal frames of organizations.** Bolman & Deal (1981/2016) has become a cornerstone in public service and administration for considering different types of organizations. These authors provide a simplified breakdown of four frames or types of organizations. These organizational frames, namely structural, human resources, political, and symbolic help business leaders and managers continually rethink and reframe their organizations.

The *structural* frame represents factory-design organizations and social architectures with clear missions, roles, goals, and tasks for technology and its environment. The *human resources* frame demonstrates family and relationship-style organizations focusing on needs, skills, and empowerment. The *political* frame exemplifies organizations of advocacy and ideology with attention to power, politics, conflict, and competition. The *symbolic* frame illustrates organizations of inspiration and culture with consideration for stories, metaphors, even heroes and ceremonies (Bolman & Deal, 1981/2016).

In the overall construction of learning cities, the Bolman and Deal organizational frames provide keen insight into the aspects of the learning-cities-for-all model, specifically academic, economic, politic, and iconic aspects (Scott, 2012). While the Bolman and Deal frames has been informative regarding organizations, it still does not directly capture all of the other considerations important to learning cities, such as experience, education, and learning.

## Weil and McGill Villages of Experience

Weil and McGill (1989) provides an exceptional assessment of experiential learning. In making sense of the broad concept, these authors conceptualize experiential learning into a four villages' framework. According to Weil and McGill, the four villages of experiential learning are 1) as assessment and accreditation of prior learning; 2) the basis for change in postsecondary institutions; 3) the basis for community action and social change; and 4) as a medium for personal growth and interpersonal development.

The immediate question is how this model distinguishes these so-called experiential learning villages across other adult-educational concepts. This question underscores a key point regarding concept clarity and the importance of applying an analytic philosophical approach. This approach is applied throughout the LCLL model, for it is the analytic philosophical perspective that can assess experiential learning across the aspects of education and learning.

As such, this model reconceptualizes the four villages' framework according to their main purposes that extend beyond the limits of the term, *experiential learning*, but associate with a broader and more adaptable term, *experience* (Chickering, 1977; Kolb, 1984). Thus, this model conceives village one: experience as educational outcome; village two: experience as learner-centered and learner-controlled; village three: experience as social change and community action; and village four: experience as interpersonal and personal interaction. The four villages are reordered in this LCLL model. Because village one address educational outcomes, such as credits for prior learning assessments (PLA), this is better placed as experiential education. Village three addresses social change and action that best align to lifelong education, given its interest in change and reform. Likewise, village two promotes learner-centered and controlled experiences that align well to the hallmark of lifelong learning that focuses on the individual learner. Given these alignments, the essence of experiential learning is arguably best viewed through village four, representing the interaction of experiences, personal and interpersonal.

## Delors Report Pillars of Education and Learning

The Delors (1996) Report has been considered the blueprint of lifelong learning, learning society, and especially learning cities. While there may be some debate as to how the four villages are represented, there should be no doubt or confusion as to how the four pillars of the Delors Report align to the related aspects of the learning cities-for-all learnership (LCLL) model. In fact, the learning cities model had been constructed upon the blueprint of the Delors Report. Other countries and organizations have adopted these pillars as factors of measuring education and learning in society (CLI, 2010). Moreover, the four pillars, given its wide acclaim, could also arguably provide a roadmap to the expressed ultimate ideals of knowledge, wealth, unity, and freedom.

Described as the four pillars of education in the report, these pillars clearly spread across the continua of education and learning. As noted, these pillars (expressed here in alignment to universal ideal) are: Learning to Know (knowledge); Learning to Do (wealth); Learning to Live Together (unity); and Learning to Be (freedom).

In the context of the LCLL model, *learning to know* is academic, relating to formal structures of education. *Learning to do* is economic, relating to the economic concerns of labor, land, and capital, especially human capital. *Learning to live together* is politic, relating to the social environment. *Learning to be* is iconic, relating to the grand image of learning that transcends lives through generations. Learning to be had been first introduced by the Faure Report (1972) and in more recent reports are considering another pillar, called *learning to change* or transform oneself and society (Lee & Jan, 2017; UNESCO, 2016) that highlights education and learning at both the individual and societal level.

## Usher, Bryant, and Johnston Social Practices

Usher, Bryant, and Johnston (1997) provide a representation of experiential struggle through an interpretative "map of experiential learning in the social practices of postmodernity." Figure 1 depicts a consumer society socialized by consumer choices. These choices are represented by four quadrants, namely *lifestyle*, *vocational*, *confessional*, and *critical*; also explained as the "social practices" of discursive/ material experience (p. 105-117).

A persuasive feature of the map does not rest solely in the name of these four consumer choices, but rather in the underlying continua or axes that develop and surround these choices, specifically the continuum of application and expression (horizontal axis) and the continuum of autonomy and adaptation (vertical axis), respectively. The learning cities-for-all learnership (LCLL) model associate application to *education*, expression to *learning*, adaptation to *experiential*, and autonomy to *lifelong*, respectively.

Each of these social practices are defined and analyzed based on their relationship to the factors of experience, knowledge, and pedagogy. While the Usher et al. (1997) description of these practices are often counter to how the LCLL model is promoted, these practices, and especially the continua, do offer insights into many of differences that exist regarding adult-educational concepts. Lastly, these authors applaud the Weil and McGill (1989) village framework of experiential learning and believe that the map of social practices matches well with the village framework. As Usher et al. (1997) explain,

*The exploration and development of the [social practices] quadrants may help to complement and expand upon the impact of the villages. Indeed, meaningful distinctions and connections can be made between these categorisations in terms of their emphases, their dynamics and complexity (p. 117).*

*Figure 1. Map of Experiential Learning in the Social Practices (Usher et al., 1997)*

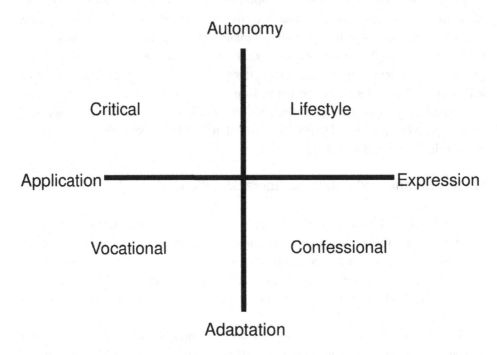

The LCLL model advances these meaningful distinctions and connections through considering the map of social practices along education and learning domains instead of application and expression. Likewise, along experiential and lifelong qualities instead of autonomy and adaptation, respectively. Given this advancement, vocational would be academic (experiential education); critical would be economic (lifelong education); confessional would be politic (experiential learning) and lifestyle would be iconic (lifelong learning). The illustration in Figure 1, will later be seen in Figure 2: Learning Cities-for-All Map (in section three of table).

## Senge Core Four Disciplines

The core four disciplines for learning organizations that Senge (1990/2006) describes leads to the quintessential fifth discipline, "systems thinking." The core four disciplines are personal mastery, mental models, shared vision, and team learning. Senge defines a discipline as a series of applied practices and principles, which provide accessible actions to a rather abstract idea of systems thinking. In order to build learning organizations, *personal mastery* requires the willingness of individuals to take responsibility for their personal growth and development; *mental models* require the openness to discover our way of thinking and reflecting upon organizational practices to gain shared understandings and patterns of change (Senge, 1990/2006). Similarly, *shared vision* invites a relationship with the organization, which is "the first step in allowing people who mistrusted each other to begin to work together" (p. 194); and *team learning*, which Senge explains will build upon personal mastery, mental models and shared vision. Team learning is the process of aligning and developing the capacity of the team members to create desirable results for the organization.

These core four disciplines build upon the culminated notion of systems thinking. For Senge, systems thinking is an approach to seeing through details and complexity and organizing them into a coherent story. A story that "illuminates the causes of problems and how they can be remedied in enduring ways" (Senge, 1990/2006; p. 124). Many leaders interested in developing learning cities have drawn upon Senge's systems thinking for learning organizations (Boshier, 2005) and these core disciplines that lead to systems thinking is an integral part of this learning cities-for-all learnership model.

## Section 3: Learning Cities' Roles, Responsibilities, and Practical Implementations

This is the last section of Table 1: *Learning Cities-for-All Learnership (LCLL) Model Components* that describes the Scott (2015) Learning Cities-for-All Aspects as a composite of the noteworthy scholarly contributions, adult-educational concepts, and ultimate ideals. At this point, some patterns should have emerged related to these components. First, that there are four essential areas that organizes all of them. Second, that these components relate to individuals, organizations, or societies at a systems level. Third, and perhaps keenly apparent for some, not all components fit agreeably within an all-inclusive model, due to different labels, terms, and definitions or opposing contexts, purposes, and more specific details.

And yet, however, these patterns provide a blueprint for the underlying structures regarding a more comprehensive view and vision of learning cities. A view/vision that pulls together attention in educational reform, economic growth, organizational learning, as well as and other individual and community change that advance learning cities for "development, innovation, and equity" (Ross-Gordon, Rose, & Kasworm, 2017; p. 400). Thus, this grand idea conceives of a learning cities-for-all, learner-leadership (LCLL) model.

## Scott Learning Cities-For-All Aspects

Scott (2015) provides a simplified illustration to all of the model components (Figure 2) through a relative learning cities-for-all map of the domains of education and learning and the qualities of experiential and lifelong. At the intermediate level, these domains and qualities form the four adult-educational concepts of experiential education, lifelong education, experiential learning, and lifelong learning, respectively. At an advanced level, these quadrants illustrate four aspects, namely academic, economic, politic, and iconic. For learning cities to become *civitas cognitionis* or the citizenship of learning, the academic offers knowledge through institutions, and the economic provides wealth through organizations. Similarly, the politic encourages unity through communities and iconic inspires freedom through learning itself.

At the basic level of the learning cities-for-all map relates to specific roles and responsibilities between cities and citizens, as well as practical implementations that can be accomplished within learning cities. Although these specific details are not shown in the map illustration (Figure 2: *Learning Cities-for-All Map*) their distinctions are noted previously (Table 1: *Learning Cities-for-All Learnership (LCLL) Model Components*).

*Figure 2. Learning Cities-for-All Map (Scott, 2015)*

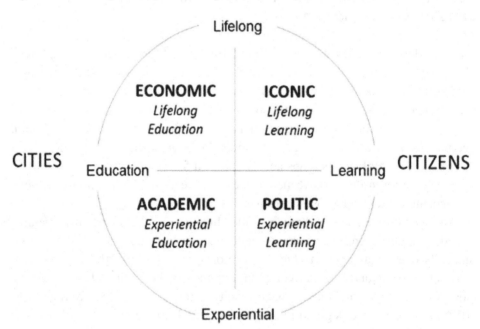

## Citizen and Cities Roles/Responsibilities

The relationship or engagement between cities and citizens requires both parties to execute respective roles and responsibilities. All citizens as well as all people are considered learners. According to the model and map, these roles/ responsibilities of learners and cities are informed by each distinctive adult-educational concept.

### Learner as Student and City as Institution

In corresponding to the experiential education (and academic aspect), learners or learner-citizens take on the role/responsibility of *student*. This view of student exists within a formal instructional structure, such as schools, colleges, and universities. However, another important view of student, comes from the Latin verb "*studere*" which means "to be eager for, keen on, or enthusiastic about" (Traupman, 1995), that moves the student beyond the traditional disciplinary pupil. The city takes on the role/responsibility of institution that provides the formal instructional structure for students and the formal setting for broad domain of education. Nonformal and informal settings of education can also be supported.

### Learner as Worker and City as Workplace

In alignment with lifelong education (and economic aspect), learners take on the role/responsibility of worker. White (1997) makes a distinction between two types of work, either "autonomous" or "heteronomous;" but claims that despite the majority of work in society being heteronomous, education can play a critical role in teaching workers to be more autonomous; thus placing work in its proper place alongside other essential aspects of living (Yorks & Scott, 2014). This view of the worker incorporates both education and economic growth. In comparison, the city as workplace takes on the role/responsibility of lifelong education that transforms businesses and organizations through what the Faure Report (1972) describes as the master concept of education. Because of the economic aspect, related economic principles such as labor, land, and capital are featured, with significant attention given to human capital (Becker, 1964), economics of education (Toutkoushian & Paulsen, 2016), and the *wealth* (Smith, 1776) of nations and societies.

### Learner as Member and City as Community

In association with experiential learning (and politic aspect), learners take on the role/responsibility of member in the community, while the city role/responsibility represents the community itself. While the Weil and McGill (1989) villages framework offer a general introduction to different views of experiential learning, Fenwick (2000) advances contemporary perspectives for the adult continuing education field to also consider (namely, constructivist, psychoanalytic, situative, critical-cultural, and enactivist).

In the context of learning cities, a partnership between members and communities may go beyond psychoanalysis or constructivist views of reflection, but instead more situated views or systems-theory (enactivist) perspectives. The critical-cultural perspective of resistance may align more to lifelong education than experiential learning for its vital attention to social change and political action. The *politic* aspect of this learning cities-for-all model should not be confused with the political. For the politic represents all people, versus the political divides them. Unity is the ultimate ideal within the learning cities model with a "unity of action and purpose" that contribute to community and collective understanding (Wong, 2002; p. 6).

### Learner as Leader and City as Learning

In orientation with lifelong learning (and the iconic aspect) learners take on the role/responsibility as leaders, and cities as learning. Like all the other arrangements placed upon adult-educational concepts (and model aspects), these roles and responsibilities are equally distinctive and builds upon each other at the same time. The learners as leaders mean taking charge of their learning with authenticity. Aspin and Chapman (2012) move the concept of lifelong learning toward its own philosophy where individuals are "autonomous agents, with complete freedom of judgment and choice" in how to make decisions about the problems they face; and about the time and resources that learners spend (p. 29). The city as learning expand lifelong learning as both economic and humanistic (Regmi, 2017). Regmi (2017) states that a humanistic form of lifelong learning "takes education and learning as a fundamental right for all individuals" (p. 679). The salient point about learners as leaders is the advancement of freedom. Freedom here is not seen as a truth, or the freedom from power, but instead as a "mechanism of power" (expressed by Foucault) whereby learners can truthfully govern themselves within the relations of power (Nicoll & Fejes, 2008; p. 6).

Cities as learning, most notably learning cities, Scott (2015) advises will require a new movement of engagement. For Scott, this engagement recognizes learning cities for "being flexible, adaptable, nourishing, and replenishing" (p. 92) and humanizes learning cities (Hibbler & Scott, 2015) as resourceful places for leisure, health, and well-being.

## Practical Implementations

Given the theoretical considerations of learning cities, this subsection addresses some of the more practical implementations of the learning cities-for-all learnership (LCLL) model as a result. Based upon prior research regarding community engagement in higher education institutions, specifically U.S. land-grant institutions (Scott, 2012), practical examples of such engagement related to mostly educational programs.

However, learning cities require more than programs or pedagogies of education but more of a comprehensive combination of resources.

For example, Cappon and Laughlin (2013) describe the Composite Learning Index (CLI, 2010) by the Canadian Council on Learning that measured lifelong learning and its progress for five years. What is important to note is that the CLI was based upon the Delors Report (1996) pillars of education (and learning). The Canadian Council operationalized the concept of lifelong learning into distinctive measures corresponding to each pillar. While the learning cities-for-all model distinguishes these four pillars (namely, learning to do, know, live together, and be) across other adult-educational concepts to be applied in the U.S., the Canadian Council's fundamental work should be noted within North America overall.

The following will describe examples within a LCLL model. These examples draw upon the CLI and other measurements advanced by organizations and countries in Europe and Asia, which have been more explicit concerning the topic learning cities and its continuing research and scholarship. For example, UNESCO (2015) provide key features of learning cities through conditions, blocks, and wider benefits for building a learning city that include political will and commitment, governance and participation, and mobilization and utilization for many varieties of learning (i.e., inclusive, revitalized, effective, modern, technological, enhanced quality, and vibrant culture). While the pillars may provide a blueprint for implementing research across metropolitan areas, the measures and data available will depend upon many other contexts, but most especially a united effort between public administrations, private organizations, and the public community.

## Programs and Projects

Programs and projects in the learning cities-for-all model concentrates on the academic aspect and experiential education. Examples are service-learning projects (Furco, 1996), or access initiative programs to educational institutions. Local plans that offer credit and credentials in formal institutions are the central focus with the overall goal of acquiring knowledge among the entire citizenry. Some adult educators describe this area for its formal setting, which is acceptable for structural and educational outcomes.

*Policies and provisions.* Policies and provisions in the learning cities-for-all model concentrates on the economic aspect and lifelong education. Examples relate to workforce policies, employment, resource allocations, equity, and the development of human capital and economic development. OECD has been a world-wide leader in viewing learning cities from an economic perspective that informs countries and administrations how to connect education-and-learning to wealth. Because there is a focus on policy design, implementation, funding, and investments, this area will be a contentious and political arena (Bolman & Deal, 1984/2016), but essential for social change and advocacy.

## Partnerships and Pacts

Partnerships and pacts in the LCLL model concentrate on the politic aspect and experiential learning. As stated earlier, the politic is not political, but rather a focus on the people showing good judgment in dealing with others, also coming together, and uniting with a shared vision for their civil society. Based upon the pillar of learning to live together, examples include volunteerism, participation in social and club organizations, and forming alliances across cultures. These kinds of partnerships also relate to the field of adult continuing education forming interdisciplinary coalitions for the purpose of advancing the community and its members.

## Pursuits and Pioneers

Pursuits and pioneers in the learning cities-for-all model concentrates on the iconic aspect and lifelong learning in a targeted way. Based upon the pillar of learning to be, this aspect, at its basic level, involves forms of expression and identity such as art, music, sports, and other aesthetic, authentic, and creative expressions. The measurement of lifelong learning comes in the development and culmination from other model aspects with a keen focus on autonomy, ownership, and freedom. From the academic aspect, knowledge develops into wisdom; from the economic aspect, wealth progresses onto entrepreneurship; from the politic aspect, unity advances into legacy.

A vital reason that this aspect is called iconic, is not to invite the iconoclasts to attack the any cherished beliefs about learning cities. But rather to highlight the *image* of learning that lasts throughout many lifetimes and generations. One of the historical descriptions of lifelong learning is that it spans across a lifetime, from cradle-to-grave. This iconic aspect invites the idea that lifelong learning lasts even beyond that. As icons are remembered way past their lifetime, so should lifelong learning: where its legacy continues in the lives of others and seen in the cities where they have lived. In this may, we can measure lifelong learning through public monuments, tributes, and memorials of pioneers, innovators, and trendsetters who have followed their pursuits, hopefully remembered and supported by their public.

Although at present, there are no formally established learning cities in America, hopefully these examples of practical implementation serve as ways to measure American cities and citizens coming together through education and learning.

# FINAL THOUGHTS ABOUT LEARNING CITIES AND ITS POTENTIAL CONNECTION TO SMART CITIES

Despite the possible benefits of learning cities and smart cities, there are many scholars that have kept these two initiatives separate and distant from each other. This chapter also intends to describe the fundamental purposes of learning cities and invite a bridge across the divide toward the ideal of smart cities. For both cities' initiatives indicate the complementary connection between lifelong learning and technology that can improve our overall quality of life. While smart cities may rely heavily on technology, infrastructure, and organizational systems, learning cities focuses on the communication, interaction, and learning that occurs within them. Although people and communities provide such learning, they must occur not just in homes and places of work, but in the entire society that requires effective governance as well as successful policy implementation.

For example, one of the signature hallmarks of lifelong learning is an ideal of a learning society. A more accurate history of the learning cities initiative comes from this global discussion. In the 1970s in the advent of computers and advanced technology, many people thought that machines would do our work for us, thus affording everyone more leisure time to learn even more. This would be the premise of a "learning society." This turned out to be a utopian view that still have not been actualized (Holford & Jarvis, 2000).

Holford and Jarvis (2000) offer four distinct ways at looking at the concept of the learning society: 1) as a futuristic/utopian society; 2) as a reflexive society; 3) as a consumer society; and 4) as the more planned society. It goes without saying that different views about a learning society will have an increasing effect, not only on the role of learning cities and lifelong learning, but also of technology and smart cities. For arguably a learning city is the learning example and the smart city is the technology example in the role of a learning society. Over time, as cities become reliable sources for lifelong learning and technology, their results would redefine the learning society for a new age. But in these current times, more progress can be made to connect lifelong learning to technology through comparing their concepts, objectives, and potential outcomes.

As a result, this chapter intends to explore the connection of learning cities and smart cities through the ideal of the learning society. Each concept of the learning society can help to connect these initiatives, exploring key characteristics. This exploration can lead to further practices, policies, partnerships, and other pursuits in learning cities and smart cities; or simply lifelong learning and technology.

# REFERENCES

Aspin, D. N., & Chapman, J. D. (2012). Toward a philosophy of lifelong learning. In *Second International Handbook of Lifelong Learning* (pp. 3–35). doi:10.1007/978-94-007-2360-3_1

Becker, G. (1964). *Human capital: A theoretical and empirical analysis with special reference to education*. University of Chicago Press.

Biao, I. (2013). The place of transformative learning in the building of learning cities in Africa. *Journal of Adult and Continuing Education, 19*(1), 3–16. doi:10.7227/JACE.19.1.2

Borkowska, K., & Osborne, M. (2018). Locating the fourth helix: Rethinking the role of civil society in developing smart learning cities. *International Review of Education, 64*(3), 355–372. doi:10.100711159-018-9723-0

Boshier, R. W. (2005). Lifelong learning. In L. English (Ed.), *International encyclopedia of adult education* (pp. 373–378). Palgrave Macmillan.

Boshier, R. W. (2018). Learning cities: Fake news or the real deal? *International Journal of Lifelong Education, 37*(4), 419–434. Advance online publication. doi:10.1080/02601370.2018.1491900

Canadian Council on Learning (CLI). (2010). *The 2010 Composite Learning Index: Five years of measuring Canada's progress in lifelong learning*. Retrieved from www.cli-ica.ca

Cappon, P., & Laughlin, J. (2013). Canada's composite learning index: A path towards learning communities. *International Review of Education, 59*(4), 505–519. doi:10.100711159-013-9374-0

Chickering, A. W. (1977). *Experience and learning: An introduction to experiential learning*. Change Magazine Press.

Choi, I., & Yang, B. C. (2012). Comparing the characteristics of lifelong learning cities in Korea and Japan: A historical sociological approach. *KEDI Journal of Educational Policy*, 183–202. http://eng.kedi.re.kr

Chourabi, H. (2012). Understanding smart cities: An integrative framework. In *45th Hawaii International Conference on System Sciences*. IEEE Computer Society. 10.1109/HICSS.2012.615

Cobb, J. (2013). *Leading the learning revolution: The expert's guide to capitalizing on the exploding lifelong education market* [Kindle version]. Retrieved from Amazon.com.

Dirks, S., & Keeling, M. (2009). *A vision of smarter cities: How cities can lead the way into a prosperous and sustainable future*. IBM Global Business Services.

Eckert, T., Preisinger-Kleine, R., Fartusnic, C., Houston, M., Juceviciené, P., Dillon, B., & ... . (2012). *Quality in developing learning cities and regions: A guide for practitioners and stakeholders*. Ludwig Maximilian University.

EPALE. (2015). *Electronic platform for adult learning in Europe*. Retrieved from https://ec.europa.eu/epale

European Commission. (2000). *A memorandum on lifelong learning SEC 1832*. Retrieved from https://arhiv.acs.si/dokumenti/Memorandum_on_Lifelong_Learning.pdf

Facer, K., & Buchczyk, M. (2019). Towards a research agenda for the 'actually existing' learning city. *Oxford Review of Education, 45*(2), 151–167. doi:10.1080/03054985.2018.1551990

Fenwick, T. (2000). Experiential learning: A review of the five contemporary perspectives of cognition. *Adult Education Quarterly, 50*(4), 243–272. doi:10.1177/07417130022087035

Florida, R. (2002). *The rise of the creative class: And how it's transforming work, leisure, community and everyday life*. Basic Books.

Fuller, S. (2018). Social democracy and neoliberalism: Beyond sibling rivalry. *Global Policy*, 10–23.

Furco, A. (1996). Service-learning: A balanced approach to experiential education. In B. Taylor (Ed.), *Expanding boundaries: Serving and learning* (pp. 2-5). Retrieved from California State University-Fresno State website: http://www.csufresno.edu/facultysl/documents/ ABalancedApproach.pdf

Hibbler, D., & Scott, L. (2015). Role of leisure in humanizing learning cities. In L. Scott (Ed.), *Learning Cities for Adult Learners* (pp. 73–82)., doi:10.1002/ace.20124

Holford, J., & Jarvis, P. (2000). The learning society. In A. L. Wilson & E. R. Hayes (Eds.), *Handbook of Adult and Continuing Education* (pp. 643–659). Jossey-Bass.

Horrigan, J. B. (2016, March). *Lifelong learning and technology*. Retrieved from https://www.pewresearch.org/

Jarvis, P. (2004). *Adult education and lifelong learning: Theory and practice* (3rd ed.). RoutledgeFalmer. doi:10.4324/9780203561560

Kearns, P. (2012). Learning cities as healthy green cities: Building sustainable opportunity cities. *Australian Journal of Adult Learning, 52*(2), 368–391.

Kolb, D. A. (1984). *Experiential learning: Experience as the source of learning and development.* Prentice Hall.

Lee, M., & Jan, S. K. (2017). Lifelong learning policy discourses on international organisations since 2000: A kaleidoscope or merely fragments? In *The Palgrave International Handbook on Adult and Lifelong Education and Learning* (pp. 375–396). doi:10.1057/987-137-55783-4

Li, C., Hao, X., & Nanchen, J. (2013). Transforming Beijing into a learning city: Practices and challenges. *International Journal of Continuing Education and Lifelong Learning, 6*(1), 37–54.

Longworth, N. (1999). Making lifelong learning work: Learning cities for a learning century. Sterling, VA: Kogan Page.

Marsick, V. J., Watkins, K. E., Scully-Russ, E., & Nicolaides, A. (2016). Rethinking in-formal and incidental learning in terms of complexity and the social context. *Journal of Adult Learning, Knowledge and Innovation, 1*(1). Retrieved from https://akademiai.com/doi/abs/10.1556/2059.01.2016.003

Martin, I. (1987). Community education: Toward a theoretical analysis. In G. Allen, J. Bastiani, I. Martin, & K. Richards (Eds.), *Community education: An agenda for educational reform* (pp. 9–32). Open University Press.

Merriam, S. B., Caffarella, R. S., & Baumgartner, L. (2007). *Learning in adulthood: A comprehensive guide* (3rd ed.). Jossey-Bass.

Nicoll, K., & Fejes, A. (2008). Mobilising Foucault in the studies of lifelong learning. In A. Fejes & K. Nicoll (Eds.), *Foucault and Lifelong Learning* (pp. 1–18). Routledge.

OECD. (2005). *Promoting adult learning.* OECD.

Osborne, M., Kearns, P., & Yang, J. (2013). Learning cities: Developing inclusive, prosperous and sustainable urban communities. *International Review of Education, 59*(4), 409–423. doi:10.100711159-013-9384-y

Pavlova, M. (2018). Fostering inclusive, sustainable economic growth and 'green' skills development in learning cities through partnerships. *International Review of Education, 64*(3), 339–354. doi:10.100711159-018-9718-x

Regmi, K. D. (2017). Habermas, lifeworld and rationality: Towards a comprehensive model of lifelong learning. *International Journal of Lifelong Education, 36*(6), 679–695. doi:10.1080/02601370.2017.1377776

Report, D. (1996). Learning: The treasure within. Report to UNESCO of the International Commission on Education for the Twenty-first Century. UNESCO Publishing.

Report, F. (1972). *Learning to be: The world of education today and tomorrow*. UNESCO.

Scott, L. (2012). *Engaged-learning: Community engagement classifications at U.S. land-grant institutions* (Unpublished doctoral dissertation). Teachers College, Columbia University, New York, NY.

Scott, L. (2015). Learning cities for all: Directions to a new adult education and learning movement. In L. Scott (Ed.), *Learning Cities for Adult Learners* (pp. 83–94). doi:10.1002/ace.20125

Scott, L., Mizzi, R. C., & Merriweather, L. R. (2021). Philosophical foundations of adult and continuing education. In T. Rocco, M. Smith, R. Mizzi, L. Merriweather, & J. Hawley (Eds.), *The Handbook of Adult and Continuing Education* (2020 Edition, pp. 11–21). Stylus.

Smith, A. (1776). *The wealth of nations*. Methuen & Co., Ltd.

Thomas, A. M. (1991). *Beyond education: A new perspective on society's management of learning*. Jossey-Bass.

Tight, M. (2001). *Key concepts in adult education and training*. RoutledgeFarmer.

Toutkoushian, R. K., & Paulsen, M. B. (2016). *Economics of higher education: Background, concepts, and applications*. Springer Nature. doi:10.1007/978-94-017-7506-9

Traupman, J. C. (1995). *The new college Latin & English dictionary*. Bantam.

U. S. Department of Health, Education, and Welfare. (1978). *Lifelong learning and public policy*. Washington, DC: U.S. Government Printing Office.

UNESCO. (2016). *Learning, sharing and collaborating: Portraits of participating cities of the first members' meeting of the UNESCO Global Network of Learning Cities* [Report]. UNESCO Institute for Lifelong Learning.

Usher, R., Bryant, I., & Johnston, R. (1997). *Adult education and the postmodern challenge: Learning beyond the limits*. Routledge.

Valdes-Cotera, R., Wang, M., & Lunardon, K. (2018). Realising lifelong learning for all: Governance and partnerships in building sustainable learning cities. *International Review of Education, 64*(3), 287–293. doi:10.100711159-018-9722-1

Wain, K. (2000). *The learning society in a postmodern world: The education crisis.* Peter Lang.

Walters, S. (2005). Learning region. In International encyclopedia of adult education (pp. 360–362). New York, NY: Palgrave Macmillan.

Wang, Y. P., & Kintrea, K. (2019). Sustainable, healthy and learning cities and neighbourhoods. *Environment & Urbanization Asia, 10*(2), 146–150. doi:10.1177/0975425319859129

Weil, S. W., & McGill, I. (1989). A framework for making sense of experiential learning. In S. Weil & I. McGill (Eds.), *Making sense of experiential learning: Diversity in theory and practice* (pp. 3–24). Society for Research into Higher Education & Open University Press.

White, J. (1997). *Education and the end of work: A new philosophy of work and learning.* Cassell.

Wong, S. (2002, April). *Learning cities: Building 21st Century communities through lifelong learning.* Travelling Scholarship [Report]. Victoria, Australia: Department of Employment, Training and Tertiary Education of the Victorian Government.

World Bank. (2011). Learning for all: Investing in people's knowledge and skills to promote development. In World Bank Group Education Strategy 2020. Washington, DC: World Bank.

Yang, J. (2012). An overview of building learning cities as a strategy for promoting lifelong learning. *Journal of Adult and Continuing Education, 18*(2), 97–113. doi:10.7227/JACE.18.2.8

Yorks, L., & Scott, L. (2014). Lifelong tools for the learner, educator, and worker. In V. C. X. Wang (Ed.), *Handbook of Research on Technologies for Improving the 21st Century Workforce: Tools for Lifelong Learning* (pp. 42–55). IGI Global.

# Chapter 4
# Large Technical Systems:
## Artificial Intelligence and Future Applications in Smart Cities

**Muhammed Can**

https://orcid.org/0000-0002-6717-2611
*University of Minho, Portugal*

**Halid Kaplan**
*University of Texas at San Antonio, USA*

## ABSTRACT

*In recent years, artificial intelligence has become a new normal in the modern world. Even though there are still limitations and it remains to be premature both in terms of applications and theoretical approaches, AI has a huge potential to shift various systems from healthcare to transportation. Needless to say, smart cities are also significant for AI's development. IoT, big data applications, and power networks bring a new understanding of how we live and what the future will be like when AI is adapted to smart cities. However, it is highly misleading to focus on AI itself in this manner. Rather, it should be considered as a part of the 'Large Technical System'. In this vein, the chapter will ask the following questions: To what extent might AI contribute the power networks of smart cities? How can LTS theory explain this evolution both in terms of technical aspects and technopolitics?*

DOI: 10.4018/978-1-7998-5326-8.ch004

## INTRODUCTION

The advent of emerging technologies be it 5G, blockchain, quantum technology or artificial intelligence has shown that they have an immeasurable potential to change our lives, if not immediately. From the autonomous cars to the health care, the more technology progresses, the more we are becoming vulnerable to malicious effects of it. Cyber domain, for instance, is a significant part of political playing ground of states and non-state actors to show prowess or exert influence on third parties. Even worse, there is no global governance scheme or regulations as to how to control and use these technologies. The gap between haves and have nots —digital divide— furthers the complexity that technology imposes upon us. This, at the end of the day leads to illusory takeaways about emerging technologies. Though politically laden comments provide a snapshot of status quo in the nexus between global politics and technology, it doesn't represent the whole reality. Rather it seems more blind men and elephant analogy that offers a little glimpse into intertwined technological systems. Artificial intelligence (AI) is one of them. Since deep learning approach has become widely used in various realms, AI discipline gained attraction from all walks of life, though the success of deep learning is a product of more than a half century old constant failures and success. Indeed, this creates fallacy or hype around a new technology. It can be seen in latest confrontation between China and the US. The main question is whether the global system is in ongoing power shift or put it differently, is it a tech 'cold war'? (Frey and Osborne, 2020; Wu et al., 2019). True, that Chinese technology policy is not innocent since it strives for diffuse authoritarian technologies throughout the world and represses its minority Uighur populations on the home front (Harsono, 2020; Shahbaz, 2018). The US technology is not also immune from these criticisms— even if they are not being used at an identical level— given predictive policing and algorithmic biases towards black people that have become more evident in the wake of George Floyd's death (Benbouzid, 2019; Hale, 2020).

The crux of the matter is what we understand from technology. That is, to what extent theoretical lenses such as Hughes' Large Technical Systems (LTS) theory help us to grasp complex relations among technology, power (political aspect) and society (Hughes, 1993). This applies to the AI-based technology development regardless of its malicious usage. In part because technology and its ramifications are path dependent that might vary at different levels. For instance, the regime type —be it liberal democracy or authoritarian— of any given country directly affects progression of technology. Furthermore, innovation ecosystem, the status of epistemic communities, collaboration between private and public sector, effective government technology strategies, ability to setting standards, research and development investments are major variables that might dramatically shift technology systems. At the end of the day, these systems are products of trajectory and paradigmatic changes, let alone being consequences of ad hoc policies or pragmatic priorities (Dosi, 198). We, therefore, investigate the AI usage in smart cities through the aspect of large technical systems. We mostly focus on Chinese AI technology development and how it affects society. Besides, we seek to find out how potential diffusion of AI usage through smart city projects might leverage authoritarian governments to sustain a grip on the power. The aim of this chapter is to provide theoretical baseline for the AI policy by using smart city applications of AI as a case study. Thus, we start with LTS theory and continue by looking at how to place AI in LTS theory. Finally, Chinese AI technologies in smart cities will be investigated through different case studies.

## 1. Large Technical Systems Theory

Over the past decades, scholars who have been studying technology, used different theoretical lenses to make technological entities meaningful for various disciplines. During the World War II technological determinism has been a dominant position for scientists and researchers that can be considered as a dire consequence of war along with the existence of nuclear weapons. Even prominent thinkers like Martin Heidegger (1954) depicted technology as a black box that can be easily exploited by who controls them. For determinists, technology seems resistant to an everlasting series of accidents, catastrophes, pending risks of obliteration related to modern weapon systems, brittle infrastructures or the diffusion of toxic artefacts and particles (Virilio, 2010). Besides, emerging technologies "were implicated in colonial domination, racism, and exploitative suppression, both practically and as a 'white mythology' has remained largely under-scrutinized in social sciences" (Mayer et al., 2014, p.5).

On the contrary, techno-optimists tend to consider technology and science as an 'enabler' to further economic conditions and human progress. For them, technology "offers better solutions to critical global challenges such as security, public health, energy, food and water supply, poverty, and climate stability (Ibid, p.4). They treat emerging technologies as neutral entities, as if they were central actor that led progress all the time. Surprisingly, taking technology for granted as a neutral phenomenon is valid for IR theories, notably social constructivism, liberalism and realism alike (Ibid). Yet as Kranzberg (1986) puts it, "Technology is neither good, nor bad, nor is it neutral". This is also valid for AI domain. It might serve malicious purposes as in spreading fake contents through deep fakes whereas it might be helpful for diagnosing diseases or it can be beneficial for the education system (Brundage, 2018; Park and Han, 2018; Roll and Wylie, 2016). Thus, pros and cons of AI is highly depended upon actors and their systems.

In his seminal book Thomas Park Hughes (1993) took a different approach and demonstrated that technology is a part of social and power relations. Hecht and

Allen notes "while for many years scholars tended to focus either on the social construction of the technological or on the technological construction of social, Hughes always emphasized both these domains simultaneously" (2001, p.2). In his theoretical approach he has always sought to explain how institutional and political relations construct the power and development of technology (Ibid). As it mentioned before, AI development and its political and social manifestations are directly related to technical systems and its trajectory. Acquiring a specific technology does not necessarily mean that they had the same trajectory and yielded same power to the countries. That is to say, developing a nuclear weapon poses different challenges to Iran such as external political resistance—sanctions, direct/indirect confrontations— while it created different implications both at political and social level on US politics. Furthermore, although developing a nuclear weapon seems to be beneficial for Iran to leverage its position in the global arena, it has suffered from this policy much more than it has enhanced political influence over the years. However, the US had a different trajectory given the fact that usage of nuclear weapons on Japan. Therefore, AI should be assessed in this aspect.

In Large Technical Systems theory, there are certain phases. These are as follows (Olsen et al., 2012, p.219):

- **"Invention phase:** A new technological system emerges around radical inventions
- **Development phase:** This nascent system is adapted to economic, political and social characteristics needed for survival in the 'use world'
- **Innovation phase:** It adds further system components relating to manufacturing, sales and service facilities, enabling the system to enter the market
- **Competition and Growth:** The system expands and adapts in competition with rival systems
- **Consolidation phase:** A system acquires so much momentum that is difficult to change, creating an appearance of autonomy from its environment
- **Transfer phase:** That may occur at any time during a system's history. "

There are also side concepts in LTS to expand and make more understandable the phases mentioned above. For instance, 'system builders' refer to a human agency or institution that might change the course of specific technology development (Ibid). 'Reverse salient' refers to "elements lagging behind and restraining total system development– and translate these into critical problems that may or may not be solved. Such reverse, salients and problems can be of a technical or non-technical nature" (Ibid, p.220). Finally, 'technological style' refers "how designs of systems and their interrelated technical and non-technical elements change when transferred to other social, natural and technical environments" (Ibid).

These phases can be applied comparatively to AI in China and US cases. Due to their different political systems, AI applications have different implications. Let's consider development phase. While China uses and applies AI-based surveillance systems to control society, US took limited approaches by deploying these systems at the police departments' disposal thanks to the structured laws and regulations on data. Put it differently, in competition and growth phase China enjoys being state capitalism whereas US relies on Silicon Valley tech giants that barely controls private sector. In transfer phase, China takes aggressive approaches under the 'Digital Silk Road' project by transferring surveillance systems —safe cities projects— whilst US takes a defensive approach to counter Chinese technology diffusion by sanctioning or establishing G7-like alliances on AI (Macaulay, 2020). 'Reverse salients' that two players encountered are different in their own systems. For instance, 'project maven' joint project of DoD and Google had been cancelled due to the wide range of criticisms. Yet Chinese tech companies like Huawei and iflytek has constantly support PLA's AI development with close cooperation. 'Technological style' of two countries are also completely different. For instance, while China focuses on specific AI technologies like computer vision, US is leading global hardware sector.

## 2. Artificial Intelligence and Large Technical Systems

It is worth emphasizing AI usage in smart cities without digging deeper into question to what extent AI can be considered as a part of large technical systems. Needless to say, AI is a major component of smart cities along with various emerging technologies such as 5G and Internet of Things (IoT). In his seminal article, Leon (2011) applies LTS theory to the Information and communications technology usage in complex city systems and argues that relations between organizations and key stake holder networks are a major factor for achieving successful results. This also applies, categorically, to the AI applications in smart cities. To understand what lies beneath the complex AI networks in smart cities that have ramifications both in social, political and economic realms, one should take into account of the history of AI along with phases what LTS theory premises.

Since AI has taken place as an academic discipline in different subjects, be it engineering or neurology, it underwent winters and summers in terms of funding, research and development, and governmental support. Following the Dartmouth Conference in 1956, AI enjoyed two decades of progression until 1973 when US congress started to criticize high spending on AI research (Haenlein and Kaplan, 2019). In the wake of James Lighthill's report on AI to the British government, support for AI had stopped both in UK and in the US (Haenlein and Kaplan, 2019).

This shows, clearly, how individual or organizational decisions might affect the trajectory of a new technology which might be seem as a 'reverse salient'. The other instance is Minsky and Pappert's book called *Perceptron* that shifted the course of deep learning approach's development. In their book they criticized the neural network approach by referring Rosenblatt's 'fallacy' and adversely affected the progression of deep learning approach until the 2010s (2017;1960). While the US and UK abandoned AI discipline other players such as Japan continued to fund research on AI throughout the 1980s that might be considered as the continuum of 'development phase'.

Perhaps the watershed moment —consolidation phase— was the Alpha GO's success against world champion Lee Sedol that attracted media coverage (Borowiec, 2016). Since then, most of the developed countries have started to heavily invest in AI to become more competitive. As a matter of fact, these aforementioned LTS theory phases were not always in order simply because while AI is still in its development phase countries transferring these technologies to third countries or while countries transferring these technologies, they are witnessing competition and growth both internal and global markets. Crux the matter of assessing AI through LTS lenses is to elaborate networks and their interactions with systems. Therefore, different phases might occur at the same time. For instance, while given country transfer technology it might confront with the reverse salient or vice versa. Today, AI is a major part of systems from electric (power networks) to the traffic systems. Therefore, AI should be evaluated on its own system through regulations, organizations, its societal effects rather than take AI for granted as a monolithic entity. This is evident in Chinese AI policy and their usage of it in smart cities. For instance, while facial recognition systems are being used to control population —or put it differently to repress the society— in China without any accountability, they are being used in a democratic system with accountability although it is possible to witness discrimination and misuse.

## 3. Artificial Intelligence and Smart Cities

Vast majority of the US states have become more dependent on AI usage in smart cities "to improve environmental planning, resource management, energy utilization and crime prevention" (West and Allen, 2020, p.9). For instance, Cincinnati Fire Department is adopting data analytics to organize medical emergency situations since it receives 80,000 requests annually, AI helps in prioritizing calls and decides means to tackle emergencies (Ibid). According to the National League of Cities, AI applications in Smart cities were quite effective combating the recent outbreak of COVID-19 virus. They stated "Smart cities have been effective in combating the pandemic by using sensors and collecting data to determine whether physical-distancing rules are being followed. For example, in Elizabeth, New Jersey, the mayor plans to deploy drones to enforce physical-distancing rules by alerting people to move away from each other if they are congregating.35 Cities like Salt Lake City, Utah are also partnering with tech companies to use smart city technology to trace the contacts of people infected with the virus to inform the community" (Yadavalli, 2020, p.25). Before delving into the how AI leverage Chinese smart city projects, it is worth looking at how AI is being used in smart cities in general. There are seven key technologies behind the majority of smart cities, those are (Kharkovyna, 2020, para.5):

- Information and Communication Technology (ICT)
- Internet of Things (IoT)
- Sensors
- Artificial Intelligence
- Cloud-based IoT applications
- Blockchain
- Geospatial Technology

In a broader sense technological ecosystem of smart cities can be divided into five distinct categories (Lea, 2017, p.4):

- **IT Players:** IP networks, tech integration, security
- **Telecom:** Broadband and internet technology, mobile telephony, monitoring and sensing
- **Governance:** E-government, open-data, citizen engagement, privacy and security
- **Building automation:** Energy management, building automation, device connectivity, monitoring and sensing, security
- **Energy and Infrastructure:** Power electronics, renewable energy, smart and micro grid, sub-station automation, T&D tech

As it can be seen from the above, smart city has contain various emerging technologies which can be considered highly complex to sustain and develop. At this point the question should be how AI can influence efficiency of smart cities or which techniques can be used? Firstly, pattern recognition can be used to boost efficiency of smart cities in cases like predicting "weather data, especially temperature and rain" (Navarathna and Malagi, 2018, p.46). Secondly, image recognition can be used in solving traffic-ridden cities' problems by implementing real time analytics (Ibid). Apart from that, AI might be beneficial in implementing automated video object detection, smart parking applications, autonomous flying objects, face detection cameras and movement for public safety, IoT solutions to manage waste, augmenting workforce knowledge and skills (Kharkovyna, 2020). Yet aside from its huge advantages, it might be used for controlling societies or creating 'feedback' societies in longer terms by the authoritarian governments. This clearly can be seen in Chinese smart city projects. This also reflects how identical technology, as in AI instance, could transform into highly opposite — in terms of purposes it serves— entity in different LTS. Therefore, it is quite significant evaluating technological entity and its trajectory, interactions between stakeholders, how it locates itself in power networks both in political and societal power dynamics.

## 4. Chinese Smart Cities and Socio-Technical Implications

From the beginning of Mao era, Chinese grand strategy in terms of technology policy has been ambitious, although Xi Jinping had to chance to materialize these dreams. The term *ganchao* refers to a phrase meaning 'catch up and surpass' has always been a mantra for CCP (Chinese Communist Party) leaders that led today's mighty Chinese technology power (Gewirtz, 2019). Until Deng Xiaoping era (1978-1992) Chinese technology policy was more inward looking due to both nature of Cold War and communist ideology. However, opening up China to the world economy dramatically affected Chinese technology policy. Agarwala and Chaudhary divides Chinese science and technology (S&T) policy in four phases (2019). The first phase occurred between 1949 and 1959 that S&T "supported the development of heavy industries along the Soviet lines" (Ibid, p.206). Second phase that was between 1959 and 1976 that "witnessed economic stagnation and ideological domination of technology projects" (Ibid). Third phase, which was from 1976 to 2001, "focused on market-driven and product-driven research" (Ibid). From the beginning of 2002 "China has aimed to develop high-technology industries and the nascent clean-energy or green technology with a focus on innovation" (Ibid). In addition to this, three distinct points can be added (Dace, 2020, para.14):

- "In its initial stages China's strategy was defined by imitation. The government protected companies such as Alibaba, Baidu and Tencent in their infancy as they adopted insights from Western Big Tech companies. The country's strategy is now one of innovation."
- "This two-stage process has seen the sector experience substantial growth. China now excels in key technologies and sectors, such as Artificial Intelligence (AI) and 5G. This has increased China's potential to expand its leverage on the international system."

- "As a result, China is spreading its own tightly controlled digital standards across the world, enabling it to project global power and leading to the emergence of conflicting global technology standards."

True that Chinese technology was mostly known as being 'copy-cat' for years, but since Xi Jinping took power it has gained momentum to become one of the most competitive innovation hub in different emerging technology realms. Made China 2025, for instance, is a well-structured initiative that aims at becoming self-sufficient in producing cutting edge technologies. This applies to the areas ranging from 5G infrastructure to the AI. More importantly, through Digital Silk Road initiative, China has started to diffuse its authoritarian technologies. For instance, China has come to terms with major African states deploying 41 different smart city projects according to the Australian Strategic Policy Institute's research (Cave et al.,2019). Not surprisingly, these agreements reveal one fact. Majority of importing states prefer technological systems from the countries that are close to their ideological mindset—authoritarian governments—which deployed and used these technologies successfully in their own system. For instance, Hillman and McCalpin (2019, para.1) argue that:

"Countries entering into Huawei "Safe City" agreements tend to share three characteristics:

**Non-liberal:** Seventy-one percent of Huawei's "Safe City" agreements are in countries with an average rating of "partly free" (44 percent) or "not free" (27 percent) by Freedom House between 2009-2018.

**Asian or African:** Fifty-nine percent of Huawei's agreements are with countries located in Asia (37 percent) or sub-Saharan Africa (22 percent).

**Middle-income:** Seventy-one percent of Huawei's agreements are in lower-middle income (42 percent) and upper-middle-income (29 percent) countries."

Perhaps following question should be how China successfully implements these technologies? To understand AI's role in Chinese smart city projects, one should consider historical and cultural basis of implementing these technologies. From the beginning of invention of paper Chinese emperors had been aware of importance —especially the power information flows— of controlling society where it seemed highly complex to do it (Andersen, 2020). In the 11th century, emperor of Song-dynasty had understood that Chinese cities had become too populated that he appointed local policy to surveil population (Ibid). This tradition continued during the civil war era. Chiang Kai-shek, for instance, shaped a policy that asking citizens to be aware of communist 'traitors' and watch their movements as much as they can (Ibid). In the wake of civil war, supreme leader Mao shifted cities outlook by transforming them into grids and embedded 'sharp eyes' to control potential threats (Ibid). Thus, today's Chinese smart city applications are not a direct reflection of technological progress, rather it is a manifestation of historical, cultural and ideological differences from the rest of the world. In the same vein, it is an obvious sign that these means and ends had become —with different technologies— a large technical system in itself. Therefore, LTS theory is a proper tool to decipher complex relations between socio-technical systems.

Perhaps the most popular example is the systems that are being used to repress Uighur minorities in the Xin Jiang region. The repression is ranging from mobile app usage to the surveillance systems. For instance, in 2014 CCP ordered private/state-backed companies —such as WeChat— to hand over data to monitor Uighurs' daily activities (Cockerel, 2019). In the following years CCP tightened its grip on Uighurs by implementing various measures. 'iFlytek' a Chinese company has been actively helping Chinese government to monitor minorities by collecting voices from calls and using its translation apps by checking which words are being used in Uighur language (Hvistendhal, 2020). Not to mention that there are words — includes awkward words and idioms as well— that have been continuously banned by CCP such as 'yellow duck' and 'may the wind fill your sails'. Apart from these, Chinese authorities mandated Uighurs to download nanny apps. As Andersen (2020, para.22) aptly puts it "The nanny apps work in tandem with the police, who spot-check phones at checkpoints, scrolling through recent calls and texts. Even an innocent digital association—being in a group text with a recent mosque attendee, for instance—could result in detention. Staying off social media altogether is no solution, because digital inactivity itself can raise suspicions. The police are required to note when Uighurs deviate from any of their normal behavior patterns. Their database wants to know if Uighurs start leaving their home through the back door instead of the front. It wants to know if they spend less time talking to neighbors than they used to".

Indeed, Xin Jiang region is an extraordinary example, and it doesn't fully represent the future AI usage in smart cities. Yet, Xin Jiang region should be considered as an 'experiment lab' in part because the state-backed company called CETC —same company who built the majority of Xin Jiang's surveillance systems— has deployed new projects in different regions from Zhejiang, Guangdong to the Shenzhen (Andersen, 2020). According to Chinese safe cities technologies and markets 2013-2022 report, Sichuan province has spent $4.2 billion to safe city project containing 500,000 surveillance cameras whereas Beijing municipal government has placed 400,000 additional cameras which corresponds 700,000 cameras in total (Homeland Security Research, 2013). Apart from that, Chinese police department uses special surveillance system that contains camera and box called 'IMSI catcher' to track population. As Mozur and Krolik puts it "Once activated, the system began to sniff for personal data. The boxes — phone scanners called IMSI catchers and widely used in the West — collected identification codes from mobile phones. The cameras recorded faces. On the back end, the system attempted to tie the data together, an examination of its underlying database showed. If a face and a phone appeared at the same place and time, the system grew more confident they belonged to the same person" (2019, para.11).

Perhaps the most significant initiative has been so far implemented by Chinese companies is the 'City Brain' project that was announced in 2016. It is a "new infrastructure built on massive data, which utilizes artificial intelligence to solve urban governance and development issues that cannot be solved by human brain (Zhang et al., 2019, p.1). It is being deployed in line with five distinct application scenarios, namely; Urban traffic checkup, urban police monitoring, urban traffic micro-control, urban special vehicles and urban strategic planning (Ibid). Many argue that City Brain would be unprecedent progress for Chinese citizens since it "could be trained to spot lost children, or luggage abandoned by tourists and terrorists. It could flag loiterers, or homeless people, or rioters" (Andersen, 2020, para.32). However, still it is on the early stages of its development although it sounds beneficial for the sake of city safety and it is still unknown whether this type of projects will end up with big brother-ish surveillance state. More importantly, once China transfer these technologies to the third countries, it is unknown to what extent it will shift daily lives of people. Therefore, technology should not be taken for granted merely good or bad. How to use these technologies and which factors might worsen or enhance complex city systems will be depended upon both who controls it and how these technologies placed themselves in socio-technical systems.

## CONCLUSION

Emerging technologies have a profound impact on societies, geopolitics, economies and many others. The advent of new approaches —exponential progress in machine learning techniques— to the AI has revealed this reality such that states rushed to regulate the usage of AI in an ethical and responsible manner. Throughout the history, technology has always been subject to fierce debates. Deterministic views treated 'thorny' existence of technology in a hasty manner whereas social constructivists held more optimist considerations. However, Thomas Park Hughes, a technology historian (1993) combined these two approaches that offered a fresh perspective to the scholars. In large technical systems theory, he argued that technology is not merely good or bad. Rather it is deeply embedded in systems that include underlying factors ranging from innovation culture, technological style to the institutions. True, that many of us missing the point how new technologies influence power relations be it society-state relations or individual-society dimension.

Today, AI is here, and its applications are vast. From autonomous cars, healthcare to the business sector, perhaps it is one of the most promising technologies along with quantum technology, biotech, IoT, Big Data analytics and many others. Yet what we understand from technology and how we use it quite challenging given the factors that affect technology policy such as innovation ecosystem, regime types, participation of citizens, R&D investments and so on.

In smart cities, AI might boost the quality of people's daily lives. It might be a quite promising tool for tackling environmental problems, and it may be a helpful to solve traffic jams. These tools are already being used to track COVID-19 contraction and proved to be effective means for governments. On the flip side of the coin, it can be used for authoritarian purposes such as repressing opponents, spying potential rivals, controlling and manipulating supporters. This is evident in Chinese case even though AI has limitations to provide full-fledged means to control what is going in cities. However, there is no global solution to control malicious usage once these technologies diffuse globally. Yet again, it should be noted that Chinese approach to the technology is complex that traced back to the foundation of Chinese civilization. At this point, LTS theory might provide theoretical lenses to understand what lies behind the complex large technical systems. More importantly, it might be beneficial for future studies to focus on how LTS theory can be applied to civil-military fusion of AI and to what extent LTS theory can explain how regime types affect the progression of AI technology.

## REFERENCES

Agarwala, N., & Chaudhary, R. D. (2019). China's Policy on Science and Technology: Implications for the Next Industrial Transition. *India Quarterly*, 75(2), 206–227. doi:10.1177/0974928419841786

Andersen, R. (2020). *The Panopticon Is Already Here*. Retrieved 6 August 2020, from https://www.theatlantic.com/magazine/archive/2020/09/china-ai-surveillance/614197/

Benbouzid, B. (2019). To predict and to manage. Predictive policing in the United States. *Big Data & Society*, 6(1). doi:10.1177/2053951719861703

Borowiec, S. (2016). *AlphaGo seals 4-1 victory over Go grandmaster Lee Sedol*. Retrieved 4 August 2020, from https://www.theguardian.com/technology/2016/mar/15/googles-alphago-seals-4-1-victory-over-grandmaster-lee-sedol

Brundage, M., Avin, S., Clark, J., Toner, H., Eckersley, P., Garfinkel, B., ... Anderson, H. (2018). *The malicious use of artificial intelligence: Forecasting, prevention, and mitigation.* arXiv preprint arXiv:1802.07228.

Cave, D., Hoffman, S., Joske, A., Ryan, F., & Thomas, E. (2019). *Mapping China's Tech Giants.* Australian Strategic Policy Institute. Retrieved from https://www.aspi. org.au/ report/ mapping – chinas – tech - giants? __ cf _ chl _ jschl _ tk __ = 5e6a d821 deb6 f569 3dd2 7937 3dc9 c27d 693d 65df – 1595 6919 65 – 0 – AVGn cFsE 7rKN JriV C4Hz Amaf 7x94 wZQx GYX8 4hXZ zKYa yARB ez - vK1V 3094 75FB 6q3R zJB2 NMY _ Udrm 2u1O rIDz jN9j bNri xNVI RW7T YTv0 spl7 kBAK 8mlRJ _ QUNN zNRy O8a0 Fhgy RuJL 6dkg 1SoA BwOq Ay0o LexV HvLe aEGY Llsw XbtP TSEh GcMa oMMV ucfC h0Ht cuCO vixh 2H9h vN _ t9sO m1JF tkrx – OTJU 82H0 QpJ1 0I86 aGPr EGbK GJ1K qdKL ZPUv l _ YDCvm _ iSgA fHfH6 _ - 23dY 53x9 ucOa E1eS OGUx W0dN agu2 NyGe iWDt _ gV-AQ

Cockerell, I. (2019). *Inside China's Massive Surveillance Operation.* Retrieved 6 August 2020, from https://www.wired.com/story/inside-chinas-massive-surveillance-operation/

Dace, H. (2020). *China's Tech Landscape: A Primer.* Retrieved 5 August 2020, from https://institute.global/policy/chinas-tech-landscape-primer

Dosi, G. (1982). Technological paradigms and technological trajectories: A suggested interpretation of the determinants and directions of technical change. *Research Policy, 11*(3), 147–162. doi:10.1016/0048-7333(82)90016-6

Efron, S., Schwindt, K., & Haskel, E. (2020). *Security Risks of China's Investments in Israel.* Retrieved 6 June 2020, from https://www.rand.org/pubs/rcscarch_rcports/RR3176.html

Frey, C., & Osborne, M. (2020). *China Won't Win the Race for AI Dominance.* Retrieved 2 August 2020, from https://www.foreignaffairs.com/articles/united-states/2020-06-19/china-wont-win-race-ai-dominance

Gewirtz, J. (2019). *China's Long March to Technological Supremacy.* Retrieved 1 June 2020, from https://www.foreignaffairs.com/articles/china/2019-08-27/chinas-long-march-technological-supremacy

Haenlein, M., & Kaplan, A. (2019). A brief history of artificial intelligence: On the past, present, and future of artificial intelligence. *California Management Review, 61*(4), 5–14. doi:10.1177/0008125619864925

Hale, K. (2020). *Amazon, Microsoft & IBM Slightly Social Distancing From The $8 Billion Facial Recognition Market*. Retrieved 2 August 2020, from https://www.forbes.com/sites/korihale/2020/06/15/amazon-microsoft--ibm-slightly-social-distancing-from-the-8-billion-facial-recognition-market/#41b125474a9a

Harsono, H. (2020). *China's Surveillance Technology Is Keeping Tabs on Populations Around the World*. Retrieved 2 August 2020, from https://thediplomat.com/2020/06/chinas-surveillance-technology-is-keeping-tabs-on-populations-around-the-world/

Hecht, G., & Allen, M. T. (2001). *Technologies of power*. MIT Press.

Heidegger, M. (1954). The question concerning technology. *Technology and values: Essential readings, 99*, 113.

Hillman, J., & McCalpin, M. (2019). *Watching Huawei's "Safe Cities"*. Retrieved 6 August 2020, from https://www.csis.org/analysis/watching-huaweis-safe-cities

Homeland Security Research. (2013). *China Safe Cities Technologies and Markets 2013-2022 Report - Cumulative 2013-2022 $138 Billion | Homeland Security Market Research*. Retrieved 6 August 2020, from https://homelandsecurityresearch.com/reports/china-safe-cities-technologies-and-markets/

Hughes, T. P. (1993). *Networks of power: electrification in Western society, 1880-1930*. JHU Press.

Hvistendahl, M. (2020). *How a Chinese AI Giant Made Chatting—and Surveillance—Easy*. Retrieved 6 August 2020, from https://www.wired.com/ story/ iflytek – china – ai – giant – voice – chatting - surveillance/ ?bxid = 5cec 2712 3f92 a45b 30f0 d63d & cndid = 5508 6070 & esrc = bounce X & source = EDT _ WIR _ NEWS LETTER _ 0 _ DAILY _ ZZ & utm _ brand = wired & utm _ campaign = aud – dev & utm _ mailing = WIR _ Daily _ 051820 & utm _ medium = email & utm _ source = nl & utm _ term = list1 _ p4

Kharkovyna, O. (2020). *Smart Cities: Applications of Artificial Intelligence in Urban Management*. Retrieved 5 August 2020, from https://towardsdatascience.com/smart-cities-applications-of-artificial-intelligence-in-urban-management-c445c414c8eb

Kranzberg, M. (1986). Technology and History:" Kranzberg's Laws. *Technology and Culture, 27*(3), 544–560. doi:10.2307/3105385

Lea, R. J. (2017). *Smart cities: An overview of the technology trends driving smart cities*. Retrieved 5 August 2020, from https://www.researchgate.net/publication/326099991_Smart_Cities_An_Overview_of_the_Technology_Trends_Driving_Smart_Cities

Leon, N. (2011). Complex city systems: Understanding how large technical systems innovation arises in cities. *IBM Journal of Research and Development, 55*(1.2), 16-1.

Macaulay, T. (2020). *US joins G7 AI alliance to counter China's influence.* Retrieved 6 June 2020, from https://sup.news/us-joins-g7-ai-alliance-to-counter-chinas-influence-2/

Mayer, M., Carpes, M., & Knoblich, R. (2014). The global politics of science and technology: An introduction. In *The Global Politics of Science and Technology-Vol. 1* (pp. 1–35). Springer. doi:10.1007/978-3-642-55007-2_1

Minsky, M., & Papert, S. A. (2017). *Perceptrons: An introduction to computational geometry.* MIT Press. doi:10.7551/mitpress/11301.001.0001

Mozur, P., & Krolik, A. (2019). *A Surveillance Net Blankets China's Cities, Giving Police Vast Powers.* Retrieved 6 August 2020, from https://www.nytimes.com/2019/12/17/technology/china-surveillance.html

Navarathna, P. J., & Malagi, V. P. (2018). Artificial intelligence in smart city analysis. In *2018 International Conference on Smart Systems and Inventive Technology (ICSSIT)* (pp. 44-47). IEEE. 10.1109/ICSSIT.2018.8748476

Olsen, J. K. B., Pedersen, S. A., & Hendricks, V. F. (2012). *A Companion to the Philosophy of Technology.* John Wiley & Sons.

Park, S. H., & Han, K. (2018). Methodologic guide for evaluating clinical performance and effect of artificial intelligence technology for medical diagnosis and prediction. *Radiology, 286*(3), 800–809. doi:10.1148/radiol.2017171920 PMID:29309734

Roll, I., & Wylie, R. (2016). Evolution and revolution in artificial intelligence in education. *International Journal of Artificial Intelligence in Education, 26*(2), 582–599. doi:10.100740593-016-0110-3

Rosenblatt, F. (1960). Perceptron simulation experiments. *Proceedings of the IRE, 48*(3), 301–309. doi:10.1109/JRPROC.1960.287598

Shahbaz, A. (2018). *The Rise of Digital Authoritarianism.* Retrieved 2 August 2020, from https://freedomhouse.org/report/freedom-net/2018/rise-digital-authoritarianism

Virilio, P. (2010). *Grey ecology* (D. Burk, Trans.). Atropos Press.

West, D., & Allen, J. (2020). *Turning point* (1st ed.). Brookings Institution Press.

White, C. (2019). *Chinese Companies Use Zimbabweans As Guinea Pigs To Identify Black Faces: Report.* Retrieved 6 June 2020, from https://nationalinterest. org/blog/buzz/chinese-companies-use-zimbabweans-guinea-pigs-identify-black-faces-report-101447

Wu, D., Hoenig, H., & Dormido, H. (2019). *Who's Winning the Tech Cold War? A China vs. U.S. Scoreboard.* Retrieved 2 August 2020, from https://www.bloomberg. com/graphics/2019-us-china-who-is-winning-the-tech-war/

Yadavalli, A., Kim, R., McFarland, C., & Rainwater, B. (2020). *State of the Cities.* National League of Cities. Retrieved from https://www.nlc.org/sites/default/files/ users/user57221/NLC_StateOfTheCities2020.pdf

Zhang, J., Hua, X. S., Huang, J., Shen, X., Chen, J., Zhou, Q., Fu, Z., & Zhao, Y. (2019). City brain: Practice of large-scale artificial intelligence in the<? show [AQ="" ID=" Q1]"?> real world. *IET Smart Cities*, *1*(1), 28–37. doi:10.1049/iet-smc.2019.0034

# Chapter 5
# Using Big Data Analytics to Assist a Smart City to Prevent Cyber Security Threats

**Fenio Annansingh**
*York College, City University of New York, USA*

## ABSTRACT

*The concept of a smart city as a means to enhance the life quality of citizens has been gaining increasing importance in recent years globally. A smart city consists of city infrastructure, which includes smart services, devices, and institutions. Every second, these components of the smart city infrastructure are generating data. The vast amount of data is called big data. This chapter explores the possibilities of using big data analytics to prevent cybersecurity threats in a smart city. It also analyzed how big data tools and concepts can solve cybersecurity challenges and detect and prevent attacks. Using interviews and an extensive review of the literature have developed the data analytics and cyber prevention model. The chapter concludes by indicating that big data analytics allow a smart city to identify and solve cybersecurity challenges quickly and efficiently.*

## INTRODUCTION

Smart cities worldwide are implementing initiatives to promote a greener and safer city environments, with cleaner air and water, better mobility, and efficient public services. These initiatives are supported by technologies like the Internet of Things (IoT) and big data analytics that forms the foundation of the smart city model. The growth of big data and the evolution of the IoT have played an essential role in the

DOI: 10.4018/978-1-7998-5326-8.ch005

feasibility of smart city initiatives. Big data offer the potential for cities to obtain valuable insights from a large amount of data collected through various sources, and the IoT allows the integration of sensors, radio-frequency identification, and Bluetooth in the real-world environment using highly networked services. IoT is an essential technology without which smart city initiatives cannot exist. The "things" of the IoT devices, sensors, applications collect the data that enables the technology solutions to be effective. For example, smart water meters reporting water quality and usage, alerting the water company of leaks or potential contamination. This highly digitalized society generates data every minute of the day. According to Juniper Research (2018), the high digitalization of cities has resulted in over one thousand five hundred and seventy-two gigabytes of global IP data transmitted every minute. 3.3 million content elements are shared on Facebook, 4.1 million searches are completed on Google, 38,194 photos uploaded on Instagram, 194,064 applications are downloaded in a minute. The enormous circulation of data adds to the size and diversity of big data. Big data analytics is used mainly for business analytics, forecasting sales and profit, understanding and targeting customers for a better relationship, and adding to business value. Similarly, big data can also be used to protect a smart city against cyber threats, prevent cyber-attacks, and advance cybersecurity and awareness. This chapter describes how big data analytics can be used to avoid cybersecurity threats in a smart city.

## SMART CITY

Today, more than 50% of people live in cities, and the UN estimates that by the year 2050, cities will be home to 70% of the world's population. To accommodate such a large population, cities have to be sustainably developed. Merely scaling up the existing resources and services is neither physically possible nor economically feasible. Instead, according to Pokric et al. (2014), services have to be automated, energy-efficient within existing infrastructure and information acquired and reused across different locations. Also, citizens' expectations are high, as they increasingly expect a better quality of life, have access to detailed information about other aspects of the city and influence various aspects of city management, development, and planning (Albino et al. 2015). Being such a complex system, with people, businesses, communities, and city services interacting with each other, the solution to a sustainable future is a smart city.

A smart city is a place where traditional networks and services are made more flexible, efficient, and sustainable with the use of information, digital, and telecommunication technologies to improve its operations for the benefit of its inhabitants. In other words, in a smart city, digital technologies translate into better public services for inhabitants and better use of resources while impacting the environment less (Mohanty et al., 2016 & Albino et al., 2015). Simultaneously, a smart city can make intelligent responses to different needs, including daily livelihood, environmental protection, transportation, public safety and city services, industrial and commercial activities. Also, it enables increased transparency and communication between governments and citizens.

A smart city represents the new trend in city development and governing by applying new technologies that enable the citizens to access and use information and applications from their city freely. The smart city concept has a different association from the people's perspective versus the technological standpoint. This is clear when countries set initiatives to become smart cities because they give different views around the smart city (Mohanty et al., 2016). It involves reducing costs and resource consumption in addition to more effectively and actively engaging with their citizens. One of the recent advancements that can potentially enhance smart city services is big data analytics. All around the world, many governments are considering adopting the smart city concept and implementing big data applications that support smart city components to reach the required level of sustainability and improve living standards.

## 1. Dealing with Data Growth

The most obvious challenge associated with big data is merely storing and analyzing all that information. It is estimated that the amount of information stored in the world's IT systems is growing by double about every two years. And enterprises have responsibility or liability for about 85% of that information (Gantz & Reinsel 2012). Some of the data is unstructured and forms part of the invisible web. Documents, photos, audio, videos, and other unstructured data can be challenging to search and analyze. To manage data growth, organizations are turning to different technologies. When it comes to storage, converged and software-defined storage can make it easier for companies to scale their hardware. However, technologies like compression, deduplication, and tiering can reduce space and the costs associated with big data storage.

## 2. Generating Insights on Time

Storing data is just not sufficient. In building smart cities, the use of big data to achieve business goals is crucial. According to the NewVantage Partners, (2017), the most common goals associated with big data projects included the following:

- Decreasing expenses through operational cost efficiencies

- Establishing a data-driven culture
- Creating new avenues for innovation and disruption
- Accelerating the speed with which new capabilities and services are deployed.
- Launching new product and service offerings

All of those goals can help the city become more competitive by extracting insights from big data and then acting on those insights quickly. Everyone wants decision-making to be faster, especially in banking, insurance, and healthcare. To achieve this, some organizations are looking to a new generation of extract-transform-load (ETL), the three database functions, and analytics tools that dramatically reduce the time it takes to generate reports. They are investing in software with real-time analytics capabilities that allow them to respond to developments in the marketplace immediately.

## 3. Recruiting and Retaining Data Analysts

To build a smart city it is inevitable to develop, manage, and run those applications that generate insights. This has increased the need for professionals with big data skills. The escalation in demand for data experts have resulted in salary increase which has impacted businesses in several ways:

- To cope with professional shortages, companies are increasing their budgets and recruitment and retention efforts.
- They are offering more training opportunities to current employees to develop the talent needed internally.
- Many organizations are looking into technological solutions and are purchasing data analytics solutions with self-service or machine learning capabilities.

These tools assist organizations in achieving their big data intelligence goals.

## 4. Integrating Disparate Data Sources

Disparate data consists of any data that are not alike and are distinctly different. They are unable to merge and provide organizations with business insight. They are of low quality and ineffective. This makes data preparation and integration difficult for organizations that collect data from more than just traditional sources. Data comes from many different places, such as social media streams, email systems, employee-created documents, and enterprise applications. Combining and reconciling this data so that it can be used to create reports can be very difficult. Many enterprises say they have not solved the data integration problem yet, although the vendors offer various data integration tools designed to make the process easier. In response, many enterprises are turning to new technology solutions. Companies have planned to invest in modern big data tools in the upcoming future. The most popular of which is a data analytics software and integration technology.

## 5. Validating Data

Data validation is similar and as vital as the idea of data integration. Organizations are receiving similar data from different systems, and the data in those different systems are prone to integration issues. For example, the e-commerce system may show daily sales at a certain level while the enterprise resource planning (ERP) system has a slightly different number. A hospital's electronic health record system may have one address for a patient, while a partner pharmacy has a different address on record. The process of getting those records to agree and making sure the files are accurate, usable, and secure is called data governance. Data governance is the fastest-growing area of concern presently. Solving data governance challenges is very complex and is usually requires a combination of policy changes and technology. Organizations often implement data governance policies and procedures. They may also invest in data management solutions designed to simplify data governance and help ensure the accuracy of data stores and the insights derived from them.

## 6. Securing Big Data

Security is also a significant concern for governments and organizations to build a smart city with big data stores. Some big data stores can be targets for hackers or advanced persistent threats. However, most organizations believe that existing data security methods are sufficient for their big data needs. Among those who do use other steps, the most popular include identity and access control, data encryption, and data segregation.

## SMART CITIES AND IoT

IoT is often a real object, broadly scattered, with low storage capability and processing capacity, to improve the reliability, performance, and security of the smart city and its infrastructures. Due to the rapid growth of the population density in urban cities, support and services are required to provide the necessities of the city residents. On this basis, there is a significant increase for digital devices, e.g., sensors, actuators, and smartphones, that drive substantial business potentials for the IoT since all devices can interconnect and communicate with each other on the Internet. The IoT prototype is subject to smart and self-configuring objects connected through a global network infrastructure (Duarte, & Ratti, 2016).

Smart cities have become more intelligent than before because of the recent developments in digital technologies. A smart city is equipped with different electronic elements employed by several applications, like street cameras for observation systems and sensors for transportation systems. Also, this can spread the usage of individual mobile devices. Therefore, by considering the heterogeneous environment, different terms, such as features of objects, contributors, motivations, and security rules, should be investigated (Álvarez et al. 2017).

The IoT is a broadband network that uses standard communication protocols, while its convergence point is the Internet. The central concept of the IoT is the universal presence of objects that can be measured, inferred, understood, and can change the environment. The IoT is enabled by the development of various objects and communication technologies such as smart devices, including mobile phones and other artifacts including appliances, landmark, monument, work of art that can integrate to provide a common target. The impact of the IoT on the life of users can be considered as its key feature (Duarte, & Ratti, (2016).

Lately, big data and IoT have enabled more innovative and creative developments for smart cities, including mobile crowdsensing and cloud computing (Sun et al. 2016). Mobile crowdsensing (MCS) represents a category of IoT applications that rely on data collection from mobile sensing devices such as smartphones. MCS applications are categorized based on the type of phenomenon being measured or mapped: environmental, infrastructure, and social (Ganti, & Lei, 2011).

- Environmental MCS applications measure natural phenomena in the environment, for example, air or noise pollution levels in a city;
- Infrastructure MCS applications measured events relating to public infrastructure, for example, traffic congestion, road conditions, parking availability, outages of public works, amongst others;
- Social MCS applications, individuals share sensed information among themselves, for example, individuals share their exercise data and compare exercise levels with the rest of the community to improve their daily exercise routines (Ganti, & Lei, 2011; Sun et al., 2016).

There are several unique advantages of MCS's. These include:

- Most mobile devices have significantly more storage, computation, and communication resources than mote-class sensors;

- They do not need additional dedicated tools to extend the existing industrial sensing system, as they use data coming from any device, especially personal devices;
- Mobile devices avoid the cost and time of deploying large-scale wireless sensor networks because of their portability.
- Human wisdom can be integrated into machine intelligence.

Cyber-physical cloud computing (CPCC) is a cyber-physical system composed of a set of cloud computing-based sensors, processing, control, and data services. It has many benefits, including efficient use of resources, modular composition, rapid development, scalability, smart adaption to the environment at every scale, reliable and resilient (Klopfenstein et al., 2019; Sun et al., 2016). Such a CPCC paradigm is fundamental for smart transportation, smart grid, smart healthcare, and smart disaster management. CPCC has the following benefits:

- Efficient use of resources
- Modular composition
- Rapid development and scalability
- Smart adaptation to the environment
- Reliable and resilient

Rotună et al., (2017) and Albino et al., (2015) describe that at the national level, there is a need to establish functional partnerships between all actors involved in a smart city ecosystem, including Public Administration, Private Companies, Professional Associations with a role in urban development and design. The collaboration between these entities will generate a coherent strategy. According to Kumar (2020) and Álvarez et al., (2017), some examples of smart city elements would be:

- **Traffic management**: Monitoring road systems will inform drivers about which route is best at any given time. Also, it will automatically manage the traffic lights to reduce congestion to the minimum, taking into account the traffic volume at certain times of the day.
- **Smart Grids**: provide the necessary amount of electricity depending on the demand. This way, power efficiency will be maximized.
- **Smart urban lighting**: these adjust the intensity of the light, depending on the people around them. Smart street lighting would also have different sensors to detect noise and air pollution levels.
- **Waste management**: Not all places generate the same kind or the same amount of waste. With smart containers and a sound fleet management

system, the routes can be tailored to any situation. This leads to efficient waste collection.

- **Smart city maintenance**: citizens can rely on smart systems to notify the City Council through their smartphones of any damages in the urban elements.

A smart city uses digital technologies or information and communication technologies (ICT) to enhance the quality and performance of public services to make the lives of citizens better (Spiro, 2006). It becomes easier to navigate for visitors and more serendipitous for locals. City officials and municipal governments are provided with a completely new way to connect with citizens and visitors and a more connected city to its people's works and feel better.

## Big Data

One of the most significant new ideas in computing is big data. There is a unanimous agreement that big data is revolutionizing businesses in the 21st century. Big data offers unprecedented insight, improved decision-making, and untapped sources of profit. According to Richards, & King, (2013) big data is the increasing size of data, the growing rate at which it is produced, and the expanding range of formats and representations employed.

Boehm, et al., (2018) argues that big data is data which "exceed(s) the capacity or capability of current or conventional methods and systems." In other words, the notion of "big" is relative to the current standard of computation. Big Data is mainly used to understand and optimize business processes, do financial trading, improve and optimize smart cities and nations, understand and target customers for better relationship management, improve healthcare, and transport services

In the USA, most government data is open access. This includes demographic as well as medical data of US citizens (Pise, & Uke, 2016). Different social networking websites such as Facebook are vast data sources that users share with the real world. Search engines such as Google provides statistics on search volume, which itself is big data. There are also financial data sets available at financial data finder, a form of big data. Log files of an application tend to increase in volume, thereby becoming a significant data source. IoT sensors and devices continuously generate data, as well.

This data is collected over time and from different sources such as web, sales, customer contact center, social media, and mobile devices. The information is typically loosely structured data that is often incomplete and inaccessible. To easily manage the data generated from such sources requires using data analytics. Big data analytics is the often-complex process of examining large and varied data sets or big data (Richards, & King, 2013). The process is used to uncover information, including hidden patterns, unknown correlations, market trends, and customer preferences that can help organizations make informed business decisions. Big data analytics also helps prevent cyber-attacks, which is one of the discussion topics of this chapter.

Big Data can be described using the 5Vs (Sagiroglu, & Sinanc, 2013) and includes:

- Volume (the era of size) examines the generation and collection of masses of data. The data scale becomes increasingly significant. The data produced is estimated in zettabytes, growing around 40 % every year.
- Velocity (the era of streaming data) focuses on the timeliness of the data. Specifically, data collection and analysis must be conducted quickly and timely to maximize the use of the commercial value of big data.
- Variety (the era of unstructured data) indicates the various types of data, including semi-structured and unstructured data such as audio, video, webpage, and text, as well as traditional structured data.
- Value (the era of the cost associated with data) focuses on data generation, collection, and analysis from different quarters. It is essential to state that today's data have some costs. The data itself can be a "commodity" that can be sold to third parties for revenue. Moreover, understanding the price or value of the data can help budget decision-makers estimate the storage cost of the data.
- Veracity (the era of data pollution that needs cleansing) There is a need to check the accuracy of the data by eliminating the noise through methodologies such as data pedigree and sanitization. This ensures data quality so that decisions made from the collected data are accurate and useful.

## Cyber Security

According to Pise, & Uke, 2016 (2016), cybersecurity is protecting information systems from theft or damage to the hardware, software, and information stored on them. A combination of methods applied to protect the reliability of an organization's security architecture is called cybersecurity. Being cyber secure means having data safeguarded against attack, damage, loss, or unauthorized access. According to Kim et al., (2018), by 2022, the cybersecurity marketplace is predictable to range US$170.4 billion. This swift market evolution is operated by an assortment of new technologies, for instance, IoT, big data, cloud-based applications, and programs. Previously, the approach taken by organizations and governments is reactive to fighting cyberthreats (Rao, 2015). This approach is expensive and complicated. The responsive approach is ineffective since there have been incidents of damaging breaches that have costs organizations a considerable amount of money.

According to Eastman(2015), most current cybersecurity threats can be classified into the following broad categories-

- Advanced persistent threats are quiet and continuous computer hacking processes.
- External software introduction, including malware and adware.
- Collect sensitive data, disrupt computer processes, and get access to private computer systems.
- Insider data theft.
- Social engineering and other forms of physiological manipulation.
- SQL injection and other code injection techniques.
- Trojan attacks.
- URL redirection or parameter tampering.

Cybersecurity threat actors may have varying degrees of financial support and motivators. Most threat actors can be categorized into these categories-

- Accidental: usually, an insider such as an employee or a contractor causes harm accidentally because of not having adequate experience.
- Opportunist. An external party uses opportunities to target known vulnerabilities in the system by employing worms, viruses, and other tools.
- Insider. Often inexperienced but can have higher-level skills who use opportunities to target known vulnerabilities in systems and policies for self-gain
- Hacktivist: External party with higher-level skills that target known vulnerabilities using DDoS attacks or malware as a path to introducing more sophisticated tools into a target system; often has a political or similar motive for action
- Professional criminal: Organized crime efforts including terrorist groups that use high-level and advanced skills to target financially relevant information

The targets and vectors for attacks also continue to evolve with new technologies. Though databases and Web sites remain traditional targets, IDC sees threats and vulnerabilities in several unique areas, including attacks on:

- Employee-owned devices
- Private, hybrid, or public clouds
- Social media and mobile devices
- The IoT where a wide variety of devices are connected to the Internet

Things like automation, machine learning, and shared threat intelligence in security architecture will help organizations keep pace with the growth of cyberattacks in the future. Machine learning can help tremendously in this regard. Machine learning can classify variants of known threats, identify patterns, and forecast the next steps of a cyber-attack. More across-the-board prevention manageable more swiftly diminishes overall cybersecurity risk to something easier to manage (Rao, 2015).

## Cloud Computation

Smart cities are a network of interconnected technologies that communicate, transfer, and analyze relevant data to maintain/improve urban operations. Today, such technologies are required in every urban infrastructure, including transportation, energy, economic and social development, traffic, environment, health, amongst others. In the real context, if smart cities wish to operate flawlessly at every level of the private and public sector, it is essential to deploy IoT and cloud computing together. Smart cities that are embracing both IoT and Cloud computing together are gaining better results. In other words, without the integration of the Cloud, it is next to impossible to visualize smart cities that can enhance public safety, promote efficient energy consumption, and develop a cohesive society while possessing the ability to track everything from waste management to congestion. Smart homes and cities cannot thrive without data fusion and mining. Managing, processing, and synthesizing mass flow of information in real-time may only be accomplished with state-of-the-art information systems architectures. Cloud computing technologies are a solid foundation to consolidate the physical infrastructure and streamline service delivery platforms.

Regarding the applications of cloud computing, there are multiple benefits. When cities develop digital infrastructure, it aids in producing enormous amounts of vital data for public and private organizations and creates a safer environment. Beyond that, smart cities also need to improve operations, increase transparency, and develop new ways to connect citizens with municipalities and businesses. Cloud computing has its applications and benefits in the same direction.

Cloud services are already a reality, and even if they are one step ahead of the legislation, a thorough analysis can identify, in most cases, solutions that cover most of the risks related to the use of a system of this type. Cloud computing is the long-awaited solution by large corporations - and not only by them - to simplify the network infrastructure required to conduct their activity and reduce equipment and maintenance costs. Despite the widely known benefits of cloud computing, the large-scale introduction of cloud computing services can generate several risks associated with data protection, particularly in what concerns the lack of control over personal data and insufficient information on how, where, and who is in charge of data processing. These risks should be evaluated when a company intends to contract a cloud computing service provider's services.

From the management and analysis perspectives, enterprises are using tools like NoSQL databases, Hadoop, Spark, big data analytics software, business intelligence applications, artificial intelligence, and machine learning to sieve through data stores to gain insights into the company's need. Simultaneously, technological aspects are not only the problem of big data, as citizens can also prove challenging. To manage data intelligence, organizations and government have to capitalize on the opportunities offered by big data. This sort of change can be tremendously difficult for cities to implement. Data fusion and mining are some of the critical aspects that smart cities require to develop. Even for a smart city to come into existence, processing, synthesizing, analyzing, and managing the mass flow of data is crucial. To ensure such changes happen consistently and efficiently, Cloud is necessary. The advancement in cloud computing supports swift delivery and consumption of data.

## RESEARCH METHODOLOGY

In today's age, cyber-crimes are growing at an exponential rate. It is estimated that cybercrime will cost $10.5 trillion annually by 2025 (Morgan, 2020). In 2015, that figure was $3 trillion. Specifically, a smart city is constructed upon different digital services, devices, and institutions is even more vulnerable to cyber-attacks. Big data analytics can be a way to combat cyber threats and create a secure smart city.

An extensive literature review was done to determine the gap in the body of knowledge. This methodology was chosen is because there are various scholarly articles published on a similar matter, which helped gain valuable insight into the research topic. Theory testing was conducted using interviews with industry experts. Five industry experts were selected across different sectors, namely (1) financial, (2) educational, and (3) technological. These industry professionals were selected as they have the credibility and experience to provide the proper direction on cybersecurity. The data generated were analyzed using open and axial coding.

Interviews were used to explore values, meanings, beliefs, thoughts, experiences, and feelings characteristic of the phenomenon under investigation (Halcomb, & Davidson, (2006. This methodology answered how big data analytics could assist a smart city in preventing cybersecurity threats. This led to theory expansion and conclusion.

### Findings

The results indicate that the key actors in securing a smart city security network are the different organizations and their employees. This is not surprising as disgruntled employees and carelessness accounts for the majority of security incidents in organizations.

Whereas big data analytics and cyber analytics tools allow organizations to recognize patterns of activity that represent network threats, the interviews indicate that not all organizations had preventive measures as they believe the current infrastructure does not support such a framework. However, not everyone is convinced of the need for data analytics since they consider that companies have solutions or mechanisms in-place that provide the same or similar capabilities as big data analytics against cyber-attacks.

This is even more complex for an entire city as the security infrastructure consists of different services, devices, and institutions. Data is generated from institutions through interactions with local citizens, civil servants, residents, students, and businesses. These individuals employ several smart devices such as phones, vehicles, televisions, amongst others. Smart citizens engage with the city's infrastructure through education, government, health, transportation, energy, and utilities. These institutions, devices, and services' interconnectivity expose the city to cybersecurity threats and vulnerabilities, proving detrimental to critical assets. Using big data analytics, a smart city can be secured from cyber threats. Consequently, this study proposes using the Cybersecurity Data Analytics Framework seen in Fig 1, where cybersecurity thinking is incorporated in the core function of the city's digital security infrastructure.

Several challenges of using big data analytics to secure a smart city infrastructure were identified and included- a massive volume of data and extraction of information from the enormous amount of data. It is also confident that the best way to protect a smart city infrastructure from cyber threats is by employing cybersecurity education and training for citizens and leaders. If the population is cybersecurity aware and has sufficient exercise, it is possible to reduce cybercrimes. Since data analytics can prevent cybersecurity threats by using machine learning algorithms, having collaboration between big data analytics and anti-virus security intelligence systems, and prioritizing alerts based on impact and severity almost certainly guarantee the chance of success. Organizations, institutions, and citizens must combine data analytics with anti-virus/anti-malware, anti-DoS/DDoS, security intelligence systems, and firewalls with big data analytics to be cyber secure.

Part of the proposed solution is the development of a cyber-prevention model, as seen in Figure 2. It is essential to detect threats and vulnerabilities, dissect the consequences and impact on the city's infrastructure and defend it from any such activities.

*Figure 1. Cybersecurity Data Analytics Framework*

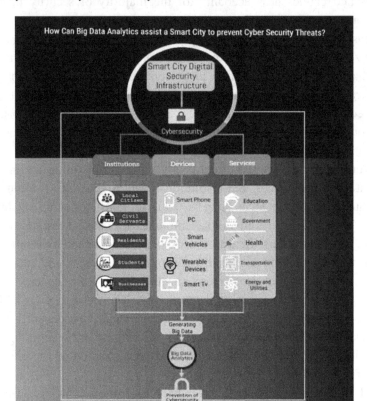

Between the layer of big data generated from smart city components, the detect function operates by ensuring mobile device security, cloud computing security, securing the Internet of things, and emerging threats. The dissect function is operating with big data analytics to analyze any anomalies. Furthermore, the defend function is working towards preventing cyber threats using big data analytics by employing techniques such as password creation, data encryption, data backup, maintenance of hardware, software, and security safeguards. Since the tools used for big data analysis operate in real-time and produce security alerts as per their severity level. The alerts are further expanded with more forensic details for fast detection and mitigation of cyber breaches. Smart cities institutions and organizations using big data analytics to contend with the continuously evolving, sophisticated cyber threats rising from the increased volumes of data generated daily. Big data analytics and machine learning combined with cyber prevention techniques allow a business and, consequently, smart cities to perform a thorough analysis of the information collected.

*Figure 2. Cyber Risks Prevention Model*

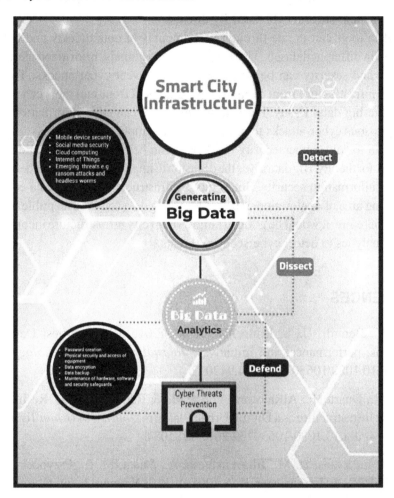

## CONCLUSION

Big Data is mainly used to comprehend and enhance business processes, refining and optimizing smart cities, understanding and targeting customers for better relationship management, transportation systems, refining healthcare systems, and much more (Pise, & Uke, 2016). Big data analytics usually means analyzing vast volumes of data and focusing on what is essential. Often, cybercriminals hide in these enormous volumes of data. This also makes it challenging to detect cyber-crimes. However, big data analytics can help in this regard by using its analytical skills.

Big data analytics can help detect abnormal behavior much earlier by using various machine learning algorithms for classification and prediction. Moreover, the collaboration between big data analytics and anti-virus security intelligence systems can help prevent cybersecurity threats.

Big data tools can iterate through vast amounts of data quickly and help find anomalies in different datasets. Upon detecting an anomaly, prioritized alerts based on impact and severity can be advantageous to prevent cyber-attacks. To defend smart city infrastructure from cyber threats, graphical front-end tools can visualize and explore big data. Lastly, big data log analytics can store information on bad actors' previous cyber-attacks to predict future attempts.

Big data to solve cybersecurity challenges can help smart cities build a robust framework for the city. Big data gives the occasion to improve situational understanding as well as information security. Smart city's infrastructure and big data concept is an emerging area of exploration, which adds to big data and is susceptible to cyber-attacks. Therefore, it would be good to build a smart city infrastructure incorporating big data analytics to detect cybersecurity threats.

## REFERENCES

Albino, V., Berardi, U., & Dangelico, R. M. (2015). Smart cities: Definitions, dimensions, performance, and initiatives. *Journal of Urban Technology*, *22*(1), 3–21. doi:10.1080/10630732.2014.942092

Álvarez, R., Duarte, F., AlRadwan, A., Sit, M., & Ratti, C. (2017). Re-Imagining Streetlight Infrastructure as a Digital Urban Platform. *Journal of Urban Technology*, *24*(2), 1–14. doi:10.1080/10630732.2017.1285084

Boehm, J. E., Evans, H. M., Jillavenkatesa, A., Nadal, M. E., Przybocki, M. A., Witherell, P. W., & Zangmeister, R. A. (2019). *2018 National Institute of Standards and Technology Environmental Scan*. NIST Publications.

Duarte, F., Ratti, C. (2016), Smart cities, big data, Internet of Things. *IEEE Standards University Magazine, 6*(4).

Eastman. (2015). *Big Data and Predictive Analytics: On the Cybersecurity Front Line*. IDC Whitepaper.

Ganti, R. K., & Lei, H. (2011). Mobile crowdsensing: Current state and future challenges. *IEEE Communications Magazine*, *49*(11), 32–39. doi:10.1109/MCOM.2011.6069707

Gantz, J. F., & Reinsel, D. (2012) The Digital Universe in 2020: Big Data, Bigger Digital Shadows, and Biggest Growth in the Far East Available from: https://www.emc.com/leadership/digital-universe/2012iview/index.htm

Halcomb, E. J., & Davidson, P. M. (2006). Is verbatim transcription of interview data always necessary? *Applied Nursing Research*, *19*(1), 38–42. doi:10.1016/j.apnr.2005.06.001 PMID:16455440

Juniper Research. (2018) Smart Cities – What's In It For Citizens? Available from: https://newsroom.intel.com/wp-content/uploads/sites/11/2018/03/smart-cities-whats-in-it-for-citizens.pdf

Kim, E., Gardner, D., Deshpande, S., Contu, R., Kish, D., & Canales, C. (2018). *Forecast Analysis: Information Security, Worldwide, 2Q18 Update*. Gartner Research.

Klopfenstein, L. C., Delpriori, S., Polidori, P., Sergiacomi, A., Marcozzi, M., Boardman, D., Parfitt, P., & Bogliolo, A. (2019). Mobile crowdsensing for road sustainability: Exploitability of publicly-sourced data. *International Review of Applied Economics*, 1–22.

Kumar, T. V. (2020). Smart living for smart cities. In *Smart Living for Smart Cities* (pp. 3–70). Springer.

Mohanty, S. P., Choppali, U., & Kougianos, E. (2016). Everything you wanted to know about smart cities: The internet of things is the backbone. *IEEE Consumer Electronics Magazine*, *5*(3), 60–70.

Morgan, S. (2020). Cybercrime To Cost The World $10.5 Trillion Annually By 2025 Cybercrime Magazine. Available from: https://cybersecurityventures.com/hackerpocalypse-cybercrime-report-2016/

NewVantage Partners Releases 5th Annual Big Data Executive Survey for 2017 (2017) Big Data Business Impact: Achieving Business Results through Innovation and Disruption. *Business Wire*

Pise, P. D., & Uke, N. J. (2016). Efficient security framework for sensitive data sharing and privacy preserving on big-data and cloud platforms. *In Proceedings of the International Conference on Internet of things and Cloud Computing* (pp. 1-5).

Rao, N.J. (2015). Cybersecurity: Issues and Challenges. *CSI Communications, 39.*

Richards, N. M., & King, J. H. (2013). Three paradoxes of big data. *Stan. L. Rev. Online*, *66*, 41.

Rotuna, C. I., Cirnu, C. E., & Gheorghita, A. (2017). Implementing Smart City Solutions: Smart City Map and City Drop. *Life (Chicago, Ill.)*, *28*, 313–327.

Sagiroglu, S., & Sinanc, D. (2013). *May. Big data: A review. In 2013 international conference on collaboration technologies and systems (CTS)*. IEEE.

Spiro, N. P. (2006). *A Competitive Model for Technology and City Planning: The Synergy of a Digital Urban Grid, a Wireless Cloud and Digital Architecture.* Ubiquitous City.

Sun, Y., Song, H., Jara, A. J., & Bie, R. (2016). Internet of things and big data analytics for smart and connected communities. *IEEE Access: Practical Innovations, Open Solutions, 4,* 766–773. doi:10.1109/ACCESS.2016.2529723

# Chapter 6
# Smart New York City:
## The Emergence of Sustainable Technological Innovations

**Wesley Palmer**
*York College, City University of New York, USA*

## ABSTRACT

*This study is an examination of the integration of information, telecommunications, mobile technology, and artificial intelligence (AI) technology in New York City's (NYC) infrastructure to maximize development and to improve the services provided to residents and their quality of life. Efficiency in service delivery is enhanced through smart technologies, and embracing innovation makes city systems efficient. The study is based on Barlow and Levy-Bencheton's smart cities theory. The research questions concern how the integration of smart technology improves the quality of life for residents and provides economic benefits for the city. The researcher surveyed 425 New York City residents to analyze the impact of smart technology on the city's systems. The findings indicated that 96% of residents experienced positive effects from smart technology on their quality of life. Smart cities have digitalized systems to enhance water supply, transportation, waste management, safety, public awareness, and health service delivery, among other essential services.*

## INTRODUCTION AND BACKGROUND

New York City is an emerging smart city that is aiming to improve the quality of life of its residents. The city mayor's office has a unit dedicated to providing innovative solutions that are designed to conserve the use, while maximizing the utility of

DOI: 10.4018/978-1-7998-5326-8.ch006

available resources. Some of the elements that make New York a model smart city are the integrated technologies applied in waste management, street lighting, street signs, bike lanes, water systems, sanitation, and air quality monitoring (Michell, 2016). According to Smart City New York, city management has embraced smart technological innovations to improve the Accelerated Conservation and Efficiency (ACE) program, an initiative that city management launched in 2013. The adoption of the program has helped conserve energy, and a reduction in electricity bills paid from taxpayers' coffers has been realized. These smart technology interventions may also help to reduce greenhouse gas emissions by approximately 80% by 2050 (Lee, Strickland, & Bienemann, 2017). Also, smart technology has been used in water meters to helped the water authorities maintain accurate records (Tobias, 2018). New York City government has also redesigned roadways to include bus and bikes lanes. The city also has designated spaces for parked cars to improve the flow of traffic and reduce time. Within the smart city development initiative, the subway system has been equipped with underground wireless signals that enable commuters to surf and chat while traveling.

The focus of this study was smart technology initiatives in New York City and their impact on the quality of life of city residents, as well as those who work and visit the city. The study sought to examine the impact on quality of life as a result of the emergence of smart systems and the economic benefits to the city. The study was conducted within the context that technological integration provides economic advantages to the city and improves quality of life. Specifically, the study sought to answer the following questions: What is the impact of smart technology integration on the quality of life of New York City residents? How does the city benefit from the implementation of smart systems?

To answer these questions, the researcher conducted an in-depth study in New York City using surveys. Five hundred surveys were distributed by hand, and 425 completed surveys were gathered and analyzed. The questions on the survey were arranged to solicit answers in the following contextual format: Do you strongly disagree, disagree, neither agree nor disagree, agree, or strongly agree. The answers and analysis helped to develop a strong qualitative study.

The findings revealed that the integration of smart technology and redesigned roadways in the city facilitate efficiency and improve the quality of life for resident, workers, and visitors. Earning the status of a smart city also helped to improve the city's economy.

# PURPOSE OF THE STUDY

The purpose of the study was to provide information about the integration of smart technology in New York City. The implementation of smart technology and the redesign of New York City as a smart city has improved service delivery in the city to ensure the population has a high standard of living (Gassmann, Böhm, & Palmié, 2019). City governments are the leading architects of transforming urban centers into smart cities; therefore, they have the burden of making the lives of city residents more comfortable. City governments realize the importance of taking the needs of its residents seriously and treating them like customers in an effort to retain professional and model residents, which is key to ensuring the sustainability of a city. In all their development plans, city governments must take into consideration the needs of the business community, academic institutions, neighborhood associations, researchers, nongovernment organizations, and residents. Throughout New York City, smart technologies are being implemented to meet the specific needs of the population. The city has opted for intelligent city systems to help improve the operations of city services. The city uses innovative technologies such as AI in creative design to enrich and create a new environmental experience for its residents. The smart city concept is citizen-driven, and all the processes are designed to improve quality of life, in terms of traffic movement, emissions reduction, and beautification (Pérez-Delhoyo, Andújar-Montoya, Mora, & Gilart-Iglesias, 2018). There is sufficient evidence that the governments of many cities, including smart cities, have opted to embrace smart technologies as technology continues to change the way people live.

# PROBLEM STATEMENT

The problem studied was that technology uses big data, which may invade residents' privacy. Smart city integration may interruption ordinary daily activities for those who do not adapt easily, and smart city technology may be susceptible to technological interruption such as system failure and hacking. In the event of a system collapse or compromise, the damage to city residents, workers, and visitors could be enormous. Smart city concepts focus on the analysis of big data to make keys decisions regarding a city's population; however, the data may not be sufficient and may result in decisions that neglect the social life systems of some residents that are essential to their well-being and to meaningful life experiences. In some cases, smart cities require the input of residents to create value and maximize the benefits of integrated systems (Schuler, 2016). If the input of residents is not considered, they may find the city systems difficult to use, which could negatively affect their quality of life. It is imperative that city governments orient the population toward digital systems in an effort to make the process easy and adaptable and thus to create a balance between the benefits and challenges across the societal divide.

## THEORETICAL FRAMEWORK

Central to this study was Barlow and Levy-Bencheton's (2019) smart city theory. Emerging concepts of the smart city theory provided insights to the study in terms of big data analytics, technological integration, system innovations, safety systems, redesigned infrastructure, and the use of digital technology as a means to provide comprehensive city services. The integration of smart city systems is a key consideration for city government as technology becomes smarter, more useful, and more available. The theoretical framework provided a succinct understanding of smart city integration; thus, a quality-of-life assessment is necessary to determine the type of impact that results from smart city integration (Schuler, 2016). The smart city assessments involved examining two main issues: (a) the quality of life of residents, workers, and visitors in terms of increased digitization, landscape redesign, and safety and (b) the invasion of privacy and identity theft.

The smart city assessment also included a critical analysis to determine the potential benefits that a smart city integrated system would add to the city's economy. The success of a smart city integrated system depends on the installation of appropriate system requirements. The analysis of the fundamental concept which is to maximize infrastructure development and improve service for the City residents, have laid the groundwork for this study. Smart city theory helps to explain the relevance of a smart city integration assessment and the impact of smart technology on stakeholders' quality of life (Tobias, 2018).

A wide range of empirical, social, academic, and scientific literature provides information on the emergence of smart cities and their global proliferation. Academic scholars and researchers have developed several conceptual arguments through an iterative process in an effort to explain the emergence of smart cities in many urban and metropolitan centers (Barlow & Levy-Bencheton, 2019). The literature reviewed presented mixed findings regarding the benefits of smart city integration. Some of the findings attributed the proliferation and integration of smart city technologies to the pervasive use of advanced technology in modern life (Michell, 2016). The focus of this research was determining smart city integration improves the quality of life for residents in urban cities.

This qualitative study followed a framework for collecting data, analyzing data, and addressing the research questions. The assessment of smart city technologies is necessary to determine the benefits and challenges involved in their use (Shelton & Lodato, 2018). The efforts to provide efficient city services and to keep pace with the changing needs of city residents in the light of modernization has created the smart city concept and led to its ongoing development.

Smart cities encourage the use of available resources to make the cities clean, productive, and safe, thus improving the quality of life of the residents. Smart cities are designed to provide centralized service delivery systems for the effective implementation and monitoring of assets. Also, the integration of smart city systems increases the rate of growth in towns and improves the provision of timely services. Smart cities offer a framework for the digitalized economy and advance the welfare of technologically advanced generations. Smart cities therefore create intelligent solutions for residents through upgraded and sustainable technologies.

## LITERATURE REVIEW

The literature review showed that 95% of New York City residents embraced the smart city integration initiative due to the improvement in the city's infrastructure in terms of underground Wi-Fi connectivity, redesigned parking spaces, bus lanes, bike lanes, park beautification, and improved safety systems. The cost of establishing smart cities is high because the smart city integration process is a continuous and long-term investment. The technology process of city integration is unique in terms of the types of technologies the city intends to use. Despite the cost of smart integration, smart digital systems make cities more user-friendly for residents and visitors (Cuzzillo & Cuzzillo, 2018).

In a smart city initiative, Bill Gates spent approximately $80 million to transform Belmont, Arizona, into a smart city; the city thus became an attractive place to live and work. According to extant literature, cities such as Tokyo, Dubai, London, and New York have spent several billion dollars to develop smart technologies due to demand (Siano, Shahrour, & Vergura, 2018). Tokyo has been improving its city system to meet the rising demands of city users and dwellers; thus, increased the cost of smart city integration exponentially. New York City recently spent $350 million for the ACE program for smart city systems to make the city more efficient (Tobias, 2018).

Researchers have contended that transforming cities into smart cities is an expensive endeavor. Although the initial cost of the ACE program is high, the benefits to New York City are greater, in that the initiative spurred economic growth and helped reduce the city's administrative, energy, water, and waste management costs. In addition, the initiative creates a healthy environment and by extension improves the quality of life for city users (Falkner, 2017).

## Benefits of Smart Cities

There are numerous benefits to city populations and economies from smart city integration. Some of the benefits include improvements to large- and small-scale business operations as well as increased job opportunities and cultural experiences. The development of a smart infrastructure in city systems is critical to economic growth. Smart cities also offer seamless communication between sensors, systems, people, and businesses (Anton, 2018). Technological innovation creates the framework to build smart cities due to the efficient processing of information in terms of tracking people's movement and resource use. Smart city systems allow smart cities to respond faster to disasters than traditional urban centers. The technology innovations that are common in most smart cities help to increase additional innovations and city revenues.

## Efficiencies of Smart Cities

Smart cities tend to be more efficient than traditional cities in providing timely solutions. Through the use of cameras and sensors, gaps in the community can be quickly identify fixed, thereby leading to a higher level of efficiency and sustainability (James, 2019). Energy conservation, which is a vital component of economic development, can also be monitored. New York City promotes efficiency through the use of solar energy generation for government and residential use. Smart city systems are digitalized; therefore, it is easy to monitor service delivery and manage data (Siano et al., 2018).

Supervising the workforce is enhanced in smart cities through the use of analytics. Thus, smart cities can meet their deadlines and prevent unnecessary delays in the provision of essential services (James, 2019). In most smart cities, traffic flow is well-organized and managed. It is also easy to access the city from smart bridges, tunnels, and highways within a short amount of time, which makes them preferred places to travel and work. Smart cities enable interconnections between people through network technology and infrastructure (Anton, 2018). Thus, efficiency improves through integrated systems that enhance the quality of life of residents and help to develop better connections and interactions by creating recreational parks that improve the urban environment.

## Cost of Smart Cities

The costs related to developing a smart city differ among academic scholars and economists. Academic scholars assess cost on the basis of environment impact, while economists assess cost on the basis of economic opportunities. The progression of smart technologies has developed over time to include smartphones, smart thermostats, smarts lights, smart homes, smart businesses, smart vehicles, and smart cities. Although these inventions bring comfort to people's lives, they all come at a cost. The primary cost of a smart city is increasing new infrastructure with technological innovations. For example, building new bridges and roads that are built across a city will increase city costs significantly (Anton, 2018). Demolishing and rebuilding toll-less systems is also expensive. Smart city systems have eliminated a lot of jobs and thus increased unemployment rates, which is also a cost to city governments. New York City recently implemented electronic tolls to alleviate traffic jams in the city and this new technology requires funding for infrastructure development.

## DATA ANALYSIS

Table 1 contains the themes that emerged from participants' answers to the survey questions based on the identification of significant categories in participants' responses.

*Table 1. Significant Themes That Answer the Research Questions*

| Themes | No. of participants (*N* = 425) | % of participants who experienced the themes |
|---|---|---|
| 1. Improved quality of life | 410 | 96 |
| 2. Efficiency in service delivery | 400 | 94 |
| 3. Improved safety | 380 | 89 |
| 4. Residents' privacy invasion | 415 | 97 |
| 5. Increase cost of living | 420 | 98 |

The initial analysis phase involved in vivo coding to locate various themes, assign broad categories, and assign titles from the interview transcripts. In the second analysis phase, the researcher applied axial coding, which involved refining the data by clustering, eliminating, and merging categories. The researcher also used selective coding to select the themes he would use to analyze, compare, and contrast the data. The five major themes that emerged that answer the research questions were improved quality of life, efficiency in service delivery, improved safety, residents' privacy invasion, and increased cost of living.

*Table 2. Descriptive Statistics*

| Improved Quality of Life | | Efficiency in Service Delivery | | Improved Safwety | | Resident' Privacy Invasion | | Increased Cost of Living | |
|---|---|---|---|---|---|---|---|---|---|
| Mean | 4.9764706 | Mean | 4.65411765 | Mean | 4.32235294 | Mean | 4.9152941 | Mean | 4.9270588 |
| Standard Error | 0.0073613 | Standard Error | 0.02309985 | Standard Error | 0.02269785 | Standard Error | 0.0135224 | Standard Er | 0.0126287 |
| Median | 5 | Median | 5 | Median | 4 | Median | 5 | Median | 5 |
| Mode | 5 | Mode | 5 | Mode | 4 | Mode | 5 | Mode | 5 |
| Standard Deviation | 0.1517563 | Standard Deviation | 0.47621566 | Standard Deviation | 0.46792811 | Standard Deviation | 0.2787717 | Standard D | 0.2603464 |
| Sample Variance | 0.02303 | Sample Variance | 0.22678135 | Sample Variance | 0.21895671 | Sample Variance | 0.0777137 | Sample Var | 0.0677802 |
| Kurtosis | 37.983577 | Kurtosis | -1.5845627 | Kurtosis | -1.42473777 | Kurtosis | 6.9941991 | Kurtosis | 8.9068844 |
| Skewness | -6.309109 | Skewness | -0.6503202 | Skewness | 0.76288214 | Skewness | -2.9935442 | Skewness | -3.2962086 |
| Range | 1 | Range | 1 | Range | 1 | Range | 1 | Range | 1 |
| Minimum | 4 | Minimum | 4 | Minimum | 4 | Minimum | 4 | Minimum | 4 |
| Maximum | 5 | Maximum | 5 | Maximum | 5 | Maximum | 5 | Maximum | 5 |
| Sum | 2115 | Sum | 1978 | Sum | 1837 | Sum | 2089 | Sum | 2094 |
| Count | 425 | Count | 425 | Count | 425 | Count | 425 | Count | 425 |
| Confidence Level (95.0%) | 0.0144691 | Confidence Level (95.0%) | 0.04540449 | Confidence Level (95.0%) | 0.04461431 | Confidence Level (95.0%) | 0.0265793 | Confidence Level (95.0%) | 0.0248226 |

The statistical inference of the data in Table 2 shows strong evidence that the integration of smart city systems into city infrastructures impact cities in positive ways. Four of the five themes fall within a narrow confidence interval, which indicates 95% certainty of the accuracy of the findings.

## DISCUSSION

### Advantages of Smart Cities

Smart cities have enhanced communications between the government and residents; hence, the government is more accountable and provides residents a platform to make complaints and recommendations. Smart cities also help foster responsible citizenship due to enhanced connectivity through websites and mobile applications (Shelton & Lodato, 2018). Further, smart cities can protect the environment and minimize carbon emissions through innovation. Finally, smart cities may help to create an environment with fewer health hazards. Technology-driven cities are staged to create employment and economic opportunities.

Residents of smart cities can participate in many income-generating opportunities that improve their standard of living. In addition, essential government services are accessible and non-bureaucratic (Khalifa, 2019). One of the advantages of smart cities is reduced pollution. In New York City, pollution reductions result from the establishment of clean industries, the development of environment-friendly buildings, and the use of clean energy resources such as electricity (Khalifa, 2019). The emergence of smart transportation systems that use electricity may reduce pollution. Smart cities are able to create environment-friendly products through waste energy systems and recycling systems. Wasted energy is reduced through smart systems, and the use of resources is rationalized. Smart energy systems that use sensors to monitor light and heat may control the temperature and comfort of homes efficiently.

## Disadvantages of Smart Cities

Some of the disadvantages of smart city integration include data security and privacy. The large volume of data collected and owned by New York City makes the city vulnerable to cybercrime and data breaches (Kitchin, 2015). Furthermore, the cost of installing and maintaining smart city technology is high; therefore, smart cities are expensive to live and work. In addition, at the pre-commercial stages, that is, before the monetization of city systems, city management face financial challenges in obtaining the appropriate resources necessary to maintain the technological fitness needed to maximize economic and social benefits (Baltac, 2019; Kitchin, 2015) Also, business models for smart city technologies remain underdeveloped.

Although New York City is among the top-ranking smart cities; the city has fallen behind in certain categories of smart city integration. For example, New York City is near the bottom of the list for social cohesion and the environment. These areas remain a great concern for the city, as they require substantial improvement. In an effort to improve in these areas, New York City created the ACE program to save energy bills and reduce greenhouse gas emissions generated by city agencies. The New York City Fire Department would benefit the most, as they operate 24 hours a day, 7 days a week (Khalifa, 2019). Installing smart lighting solutions helped agencies that adopted the ACE program reduce energy use by up to 3 million kilowatt-hours. The ACE program also helps reduce greenhouse gas emissions by up to 520 metric tons of carbon dioxide each year.

City budget constraints may prevent essential components from facilitating the process in terms of providing technical training for smart technology staff, administrators, and users. Poor and untimely implementation could affect the success of smart city integration. For example, the installation of millions of sensors throughout New York City has become problematic, as too many devices are interfering with wireless and telecommunications (James, 2019). In addition, rush hour traffic is difficult to manage in cities, which minimizes technological benefits. Smart city integration has not led to a significant decrease in air pollution (Hatem, 2017). Thus, poor air quality could affect certain business sector such as food processing plants which is susceptible to air pollutions. In addition, interpreting data represents a major challenge in a smart city due to the diverse population and the large number of activities involved. Smart cities often experience the lack expert's assistance to interpret and use data correctly.

## Use of Artificial Intelligence in Smart Cities

New York City has adopted AI because it offers smart services that go beyond human ability, especially in law enforcement. AI is used in smart cities to analyze big data. In addition, AI helps to address the challenges associated with a large urban population that ranges from traffic jams, crimes, and fires and medical emergencies. AI helps organize critical service delivery systems such as 911 dispatchers (Özdemir & Hekim, 2018). AI is also used in various agencies to provide efficient service through the integration of algorithms and the configuration of a computer network that connects city users.

AI enhances efficiency in many applications where computer systems are required to store and process large amounts of data. The primary goal of AI in smart city integration is to provide technical solutions that integrate human and machine interventions (Batty, 2018). AI simulates human intelligence in its processes to evaluate issues and match them with appropriate and well-defined answers. In smart cities, AI helps to analyze complex urban problems that require a high level of comprehension and assessment (Baltac, 2019). AI is used in many metropolitan cities, including London, New York, and Tokyo, to manage traffic and prevent congestion within the Central Business District. In some the smart cities, AI is used to reduce the waste of essential resources through efficient scheduling and routing of traffic.

## LIMITATIONS OF SMART CITIES

Most smart cities have not been able to maximize their potential due to several issues. The influx of people into cities in pursuit of a better life has brought several challenges to smart cities. Some cities are not designed to cater to large populations; thus, over population burdened the infrastructure (Falkner, 2017). To operate efficiently, smart cities require multiple sensors, which are costly. Therefore, it is impractical to have sufficient sensors to monitor the large number of city residents. The situation becomes even more complicated in cities that often experience influxes of new residents, which makes it challenging to determine the number of detectors required at a given time.

## CONCLUSION

San Francisco is leading the development of innovation and creativity in smart cities. The city has well-developed innovations that have made its parking system one of the best in the United States, Europe and Asia. San Francisco has also been able to initiate green projects that focused on environmental conservation. The city of San Francisco has been transformed, and researchers have recognized the city as a sustainable smart green city (Lee & Hancock, 2012). New York City, Tokyo, Dubai, London, and Ontario have also made significant progress in their smart city integration efforts as well. Big data analytics and the availability of cutting-edge technologies are driving cities out of their traditional modes of operation. The integration of smart infrastructure integration and development in New York City has resulted in an improved quality of life, efficient service delivery, and improved safety for city residents, workers, and visitors. The emergence of smart cities has revolutionized city operations and services. Thus, creates a more efficient and robust experiences for residents and visitors. The installation of smart maps and electronic audio street crossing announcers, have improved the ambient environment of cities. Hence, the stage is set for reduce accidents, enhance safety, time savings, and reduction is city budgets as well as financial and human resources.

## REFERENCES

Anton, R. (2018). *Intelligent communication and patterning in smart cities.* Assistive Technologies in Smart Cities. Https. doi:10.5772/intechopen.79629

Baltac, V. (2019). Smart cities—A view of societal aspects. *Smart Cities, 2*(4), 538–548. doi:10.3390martcities2040033

Barlow, M., & Levy Bencheton, C. (2019). *Smart cities, smart future: Showcasing tomorrow.* Wiley.

Bassi, A. (2016). Looking at smart cities with an historical perspective. *Designing, Developing, and Facilitating Smart Cities,* 3–15. doi:10.1007/978-3-319-44924-1_1

Batty, M. (2018). Artificial intelligence and smart cities. *Environment and Planning. B, Urban Analytics and City Science, 45*(1), 3–6. doi:10.1177/2399808317751169

Cuzzillo, T., & Cuzzillo, T. (2018, March 28). *Who pays for smart cities?* https://www.datadoodle.com/2018/04/12/who-pays-for-smart-cities/

Falkner, N. (2017, May 10). A smart city is more than international ratings: A smart city works for you. So what do you want? *The Advertiser*. https://www.adelaidenow. com.au/

Gassmann, O., Böhm, J., & Palmié, M. (2019). The future of cities and the concept of smart cities. *Smart Cities*, *3–4*, 3–4. Advance online publication. doi:10.1108/978-1-78769-613-620191007

James, E. (2019). Smart cities: The future of urban development. *Forbes*. https://www.forbes.com/sites/jamesellsmoor/2019/05/19/smart-cities-the-future-of-urban-development/#72a774662f90

Khalifa, E. (2019). Smart cities: Opportunities, challenges, and security threats. *Journal of Strategic Innovation and Sustainability*, *14*(3), 2019–2079.

Kitchin, R. (2015). Making sense of smart cities: Addressing present shortcomings. *Cambridge Journal of Regions, Economy and Society*, *8*(1), 131–136. doi:10.1093/cjres/rsu027

Lee, J., Strickland, C., & Bienemann, J. (2017). *Reducing greenhouse gas emissions attributed to the building sector in New York City*. American Society of Civil Engineers. *International Conference on Sustainable Infrastructure*, New York, NY. 10.1061/9780784481202.031

Lee, J. H., & Hancock, M. G. (2012). Toward a Framework for Smart Cities: A Comparison of Seoul, San Francisco and Amsterdam. *Stanford Program on Regions of Innovation and Entrepreneurship*, *1*(1), 1-22. https://sprie.gsb.stanford.edu/people/Jung-hoon_Lee/

Michell, N. (2016, November 23). *New York awarded 2016 Best Smart City*. https://cities-today.com/new-york-awarded-2016-best-smart-city/

Özdemir, V., & Hekim, N. (2018). Birth of Industry 5.0: Making sense of big data with artificial intelligence, "the Internet of Things" and next-generation technology policy. *OMICS: A Journal of Integrative Biology*, *22*(1), 65–76. doi:10.1089/omi.2017.0194 PMID:29293405

Pérez-Delhoyo, R., Andújar-Montoya, M. D., Mora, H., & Gilart-Iglesias, V. (2018). Citizen participation in urban planning-management processes: Assessing urban accessibility in smart cities. *Proceedings of the 7th International Conference on Smart Cities and Green ICT Systems*. 10.5220/0006704202060213

Schuler, D. (2016). Smart cities + smart citizens = civic intelligence? *Human Smart Cities*, 41–60. doi:10.1007/978-3-319-33024-2_3

Shelton, T., & Lodato, T. (2018). From smart cities to smart citizens? *Creating Smart Cities*, 144–154. doi:10.4324/9781351182409-11

Siano, P., Shahrour, I., & Vergura, S. (2018). Introducing *Smart Cities*: A transdisciplinary journal on the science and technology of smart cities. *Smart Cities*, *1*(1), 1–3. doi:10.3390martcities1010001

Smart City New York. (n.d.). *Cooperation to Innovation*. https://mobility.here.com/smart-city-new-york-cooperation-innovation

Tobias, M. (2018). *How New York is becoming a smart city*. https://www.ny-engineers.com/blog/how-new-york-is-becoming-a-smart-city

# Chapter 7
# Smart Parking:
## The Cornerstone of a Smart City

**Fenio Annansingh**
*Department of Business and Economics, York College, City University of New York, USA*

## ABSTRACT

*With the increase of urban population and traffic congestion, smart parking is a strategic, economic, environmentally friendly solution for cities looking to remain connected. A sustainable parking system parking is connected in some way to every facet of the city that is water, waste, energy, and transportation. With the information and communication technology evolution and the development of the internet of things, drivers can more efficiently find satisfying parking spaces with smart parking services. This research adopts a survey approach by employing the use of questionnaires. From the questionnaire, descriptive data analysis is used to synthesize, analyze, and interpret the data. The result elicits user requirements and constraints for the development of a mobile app solution that will eliminate unnecessary traffic and ensure the maximum utilization of municipal parking facilities. These user requirements will determine the design and development of a mobile application that saves time, reduce the environmental impact, and improve the quality of life.*

## INTRODUCTION

About 70% of the world's population, over six billion people, will live in cities and surrounding regions by 2050. To cope with these demands cities need to be smart. A smart city is driven and enabled technologically by the Internet of Things (IoT).

DOI: 10.4018/978-1-7998-5326-8.ch007

The IoT is an evolution of the current ubiquitous network of interconnected objects that not only harvests information from the environments and interacts with the physical world but also uses existing Internet standards to provide services for data transfer, analytics, and applications (Jin et al., 2014, Sha, et al. 2020).

Parking challenges faced in cities and urban areas indicate a gap between parking demand and the number of available parking spaces. This gap is due to several reasons:

- Several cities were planned with narrow streets and less traffic.
- Increase in population densities of these cities.
- There is a high concentration of activities and commercial facilities such as with office buildings.
- A failure of the mass transit system offered in the city. Therefore, citizens depend on private transportation.
- There are no or few allocated parking spaces (Ibrahim, 2017).

Transportation systems do not just move people around. They are also catalysts for moving cities towards a smarter solution. Quite often, between state-level inertia and the shortage of investment in infrastructure and public transportation efforts, several cities face gridlock when it comes to transportation reform. Consequently, many individuals rely on private means of transportation and require parking, which can be problematic in a city such as N.Y. Studies (Shoup, 2006; Vishnubhotla et al., 2010; Pierce and Shoup, 2013) show drivers spend an enormous amount of time and resources seeking parking. For example, drivers often spend over 20 minutes seeking parking in city centers, accounting for as much as 30% of the traffic congestion (Byrd, 2014). During weekdays this figure can increase as high as 54%. Shortage of parking space, high parking fees, and traffic congestion resulting from drivers searching for a parking place are just a few examples of everyday parking problems.

To solve these parking issues, cities and residents are looking towards technology for assistance. Current parking systems that deliver timely information about available parking spaces require sensors to be deployed in the parking areas to monitor occupancy, quick data processing units and, practical insights from data collected over various sources. There are many parking applications currently in existence that provide similar services. These applications are costly and have not received widespread acceptance. The reason is twofold: First, providing real-time parking availability information requires knowing in real-time when a user vacates a parking space. Second, such an application needs a significant user rate to be successful. Hence, this research aims to identify user needs in developing a community-based social parking application where users will assist/notify other users' parking space availability. The study seeks to close the gap between software developers of such parking applications and uses of the system. Thus, it aims to capture the requirement specification for a real-time parking system that loosens the need for specialized infrastructure, relying instead on the smartphone's sensors and the ubiquitous Wi-Fi and cellular infrastructure. Therefore, this paper discusses the expectations and needs of drivers of smart city parking.

## Problems with Parking in New York City

New York City metropolitan region has over 20 million people, scattered throughout 25 counties in three boroughs. The city hosts up to 11 million passenger cars in addition to commercial and freight vehicles. New York City is said to have the second-worst traffic congestion in the U.S, suffers from air pollution, and ranked worst on commuting times. The congestion experienced by drivers restricts freedom of mobility, which leads to undue delay or frustration. These traffic bottlenecks create a colossal waste of resources and diminish productivity and well-being.

However, the city boasts much on-street free parking, which is available to drivers in different areas. In vicinities with meters, the prices are usually low and independent of the demand for parking. This creates a problem where drivers are circulating in a specific area looking for free or affordable parking. In some instances, drivers may double park and wait for a particular parking location, further exacerbating the congestion problem. Approximately 30% of a city's traffic results from drivers searching for a parking space (Gautam, 2018). In New York, the average time spent on parking is about 17 hours a year (USA Today, 2017). The hunt adds up to an estimated $345 per driver wasted in time, fuel, and emissions, costing drivers $4.3 billion. Likewise, the average cost of parking for two hours in NYC is $33. In response, this chapter proposes a free parking application capable of providing drivers with real-time parking availability information.

## REVIEW OF THE LITERATURE

### Smart City

Most urban infrastructures are ad-hoc structures and services, which emerged over time in response to businesses, residents, and commuters' needs. No utility, service, activity, or facility currently can be monitored, measured, and managed through a combination of devices connected to a computer network. A smart city incorporates web connectivity, analytics, mobile solutions, sensors, data collection, and other technology. It can include surveillance systems utilized by law enforcement, smart congestion-mitigating traffic systems, LED streetlights equipped with motion sensors, smart grids, and intelligent water systems. Smart cities contain a myriad of objects that receive, collect, and transmit data. Along with data analytics, these data collection tools allow for the creation of innovative products and services, such as a social parking mobile application (Neirotti et al., 2014; Su et al., 2011; Ibrahim, 2017).

The smart city structure has several layers of perception, network, and application, which can assist with the design by making the city increasingly appreciable, measurable, interconnected, interoperable, and intelligent (Su et al., 2011). While smart cities often rely on ICT solutions, they are considered just one of the various resources for projects and approaches required for urban planning and living.

ICT-based solutions, however, are just one of the resources required for projects and approaches to urban planning and living that have the aim of improving the economic, social, and environmental conditions of a city. Cities that are better equipped with ICT systems are not necessarily smarter. Likewise, the number of "smart" initiatives launched by a municipality is not an indicator of city performance or success but instead based on a strong relationship with the citizens, government, and the private sector. Therefore, the city's success depends on building positive relationships than completing a single project.

Smart cities consist of IoT, cloud computing, software solutions, user interfaces, and communication networks. The connection of these devices generates vast volumes of data, which, when analyzed, facilitates improving both public and private sector efficiency, enabling economic development and improving citizen's lives.

## Internet of Things

Creating smart cities is now becoming possible with the emergence of the IoT. However, one of the critical features required for smart cities' development is car parking facilities and traffic management systems. For years, parking management systems have been among the city's vital concerns. Some cities have carried out studies on the smart parking concept and the impacts these systems can have on the socio-economic, political, and environmental climate.

The IoT is a communication model in which objects are equipped with microcontrollers, transceivers for digital communication, and the appropriate protocol stacks, which allows them to communicate with other devices and the users (International Telecommunication Union, 2014). The IoT concept seeks to make the Internet more immersive and pervasive by enabling increased accessibility and interactivity with several devices such as surveillance cameras, monitoring sensors, and vehicles. It fosters the development of applications that can provide new services to citizens, organizations, and government institutions and consequently finds application in several domains, such as home and industrial automation, healthcare, intelligent energy management, and traffic management. The use of the

IoT paradigm in an urban context is interesting. It directly results from the strong push of public institutions and governments to adopt ICT solutions to manage public affairs, thus creating the smart city concept (Barriga, 2019). Urban implementation and utilization of IoT make several benefits in managing and optimizing traditionally public services, such as transport and parking, lighting, surveillance and maintenance of public areas, preservation of cultural heritage, and garbage collection.

With the ever-increasing number of private car users, parking and traffic congestion problems are solvable if drivers are informed in advance about the available parking spaces at and around their intended destination. Recent advances in creating low-cost, low-power embedded systems are helping developers to build new applications for IoT. These developments present an opportunity for smart cities to undertake actions to enhance the efficiency of available parking resources, reducing searching times, traffic congestion, and road accidents. With the advanced developments in sensor technology, many smart cities have opted to deploy various IoT-based monitoring systems (Khanna and Anand, 2016; (Sha et al., 2020). The IoT system architecture comprises three layers: the perception layer, the network layer, and the service or application layer.

## Perception Layer

It is the lowest layer of the conventional architecture core layer of IoT. The primary function is to gather useful information/data of the physical world or environment.

## Network Layer

The transport layer is also responsible for connecting to other smart things, network devices, and servers. It includes access and core network, provides transparent data transmission capability. This layer provides an efficient, robust, trusted network infrastructure platform and large-scale industrial application.

## Service/Application Layer

This layer is responsible for delivering personalized applications specific to the user. The primary responsibility of the application layer is to bridge the gap between users and applications. It includes data management and application service sub-layer. The data management layer processes complex data and uncertain information, such as restructuring, directory service, and cloud-computing technologies. The application service sub-layer transforms information into content and provides an excellent user interface for enterprise applications and end-users. IoT devices would be unable to share data and information without application layer protocols either from device-to-device or device-to-server.

## IoT Technologies

According to Lee and Lee (2015). These are the five IoT technologies are widely used for the deployment of successful IoT-based products and services:

## Radio Frequency Identification (RFID)

RFID technology identifies the animate or inanimate use of radio waves and enables wireless data transmission. It is used to store more data than traditional barcodes. RFID allows for the automatic identification and capture of data using radio waves, a tag, and a reader. The tag contains data in a global RFID-based item identification system called the Electronic Product Code (EPC). Wireless sensor networks (WSN) are comprised of spatially distributed autonomous sensor-equipped devices. They monitor the physical or environmental conditions and can work with RFID systems to track the status of devices such as their location, temperature, and movements. An RFID system generally consists of tags (transmitters/ responders) and readers (transmitters/receivers). The tag uses a microchip connected with an antenna to identify objects. The RFID reader communicates with the RFID tag through radio waves. RFID technology's main benefit is the automated identification and data capture function, which reduces the cost of the already existing systems such as bar codes (Jia et al., 2012).

Three types of RFID tags are generally used. Passive RFID tags rely on radio frequency transferred from the reader to the tag and are typically powered by electromagnetic energy transmitted from an RFID reader. Examples of passive RFIDs are seen in supply chains and file tracking. Active tags are battery-powered and continuously broadcast a signal. They are commonly used as "beacons" and can contain external sensors to monitor temperature, pressure, hospital laboratories. The semi-passive tag operates similarly to the passive tag but uses batteries to power the microchip.

RFIDs have several applications in retail, logistics, and supply, manufacturing, and transportation. Therefore, RFID technology is ideal for automatic vehicle identification that requires no personnel. RFID technology can be utilized in smart city applications for a smart city to monitor and track physical objects while steady or moving. The status of such items is collected along with their unique identification number for further processing.

## Middleware

Middleware software is a layer interposed between software applications to perform communication outside of the operating system. Middleware technology transfers information from and between programs in a distributed environment, making it independent from communication protocols, O.S., and hardware. It also facilitated common uses such as data management, application services, messaging, authentication, and API management. Using middleware is ideal for IoT application development. Most IoT middleware follows a service-oriented approach to support an unknown and dynamic network topology.

## Cloud Computing

Cloud Computing can access a shared pool of configurable resources owned and maintained by a third party via the Internet. The "cloud" comprises hardware, computers, storage, networks, applications, interfaces, and services that provide users access to infrastructures, computing power, applications, and services on demand, which are independent of locations. It represents a convergence of two significant developments in information technology: I.T. efficiency and business agility. I.T. efficiency embraces green computing, whereby computing resources are used more efficiently. Business agility indicates that businesses can use computational tools that can be deployed and scaled rapidly by reducing the need for massive investments (Dillon et al., 2010). The IoT generates an enormous amount of data from devices connected to the Internet and, consequently, requires ample data storage and immense processing speed to enable real-time decision-making. Cloud computing provides the solution for coping with substantial data streams and processing them for an unprecedented number of IoT devices in real-time (Arora et al., 2013). Specifically, the benefits of cloud computing are:

- reduces the cost of hardware.
- lowers the cost of entry for small companies entering into market segments that are generally dominated by larger corporations.
- provides access to hardware resources with no upfront capital investments, leading to a faster entry time to market in many businesses.
- lowers the I.T. barriers to innovation, as can be with online applications such as Facebook and YouTube.
- allows for the effortless scalability of organizational services – which are increasingly reliant on accurate information. Therefore, the user gains the maximum capability of computing while having the minimum hardware requirement.

- allows for the development of new classes of applications and delivers services such as parallel batch processing, and business analytics

## IoT Application Software

The IoT applications allow reliable device-to-device and human-to-device interactions to occur. IoT applications need to ensure that data/messages received are acted upon promptly and adequately. Device-to-device applications do not always require data visualization. Increasingly, human-centered IoT applications allow the display to present information to end-users in an intuitive and easy-to-understand way. It also allows interaction with the environment. IoT applications need to be built with intelligence so devices can monitor the situation, identify problems, communicate with each other, and potentially resolve issues without the need for human intervention (Lee and Lee, 2015).

## Wireless Sensor Networks (WSN)

Wireless Sensor Networks (WSNs) aims to gather environmental data. They are self-configured and infrastructure-less wireless networks used to monitor physical or environmental conditions and cooperatively pass data through the system to a central location or sink where it can be observed and analyzed. A sink functions as an interface between users and the network. Required information is retrieved from the network by injecting queries and gathering results from the sink. Typically, a wireless sensor network contains hundreds of thousands of sensor nodes. These nodes communicate using radio signals and are equipped with sensing and computing devices, radio transceivers, and power components. The individual nodes are inherently resource-constrained since they have limited processing speed, storage capacity, and communication bandwidth. Therefore, many nodes, limited battery power, and the data-focused nature of routing make routing a challenging problem in WSN (Kumar et al., 2020). Applications of WSN include tracking, monitoring, surveillance, environmental tracking, building automation, control system, and military (Beom-Su et al., 2017).

## Smart Parking

Parking is a $30 billion-a-year industry (Suqi, 2020). Smart Parking combines technology and human innovation to achieve faster and easier parking of vehicles using as few resources as possible—such as fuel, time, and space. There is a large variety of parking lots available for public use, namely street and off-street. On-street parking is convenient and offers access to nearby locations. Off-street parking spaces can accommodate large amounts of vehicles and are either operated by local authorities or private companies. Various payment methods and technologies are employed for both parking systems. For on-street spaces, meters that accept coins or cards are widely used.

Parking and transportation are both essential in the movement of people and goods. Both parking and traffic congestion are constant sources of driver frustration. Bottlenecks in parking and traffic management are not always limited to peak times. Smart parking technology is crucial for easing traffic congestion in cities. A smart parking application will help propel smart cities and address concerns and problems in several ways (Gautam, 2018).

- It will not help create additional parking spaces but make it easier for drivers to locate existing ones. Therefore, it will reduce the time spent searching for parking. Drivers cruising and searching for parking worsen traffic since they are driving slower than others. They also are more likely to get into an accident from being distracted.
- The technology employs sensors, street lights, and navigation systems to communicate information to drivers and parking lot operators or other drivers. Drivers use real-time data to find the nearest parking or the least congested route to available parking.
- Using sensors that detect empty spaces, this smart parking technology can help drivers locate vacant spots rather than searching for them. Therefore drivers become less distracted and can plan their parking maneuvers and warn the driver behind about their intentions.
- It also reduces traffic congestion and cruising time by locating and making the process of parking faster. The smart parking technology can ensure that drivers always have the latest information and save commute time. Using the latest IoT advances, sensors can be synced to a cloud platform that feeds the data into a mobile app. These applications, in conjunction with GPS, provide directions to the next available parking location.
- Smart parking can ease traffic through instant payment from mobile devices, this making a parking space available to the next driver faster.
- It can also help city planners to identify inefficiencies through parking duration and downtime. Real-time information on the parking duration helps law enforcement identify unusual, illegal parking activities or high-risk violations such as cars illegally parked next to fire hydrants.

# RESEARCH METHODOLOGY

This research adopts a survey method. Surveys are grouped into two broad categories questionnaires and interviews (Evans, and Mathur, 2005). This study employed questionnaires as the primary method of data collection. The questionnaires consisted of both open and closed-ended questions.

Closed-ended questions offer a limited number of responses and are intended to provide a precise, clearly identifiable, and easily classified explanation. An open-ended question allows the respondent to express their opinions freely on a given subject. Such questions are non-directive and allow respondents to answer at their convenience (Fowler, 2013).

A representative of the driving population of NYC who demonstrate the required characteristics and whose inputs can be generalized and applied to the larger population was targeted. There are two types of sampling techniques:

- Probability Sampling: Every individual of a target population has an equal opportunity to be a part of a selected sample.
- Non-probability Sampling: the sample is chosen based on the researcher's judgment, experience, and knowledge and not randomly.

In this case, probability sampling was employed, and two hundred and sixteen valid responses were recorded.

This study used an online platform where a form was created and the link sent to participants. The online survey was designed to be executed by multiple platforms and browsers, prevent multiple submissions, and provide prompt feedback upon completion. There are several advantages of online surveys, including (Wright, 2005; Evans, and Mathur, 2005):

- Access: the Internet provides access to groups, communities of practice that exist online, and individuals who would be challenging, if not impossible, to reach.
- Time: Online surveys save time as data collection and analysis can occur in real-time
- Cost-efficient: Online surveys are cheaper to execute due to the minimum required resources.
- Required completion of answers: online surveys can force respondents to answer a question before advancing to the next question or completing the study. This eliminates non-responses.

- Flexible: Online surveys are flexible as they can be delivered in several formats, such as an e-mail with an embedded investigation, an e-mail with a link to a survey URL or web site.

Therefore, to address the issue of user requirements for the development of the mobile application, the survey considered the following questions:

- What impact does parking have on the connectedness of a city?
- Which features are essential in creating a smart city?
- What are the understandings of the challenges specific to parking in NYC?

## Data Analysis

From the questionnaire, descriptive data analysis was employed to synthesize, analyze, and interpret the data. Descriptive data analysis helps to describe, show, or summarize data in a meaningful way. This includes a univariate and bivariate analysis that utilizes correlations, graphs, and charts. Microsoft Excel was employed to facilitate data analysis.

## PRESENTATION AND DISCUSSION OF THE FINDINGS

The participants were all from New York City and were randomly selected based on their willingness to participate in the study.

## What Impact Does Parking Have on the Connectedness of a City?

Cities consist of the physical, tangible, mostly immovable structures and social components of people, institutions, workplaces, public transport, and the information networks garnered from smartphones, mobile devices, IoT, and traffic lights. These infrastructures help with the city's connectedness, enabling public participation while creating transparency and citizens' empowerment. Hence connectedness is key to understanding user requirements and developing a smart parking application.

The results show that the primary transportation mode for 67.1% of participants was private vehicles; 58.3% used public transit, and 7.9% practiced carpooling. The primary purpose of traveling was 86.6% for work, 56% for entertainment and socialization, and 7% for college/school. In terms of the need for parking, 69.4% of commuters used on-street parking. Parking remains a daily struggle. The results show that drivers need to search for available parking, which increases the number of vehicular traffic on the road and harms citizens' quality of life.

Since participants identified affordability as key to determining the selection of a particular parking location, then having a system that identifies the cost of a specific area and reduces the adverse effects of searching for cheaper space is most desirable. It will also cut the cost to drivers yearly. The results indicate that over 25% of participants paid between $5-$15 per day for parking. This cost burden falls primarily on the individual drivers, where 77.8% claimed they paid out of pocket, and employers funded 11.6%. This can add up to a significant amount over time.

*Figure 1. Time Spent Seeking parking*

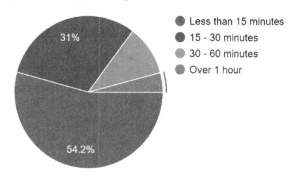

The duration of time drivers spend seeking parking has significant implications for developing a smart parking solution from the literature review. As seen in Figure 1.0, the study results indicate that NYC drivers, on average, spend less than 15 minutes (54.2%) seeking a suitable parking space, whereas 31% spend between 15-30 minutes and 10.6% spend between 30-60 minutes. This continuous search for parking results in lost time, wasted fuel, traffic congestion, thus imposing a cost to the individual, other drivers, and users of different transportation modes. In addition to the loss of time and fuel cost, drivers often make overpayments to avoid getting a ticket. Parking fines in cities also tend to expensive. These factors influence the city's connectedness as they determine how, when, and where people travel. Having an efficient transportation system and reliable parking solution helps develop a collaborative ecosystem that enables smart and connected communities to meet citizens' emerging needs while minimizing the environmental effects of rapid and sustained growth.

In addition to a functional digital infrastructure, the interconnection and ease of movement between different city areas are critical to achieving its desired success.

To assists with the city's connectedness, a reliable and free parking solution must consist of the following functionalities:

- Search – Users enter the vehicle location details using GPS to find the nearest available parking spot.
- Compare– Users compare parking options, which allows price and proximity comparison.
- Drive and Locate–The in-built navigational functions provide direction to an available parking spot.
- Park– users are park the car in the allotted slot.

Data from this and similar mobile applications can be captured across the city and sent to various connectivity platforms ready such as IoT and hosted in the cloud. Connected with other devices, drivers, citizens, and businesses can interact and communicate with each other.

## Which Features are Essential in Creating a Smart City?

For any city to be considered smart, there are crucial features required to improve individuals' quality of life in the area. A smart city should increase sustainability and create economic benefits and provide utilities security and safety. The following are essential for the success of any city:

- The use and promotion of digital technology, information, and data to enhance and improve its infrastructure and services.
- Increase access to e-government services, thus increasing accountability, transparency, and involvement of citizens. In addition to online services, physical access to government buildings should be within easy public transportation reach and with facilities for individuals with disabilities.
- Access to public transportation increased pedestrianized and cyclist zones, and intelligent parking solutions and management.
- Infrastructure should reduce the amount of waste generated and promote greener operational models.

To satisfy these demands for creating a smart city requires reliable digital connectivity, which allows for the real-time communication of connected devices. These projects must involve integrating technologies with operational techniques, inter-departmental coordination, and communication between different stakeholders.

## What are the Understandings of the Challenges Specific to Parking in NYC?

Parking is a significant problem, yet it is a common issue for many cities worldwide. The lack of adequate city parking infrastructure often led to dissatisfaction among drivers, resulting in lost revenue for businesses as they are often frustrated from their journey. In addition to the loss of revenue, some of the issues identified with parking in NYC were as follows:

• Not enough parking space near crucial infrastructure;
• Inefficient or flawed parking management system;
• Lack of immediate awareness of available parking spaces;
• Time and petrol used to find free or available parking spaces.
• Traffic congestion centered around poorly executed parking structures.
• Poor parking price models where drivers are required to pay a specific period for a set price. Parking prices are often exorbitant
• The environmental and physical impact of driving around seeking parking

The main reason for selecting a parking location was proximity (44%) to the intended destination and affordability(42.1%). Drivers spend a substantial amount of time searching for empty parking slots in an attempt to find a nearby yet affordable space to park for work in an office building. These individuals looking for a parking space prefer a real-time smart parking app that will guide them to the nearest vacant space. Reliable, real-time data that allows drivers to choose between free or paid parking and on-street or commercial parking will reduce the city parking woes. Employing cost-effective parking management and guidance solutions will increase revenue generation for a city, as existing parking spaces are appropriately monetized and efficiently managed. Drivers' awareness of parking spaces reduces traffic congestion and increases their willingness to pay for valuable public space and service.

## CONCLUSION

City parking is becoming increasingly tricky as urban areas become more populated and the number of vehicles on the road increases. Finding free or even cheap parking is increasingly challenging. Having a system in place that makes it faster, cleaner, and more reliable to find vacant parking helps the city's connectedness and progression to a smart city. Technology, particularly the integration of IoT and RFIDs that collect information and transmit it back to a central platform, is essential for developing a mobile application. Through data analytics, drivers can have access to real-time parking information on their mobile phones. A free or cheaply acquired guided mobile application can increase efficiency and make cities more attractive places to live and work. If benefitted from wide user acceptance, such an application would reduce congestion in dense neighborhoods, traffic casualties and encourage environmentally-friendly development. Therefore, a smart parking mobile application will transform journey planning from fragmented systems to an integrated solution that will revolutionize mobility, reduce environmental impact, and improve city dwellers' quality of life.

## REFERENCES

Arora, R., Parashar, A., & Transforming, C. C. I. (2013). Secure user data in cloud computing using encryption algorithms. *International Journal of Engineering Research and Applications*, *3*(4), 1922–1926.

Barriga, J. J., Sulca, J., León, J. L., Ulloa, A., Portero, D., Andrade, R., & Yoo, S. G. (2019). Smart Parking: A Literature Review from the Technological Perspective. *Applied Sciences (Basel, Switzerland)*, *9*(21), 4569. doi:10.3390/app9214569

Beom-Su, K., HoSung, P., Kyong Hoon, K., Daniel, G., & Ki-Il, K. (2017). *A Survey on Real-Time Communications in Wireless Sensor Networks*. doi:10.1155/2017/1864847

Byrd, B. (2014). *Modernizing Public Parking To Improve Transportation And Strengthen Democracy In New York City*. White Paper By Senior Fellow For Economic Development Columbia University. Available from http://rooseveltforward.org/wp-content/uploads/2015/10/BritByrd.WhitePaper.Web_.pdf

Dillon, T., Wu, C., & Chang, E. (2010, April). Cloud computing: issues and challenges. In *2010 24th IEEE international conference on advanced information networking and applications* (pp. 27-33). IEEE. 10.1109/AINA.2010.187

Evans, J. R., & Mathur, A. (2005). The value of online surveys. *Internet Research*, *15*(2), 195–219. doi:10.1108/10662240510590360

Fowler, F. J. Jr. (2013). *Survey research methods*. Sage Publications.

Gautam, S. (2018). *Benefits of Smart Parking: How Smart Parking Reduces Traffic*. https://www.parking-net.com/parking-industry-blog/get-my-parking/how-smart-parking-reduces-traffic#:~:text=Smart%20parking%20can%20reduce%20traffic,can%20help%20drivers%20locate%20spots

IbrahimH. E. (2017). Car Parking Problem in Urban Areas, Causes and Solutions 1st International Conference on Towards a Better Quality of Life. Available at https:// ssrn.com/abstract=3163473 doi:10.2139srn.3163473

International Telecommunication Union. (2014). *World Telecommunication Development Conference (WTDC-14).* Final Report; International Telecommunication Union.

Jia, X., Feng, Q., Fan, T., & Lei, Q. (2012). RFID technology and its applications in the Internet of Things (IoT). *2012 2nd International Conference on Consumer Electronics, Communications and Networks (CECNet)*, 1282-1285. 10.1109/ CECNet.2012.6201508

Jin, J., Gubbi, J., Marusic, S., & Palaniswami, M. (2014). An information framework for creating a smart city through the Internet of things. *IEEE Internet of Things Journal, 1*(2), 112–121. doi:10.1109/JIOT.2013.2296516

Khanna, A., & Anand, R. (2016, January). IoT based smart parking system. In *2016 International Conference on Internet of Things and Applications (IOTA)* (pp. 266-270). IEEE. 10.1109/IOTA.2016.7562735

Lee, I., & Lee, K. (2015). The Internet of Things (IoT): Applications, investments, and challenges for enterprises. *Business Horizons, 58*(4), 431–440. doi:10.1016/j. bushor.2015.03.008

Lin, T., Rivano, H., & Le Mouel, F. (2017). A Survey of Smart Parking Solutions. *IEEE Transactions on Intelligent Transportation Systems, 18*(12), 3229–3253. doi:10.1109/TITS.2017.2685143

Neirotti, P., De Marco, A., Cagliano, A. C., Mangano, G., & Scorrano, F. (2014). Current trends in Smart City initiatives: Some stylized facts. *Cities (London, England), 38*, 25–36. doi:10.1016/j.cities.2013.12.010

Pala, Z., & Inanc, N. (2007, September). *Smart parking applications using RFID technology. In 2007 1st Annual RFID Eurasia.* IEEE.

Pierce, G., & Shoup, D. (2013). Getting the prices right: An evaluation of pricing parking by demand in San Francisco. *Journal of the American Planning Association, 79*(1), 67–81. doi:10.1080/01944363.2013.787307

Sha, K., Yang, T. A., Wei, W., & Davari, S. (2020). A survey of edge computing-based designs for IoT security. *Digital Communications and Networks, 6*(2), 195–202. doi:10.1016/j.dcan.2019.08.006

Shoup, D. C. (2006). Cruising for parking. *Transport Policy*, *13*(6), 479–486. doi:10.1016/j.tranpol.2006.05.005

Su, K., Li, J., & Fu, H. (2011, September). Smart city and the applications. In *2011 international conference on electronics, communications, and control (ICECC)* (pp. 1028-1031). IEEE.

Suqi, F. (2020). *A Space for Parking in the Future of Mobility*. City Tech Collaborative. Available at: https://www.citytech.org/a-space-for-parking-in-the-future-of-mobility

Vishnubhotla, R., Rao, P. S., Ladha, A., Kadiyala, S., Narmada, A., Ronanki, B., & Illapakurthi, S. (2010). ZigBee based multi-level parking vacancy monitoring system. In *2010 IEEE International Conference on Electro/Information Technology* (pp. 1-4). IEEE. 10.1109/EIT.2010.5612133

Wright, K.B. (2005). Researching Internet-based populations: Advantages and disadvantages of online survey research, online questionnaire authoring software packages, and web survey services. *Journal of Computer-Mediated Communication*, *10*(3).

# Chapter 8
# Smart Cities, ICT, and Small Businesses in the USA

**Lloyd Amaghionyeodiwe**
*York College, City University of New York, USA*

## ABSTRACT

*The phenomenon of smart cities is not new in the literature, and one of the definitions emphasizes the use of information and communication technologies (ICTs) to improve quality of life and efficiency of services. To this end, IT systems become crucial and essential to a city's quest to be "smart." Thus, many organizations including SMEs have developed and utilized networks to facilitate their operations, transactions, and business functions. Given the role of small businesses in an economy and their quest operate in a smart environment and using surveys from organization, this study examines how smart these small businesses are by looking at their ICT usage. The study found that inasmuch as these small businesses improved in their usage of ICT, they are now faced with the risk of cyberattack, and while many of these businesses are virtually doing nothing to curb this, it becomes pertinent for an awareness to be put in place to help these small businesses realize the need for risk management especially as it relates to cyberattacks.*

## INTRODUCTION

There is no proper or official definition of what a smart city is. According to Schaffers, (2012), the concept of smart cities has emerged during the last few years to describe how investments in human and social capital and modern ICT infrastructure and e-services fuel sustainable growth and quality of life, enabled by a wise management of natural resources and through participative government. In literature the term smart

DOI: 10.4018/978-1-7998-5326-8.ch008

city is used to specify a city's ability to respond as promptly as possible to the needs of citizens, (Essays, UK. (2013). According to Muente-Kunigami and Mulas (2015), Smart cities can be viewed from two perspectives namely "a technology-intensive city, with sensors everywhere and highly efficient public services, thanks to information that is gathered in real time by thousands of interconnected devices". And secondly, "a city that cultivates a better relationship between citizens and governments - leveraged by available technology. They rely on feedback from citizens to help improve service delivery and creating mechanisms to gather this information".

A technical report by the International Telecommunication Union (2014), as cited by Al-Nasrawi, Adams, and El-Zaart (2015), considered and analyzed about 120 definitions of smart city from different studies and based on tier analyses, they came out with a comprehensive definition that encompasses the following: Improve the quality of life of its citizens; Ensure tangible economic growth such as higher standards of living and employment opportunities for its citizens; Improve the well-being of its citizens including medical care, welfare, physical safety and education; Establish an environmentally responsible and sustainable approach which "meets the needs of today without sacrificing the needs of future generations"; Streamline the physical infrastructure based services such as transportation (mobility), water, utilities (energy), telecommunications, and manufacturing sectors; Reinforce prevention and handling functionality for natural and man-made disasters including the ability to address the impacts of climate change; Provide an effective and well-balanced regulatory, compliance and governance mechanisms with appropriate and equitable policies and processes in a standardized manner. Thus, an all-inclusive definition of a smart city states as follows "A smart sustainable city is an innovative city that uses information and communication technologies (ICTs) and other means to improve quality of life, efficiency of urban operation and services, and competitiveness, while ensuring that it meets the needs of present and future generations with respect to economic, social and environmental aspects".

The concept of a smart city evolved as a solution to the challenges imposed by growing urbanization, digital revolution, and the demands of society for more efficient and sustainable urban services and the improvement of quality of life. Thus, accessibility to an efficient communications platform and technology infrastructure are important factors of a smart city though the effect of the technology infrastructure might be less if the human infrastructure is not built. Building a human infrastructure is important as well as technology infrastructure. Consequently, there is the need to educate people in building a smart city in these technologies. In this regard, two closely related technology frameworks are the Internet of Things (IoT) and big data (BD). They help make smart cities efficient and responsive. Big data offer the potential for cities to obtain valuable insights from a large amount of data collected through various sources, and the IoT allows the integration of sensors, radio-frequency identification, and Bluetooth in the real-world environment using highly networked services. IoT is an essential technology without which smart city initiatives cannot exist. The "things" of the IoT devices, sensors, applications collect the data that enables the technology solutions to be effective.

The technology has matured enough to allow smart cities to emerge. Businesses and organizations require and deal with a lot of data, which are collected for intelligence purposes. These data are sourced from various sources that include business performance metrics, data mining of consumers and users, and other descriptive sources. This can be related to business intelligence (BI), which combines business analytics, data mining, data visualization, data tools and infrastructure, and best practices to help organizations to make more data-driven decisions, (Tableau.com (n.d)). Furthermore, BI makes use of internal data to analyze their own operations or workforce in a bid to make better decisions in the future. It helps to create a comprehensive view of a business to help people make better, actionable decisions. In the process of building a smart city business intelligence holds a vital part to improve the services. Business intelligence includes data analytics and business analytics but uses them only as parts of the whole process (Tableau.com (n.d)). These are used to track business performance against their goals. In doing this, they gather the necessary data, analyze it, and determine which actions to take to reach their goals. There are many self-service business intelligence tools and platforms that are used by businesses to achieve their goal and these tools and platforms help streamline the analysis process. This makes it easier for people to understand their data without the technical know-how to dig into the data themselves.

According to Cisco (2006) in the present-day world, IT systems are essential and indispensable and most organizations, including SMEs, have networks to facilitate their operations, transactions and business functions. The implication of this is that a substantial amount of information that exists within these organizations is in an electronic format as such, it becomes very important that SMEs should maintain the operational status of such a network, as any disruption of the flow of information or any occasion that one of the elements that constitute it becomes unavailable, may immediately mean loss of capital and reputation (Camp 2006). In the USA, the role of small businesses in enhancing the smartness of the city cannot be underestimated. This is given the role they play in enhancing economic growth and development. But the question is whether these SMEs can utilize these business intelligent tools to help promote their operations, growth, and performance, thereby enhancing the effectiveness of a city being "smart"? This is the aim of this study. This study utilizes Atkins and Lowe (1997) definition of SMEs which was defined as organizations with less than 200 employees. Also, recently many small businesses use the internet for many reasons especially using their websites to advertise and sell their products as well as create awareness public awareness as to what they do. Apart from the cost, this may come with a consequence/risk which includes cyberattack. And with many big businesses committing more resources to and having more understanding about cyber security, cyber attackers appear to have shifted more focus on small businesses. This is the focus of this study.

## LITERATURE REVIEW

### The Concept of Smart City

The concept of smart city is not new in the literature. There are a lot of studies on smart cities but yet there is not agreed definition of what a smart city is. For instance, Center for Cities (2014) there is a lack of consensus on what 'smart' means and how cities should approach this agenda as becoming 'smart' means different things to different audiences. Some specific definitions include those of the United Kingdom Department for Business, Innovation and Skills (BIS) which considers smart cities as a process rather than a static outcome, in which increased citizen engagement, hard infrastructure, social capital and digital technologies make cities more livable, resilient, and better able to respond to challenges, (BIS, 2013). IBM defines a smart city as "one that makes optimal use of all the interconnected information available today to better understand and control its operations and optimize the use of limited resources", (Cosgrove and Al, 2011)., Cisco defines smart cities as those who adopt "scalable solutions that take advantage of information and communications technology (ICT) to increase efficiencies, reduce costs, and enhance quality of life", Falconer and Mitchell (2012).

According to Samih, (2019), the various authors, in their attempts to explain and describe the features of a smart city, indicated that the smart city has six possible characteristics: smart economy, smart people, smart governance, smart mobility, smart environment, and smart living. This can be represented in figure below:

Nam and Pardo, (2011) in their study titled "Conceptualizing smart city with dimensions of technology, people, and institutions" offers strategic principles aligning to the three main dimensions (technology, people, and institutions) of smart city: integration of infrastructures and technology-mediated services, social learning for strengthening human infrastructure, and governance for institutional improvement and citizen engagement. This was represented as:

Al-Nasrawi, Adams, and El-Zaart (2015) stated that a city is smart when investments in human and social capital, together with ICT infrastructures, boost sustainable growth and enhance the quality of life. Their study listed key dimensions of smart and sustainable cities based on various other studies in the literature. These they summarized as:

*Figure 1. Characteristics of a Smart City*
*Source: Adapted from Samih, (2019).*

*Figure 2. Fundamental components of a Smart City*
*Source: Adapted from Samih, (2019).*

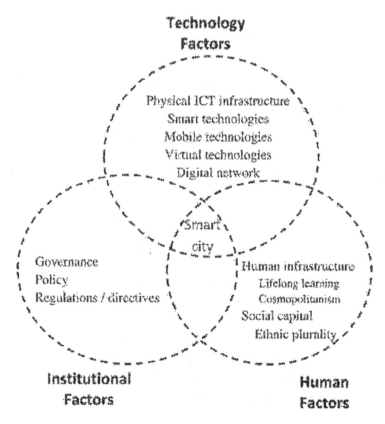

*Table 1. Key Dimensions of a Smart City*

| Key dimensions of a smart city | Source |
|---|---|
| Economic (GDP, sector strength, international transactions, foreign investment) Human (talent, innovation, creativity, education) Social (traditions, habits, religions, families) Environmental (energy policies, waste and water management, landscape) Institutional (civic engagement, administrative authority, elections) | (Barrionuevo et al., 2012) |
| Management and organizations Technology Governance Policy context People and communities Economy Built infrastructure Natural environment | (Alwadhi et al., 2102) |
| Technology Economic development Job growth Increased quality of life | (Eger, 2009) |
| Economy Mobility Environment People Governance | (Giffinger et al., 2007) |
| Human capital (e.g., skilled labor force) Infrastructural capital (e.g., high-tech communication facilities) social capital (e.g., intense, and open network linkages) Entrepreneurial capital (e.g., creative and risk-taking business activities) | (Kourtit and Nijkamp, 2012) |
| IT education IT infrastructure IT economy Quality of life | (Mahizhnan, 1999) |
| Economic socio-political issues of the city Economic-technical-social issues of the environment Interconnection Instrumentation Integration Applications Innovations | (Nam and Pardo, 2011) |
| Quality of life Sustainable economic development Management of natural resources through participatory policies Convergence of economic, Social, and environmental goals | (Thuzar, 2011) |

Source: Adapted from Al-Nasrawi, Adams, and El-Zaart (2015)

According to Hamid, Jhanjhi, Humayun, Khan, and Alsayat (2019) the increasing need and implementation of Information Communication Technologies (ICT) in urban infrastructure have led to greater attention in smart cities. Smart cities make use of ICTs to enhance: the quality of life of citizens by paving the way to improve local economy, enhance transport system and transport management thereby providing conducive environment to build strong relationships together with public authorities.

Simić, Vucetic, Kee, and Stanković (2019) opined that the phenomenon of Smart City had its around-twenty-year development path influenced by changes in technological, social, and business environment. Big Data, together with Internet of Things and Cloud Computing, has tremendous and profound impact on the changes of Smart City, transforming its shape and achievable goals and redefining its requirements and challenges. Cedeño,Papinniemi, Hannola, and Donoghue (2018) stated that businesses are always looking for increasing profitability and higher economic outcomes, thus companies need more and more to cooperate with each other to develop new innovative business models based on smart and digital services. In this regard IoT becomes very vital to business likewise Park, Pobil, and Kwon, (2018) stated that IoT technologies contribute significantly to most of the detailed aspects of smart city technologies and infrastructure. Because the fundamental concepts and ideas of IoT technologies are shared with those of smart city technologies and infrastructure, many business opportunities and extensive growth potential exist.

In all, there is no proper explanation of how to define a smart city, generally speaking a city based on information or computer technology can be considered as Smart City. The information technology is the basis of the entire city, its property, its medium of communication and other facilities.

## Internet of Things, Small Businesses, and ICT Usage

The role of Internet of Things (IoT) in the definition of smart cities and smart businesses cannot be overlooked. Similarly, the relationship between IoT and internet use cannot be divorced. The IoT is all about prolonging the power of the internet much beyond electronic devices such as desktops, laptops, and smartphones to a whole lot of other systems, procedures, and environments. The concept is to connect the internet to all possible things in the world and to enhance communication, (Biswas, 2020). While many small businesses strive to be smarter by using more of the internet in their daily operations, the role of IoT in these businesses cannot be underplayed.

Moeuf et al., (2018) study was on the industrial management of SMEs in the era of Industry 4.0. According to them, Industry 4.0 provides new paradigms for the industrial management of SMEs. Supported by a growing number of new technologies, this concept appears more flexible and less expensive than traditional enterprise information systems such as ERP and MES. However, SMEs find themselves ill-equipped to face these new possibilities regarding their production planning and control functions. Their results show that SMEs do not exploit all the resources for implementing Industry 4.0 and often limit themselves to the adoption of Cloud Computing and the Internet of Things. Likewise, SMEs seem to have adopted Industry 4.0 concepts only for monitoring industrial processes and there is still absence of real applications in the field of production planning.

A study by Biswas (2020) as reported in Keap Business Success Blog (2020), on the Internet of Things, every device and every system are connected and can be broadly classified under the following three categories namely: Systems that collect data and then send it: sensors of any type such as temperature sensors, motion sensors, etc. fall under this category. Secondly, systems that receives data and act upon such as printers, which obtains information and prints documents, or the car door that opens on receiving a signal from the key fob. And lastly, systems that can do both. The actual power of IoT arises when devices can do both, that is, collect data, send it, and receive it and act upon it. For example, motion sensor, which not only senses when someone steps in the vicinity but also sends a notification on your mobile to alert you.

Furthermore, Keap Business Success Blog (2020), stated some of the benefits of IoT to include:

- Better measurement of productivity: Managers can understand how operations are flowing from data produced by the sensors positioned in construction systems, assembly lines, warehouses, and transport. This vast data helps them to monitor the business vigilantly and take necessary steps to improve their performance. With the real-time data that flows in from data centers, production units, sensors, and IoT systems, the leaders are more aware of their current position vis-à-vis the industry standard. And with better insights into their company's performance, they can plan their future scope and innovations more competently.
- A better understanding of the market: Analysts now prefer to use real-time data than rely on information that has been collected in the past. The market is so volatile that every single moment counts and every reaction of customers' matter. Companies want to get a better understanding of customer behavior for instance, they want to know exactly how the customers behave in the marketplace, or when they see some new product being launched. Cameras are used mostly for this example is the on-floor cameras, when synced to cognitive intelligence or analytic systems, give retailers better insight into customer reactions to sales floor promotions and analyze future strategies accordingly.
- Business expansion: Internet of Things is giving a new shape to the industries. Breaking all boundaries, open sources can support nearly any system in any environment from any industry and have the prospect of transforming current business models. Companies can now utilize the data to pave their path towards a broader horizon. They can use the vast information for innovation and can participate in markets of any industry, appeal to new customer segments, and create new opportunities for revenue.
- Enhanced customer service: With IoT, it is possible for companies to collate real-time data, which they can work upon quickly to resolve any issues and requests even before the customers raise them. Real-time feedback on the fingertips of the analysts and the rational intelligence in IoT enabled systems help in enhancing customer experiences by discovering new insights about their purchasing habits.
- Increased efficiency: The growth of the Internet of Things across different parts of the company and its networks can improve the digitization of processes, which in turn can help in cost-cutting. With IoT information from all around the globe, it can be on the palmtop with one touch. Data is more

accurate, and decisions are more informed. Thus, the overall efficiency of an organization increases by leaps and bounds.

## The Role and Usage of IoT in Small Business

Spors, (2014) advocated that the concept of IoT could very well revolutionize small businesses in the following ways: Being able to connect more devices to the Internet will allow businesses greater intelligence and the ability to bolster the efficiency and effectiveness of their operations. Thus, many small businesses will likely install "smart" machines and devices that can be hooked up to the Internet like installing point-of-sale scanners on a retail floor. These are connected to warehouse systems and analytics software at headquarters for industry-leading efficiency in inventory. Furthermore, he stated that the Internet of Things does not just offer greater efficiency, it also opens many business opportunities and revenue streams to these small businesses. This can change businesses and consumers' view and approach to business and the world thus, their need for new devices and services that help them navigate this changing, ultra-connected landscape. These notwithstanding, Kelly (2014) noted that one drawback to this ultra-connected world is cybersecurity. To him, the more data that is collected online inevitably means there's greater potential for thieves to hack into online data troves and steal valuable and sensitive business information.

Dotzler, (2018) listed five ways the Internet of Things (IoT) is transforming small business. This includes Remote Monitoring, that is, the IoT allows organizations to remotely monitor various parts of their operations to allow production to continue around the clock, even if workers are not on the factory floor. Also, many smaller job shops are leveraging automation to gain a competitive advantage. Another way relates to Inventory Management, - before now, the use of bar-coding systems in inventory management has been in use for years. Some of these tracking systems, however, still required someone to physically scan individual parts to get an accurate count or location. But with IoT, warehouses and retail settings are becoming "smarter" as sensors come into play. He stated that "cost-effective RFID chips can be placed on products and remotely connected to technology to create real-time visibility into product locations and quantities. Built-in GPS can even allow an organization to pinpoint an item's location during shipping". The third way is mobility - many small businesses are with IoT can now work remotely, where workers or employees can collaborate and engage with each other no matter where they are located. IoT also enhances payments on the go – in this case, many SMBs use mobile devices to conduct business with IoT devices that connect to a smartphone to process payments on the go. Other ways that IoT influences the conduct of business for SMEs are through video conferencing apps and interactive whiteboards. Finally, the adoption of IoT can help improve overall efficiencies and productivity. The adoption of IoT, will come with big data can help improve day-to-day operations. For instance, scheduling meetings becomes more efficient when data regarding room occupancy and employee logistics is more visible while automatic reordering of office supplies based on tracked usage can cut down on waste and save time and machine data can be used to identify opportunities for improving startup times or which shifts have greater output in a manufacturing facility. Energy efficiency can also be improved with smart lighting and heating systems that adjust automatically based on activity in a room. Dotzler, (2018) concluded that many SMEs have limited IT staff, and this can be an impediment in terms of ensuring secure connections for SMEs, thus, there is the need to have the right infrastructure and expertise to integrate the IoT within the business.

According to Brown (2019), as cited in Jones, and Graham (2020), small businesses must adopt these technologies to be competitive. It would enable them to automate tedious, time-intensive processes, and interact with customers more effectively via personalized interactions. He recommends several ways that small businesses can cost-effectively use IoT technologies. More specifically, Brown (2019), state that "the benefits for businesses and consumers are similar in terms of the ability to share and receive information as well as minimize some time-consuming tasks through automated functionality. There is also a greater level of personalization that can be achieved thanks to machine learning that the devices use to improve various interactions and experiences". One easy adoption would be using a virtual assistant like Google Assistant and Siri. This he said will add productivity and efficiency to SMEs workdays by saving time looking things up, from a payroll question to fact-checking, and helping with scheduling meetings, changing appointments, and reordering office supplies. It also helps small businesses in tracking time, enhancing productivity and collaboration. Brown (2019) opined that when small businesses connect their computers and mobile devices, it provides a way for them to understand precisely how much time each person is spending on a project, including individual and collaborative time. This helps them to better understand who and what is impacting the ability to achieve greater productivity. Finally, he stated that IoT usage will help small businesses to collect more detailed business insights. He hinted that "Many small businesses could never afford to get access to the data they needed about their customers. Plus, if they did make a significant investment in third-party data, what they received still might not have provided the information necessary to create a better customer experience. However, if you connect to customer IoT devices, you will be able to receive direct information about your customers and their preferences. In return, you can deliver the personalization they expect".

Jarvis (2019) stated that there is no debate about the fact that IoT has reached the pinnacle of inflated expectations of emerging technologies. Organizations including small businesses are now able to overcome some significant challenges like data and information management issues, lack of inter operable technologies, security and privacy concerns, and the skills to manage IoT's growing complexity. Jones, and Graham (2020), explored the emerging role of the IoT in small businesses, the impact on their ability to compete in a rapidly changing digital environment, and their awareness, attitudes, perceptions, and willingness to adopt it. Their study utilized an initial exploratory approach based on a review of case studies in the literature, interviews with several economic development personnel and a few small and medium-size business managers. They opined from their study's findings that benefits from the use of the IoT include increased efficiency in operations and reduced costs in businesses. However, most of the small businesses interviewed did not have much or any awareness of what IoT technologies were or their potential benefits. The use of IoT by small businesses helps them to make core activities of value creation more effective, the implementation of IoT solutions enables manufacturing SMEs to manage information flows better, thereby improving management and control (Moeuf, et al., 2018; Müller et al., 2018).

Nichols, (2020) stated that what the IoT can do varies depending on resources and business type. For small and medium sized businesses (SMBs), the advantages of IoT can be categorized into efficiency and cost-effectiveness. In terms of efficiency, small and medium sized businesses moving packaged goods need to optimize their warehouse organization to maximize efficiency. IoT devices like radio frequency identification (RFID) tags can help with that. These tiny sensors let employees find and track goods throughout the entire logistics chain. In terms of cost-effectiveness, IoT versions of standard workplace equipment often represent a substantial cost reduction over time. For instance, mundane gadgets like smart thermostats offer savings by reducing energy use and providing real-time monitoring tools. In terms of Implementing the IoT in SMBs, he stated that IoT technology can offer SMBs a lot of the same advantages as it does to larger corporations though, the rate and scale of adoption is not the same. Notwithstanding, the fact that IoT can lower costs, some business owners may worry about the initial expense of buying and installing these devices.

## ANALYSIS OF SMALL BUSINESS AND ICT USAGE

## Method and Data Source

In assessing how smart small businesses are in the USA, we looked at their ICT usage and used the data from surveys conducted by various organizations. Additionally, this study utilized mostly qualitative research method. This method primarily involves collection of quantitative data and its analysis using percentages, charts, and trend analysis. In conducting this study, data from the 2019 survey of technology and was used. This survey was conducted on-line from March 3 to April 7, 2019 among 551 small-business owners (both members and nonmembers of NSBA) representing every industry in every state in the nation. Also, some publications were accessed, and they also served as a complementary source of data for the study. The survey covered a wide spectrum of small businesses namely: Professional, Scientific and Technical Services (34%); Manufacturing (9%) ; Construction (7%) ; Information (7%); Other Services (except Public Administration) (7%); Retail Trade (5%); Health Care and Social Assistance (4%); Agriculture, Forestry, Fishing and Hunting (3%); Educational Services (3%); Real Estate, Rental and Leasing (3%); Transportation and Warehousing (3%); Wholesale Trade (2%); Arts, Entertainment, and Recreation (2%); Management of Companies and Enterprises (2%); Finance & Insurance (2%); Administrative and Support, Waste Management and Remediation Services (2%); Accommodation and Food Services (1%); Public Administration (1%); And Utilities (1%). Furthermore, most of these businesses were Limited Liability Companies (LLCs) (34%); S-Corporation (32%); Corporations (18%); Sole proprietorship (12%) and Partnership (3%). In terms of gross sales or revenue, majority of these small businesses were making less than $100,000 in a year.

## Survey Result and Analysis

And in line with being smart in a smart environment, many of these small businesses have shifted to the use of more technology in their daily activities. For instance, this survey reported an expected increase in utilization of technology, specifically smart phones, high-speed internet, cloud computing and nearly every online business management platform. Most small businesses now allow their employees to telecommute, with nearly half saying they offer it on a regular basis to employees. More, specifically, table 2 indicated that most the firms (94%) utilize smart phone and/or cell phone while 87% and 68% of them use laptop and desktop computers, respectively.

Data from the survey shows that most of their employees (69%) telecommute and this was a higher percentage when compared to the 2013 and 2010 figure as reported in the survey. This figure was 60% in 2013 and 56% in 2010, representing an increase rate of 23% from the date 2010 data. Furthermore, table 3 indicates which of the business activities that these firms conduct online. From the table, managing banking accounts, purchasing supplies, and Paying bills or utilizing electronic bill pay were dominant as they constituted 88%, 85% and 83% respectively. Other activities of interest include: Document Sharing (70%); Conducting phone calls or teleconferences (like skype or VOIP) (68%); Conducting meetings (like WebEx) (59); Payroll management (55%); Project management (42%) and– customer relationship management (39%).

*Table 2. Type of Devices being used regularly for business*

| Device Type | Percentage |
|---|---|
| Smart phone / cell phone | 94 |
| Laptop computer | 87 |
| Desktop computer | 68 |
| Land-line phone | 50 |
| Tablet | 41 |
| Fax machine | 31 |
| Smartboard | 3 |
| Other | 5 |

Source: National Small Business Association (2019) Technology and Small Business Survey in the U.S.

*Table 3. Technology and Business Activities*

| Business Activities | Percentage |
|---|---|
| Manage banking accounts | 88 |
| Purchase supplies | 85 |
| Pay bills or utilize electronic bill pay | 83 |
| Document Sharing | 70 |
| Conducting phone calls or teleconferences (e.g.: skype or VOIP) | 68 |
| Conducting meetings (e.g.: WebEx) | 59 |
| Manage payroll | 55 |
| Project management | 42 |
| CRM – customer relationship management | 39 |
| HR apps | 21 |
| Other | 10 |

Source: National Small Business Association (2019) Technology and Small Business Survey in the U.S.

In undertaking these activities, majority of these firms make use of cable internet (46%). Other forms of internet service that these businesses use is: Broadband (24%); Fiber (24%); DSL (14%); Not Sure (7%); AirCard (3%); Satellite (3%) and others (3%). Many of these firms also use cloud computing as can be seen from table 4. This was a significant improvement to what was obtained in 2010 where only 5% of the firms made use of cloud computing technologies.

The survey also indicated that majority of these firms maintain an online presence for their business, while those that do not believe that it is not needed and essential for their business. This can be the reason why many of the small businesses sell their products or services on-line. In line with this, less than one-in-ten small businesses utilize platforms like Amazon or E-Bay to sell their products and/or services. Precisely, 80% of the firms sell their products or services online through their website while 18% do same through trade-specific portal, (see table 5). Only 9%, 8% and 2% make use of Amazon,

E-bay and Craigslist in their respective sale of their products or services online. This notwithstanding, many (39%) of those that do not have a website claimed that it was not needed for their business while 25% claimed that they do not own a website because it is too difficult to create and maintain.

*Table 4. Business usage of Cloud Computing Technologies*

| Response | Percentage | | |
|---|---|---|---|
| | **2019** | **2013** | **2010** |
| Yes | 62 | 43 | 5 |
| No | 32 | 57 | 95 |
| Not Sure | 5 | - | - |

Source: National Small Business Association (2019) Technology and Small Business Survey in the U.S.

*Table 5. Medium of Sale for Products or Services On-line*

| Medium of Sale | Percentage |
|---|---|
| Through my website | 80 |
| Trade-specific portal | 18 |
| Online distributor | 10 |
| Amazon | 9 |
| E-bay | 8 |
| Craigslist | 2 |
| Etsy | 1 |
| Other | 22 |

Source: National Small Business Association (2019) Technology and Small Business Survey in the U.S.

For those firms that do not sell their products or services online, 85% maintained that they do not need it for their business as such they do not have any products or services that can be sold on-line while 5% claimed that they do not know how to use it and they are not comfortable with it. Others claim that they do not have back-office to handle fulfillment (3%), it is too expensive (3%), and they use a distributor to sell their products online (2%). The survey further indicate that most small-business owners are using some kind of social media for business networking, with Facebook and LinkedIn being in the lead, (see table 6). This usage can be concomitant with what activity that firms most commonly use social media for. For instance, 67% were using social media for Business networking while 23% used it for keeping in touch with friends, 2% used it for political advocacy and 8% used it for other purposes.

*Table 6: Social Media Platforms utilized by Firms*

| Social Media Platforms | Percentage | |
|---|---|---|
| | 2019 | 2013 |
| Facebook | 67 | 50 |
| LinkedIn | 62 | 57 |
| Twitter | 42 | 26 |
| YouTube | 28 | 19 |
| Instagram | 28 | 2 |
| Google+ | 21 | 24 |
| None – I do not use social media | 17 | 27 |
| Blogs | 11 | 10 |
| Pinterest | 10 | 6 |
| Vimeo | 6 | - |
| Wikis | 5 | 3 |
| Snapchat | 4 | - |
| Other | 3 | 2 |
| Foursquare | 1 | 2 |

Source: National Small Business Association (2019) Technology and Small Business Survey in the U.S.

In responding to the question on how important technology is, and keeping up with new technology, to the success of your company, 74% indicated that technology is very important to them, 22% claimed that it was somewhat important while 3% maintained that it is not very important. Likewise, taking appropriate security precautions was one of the biggest challenges that the firms faced with their company's use of technology (24%). This was followed by Cost of needed upgrades to technology (27%), Time it takes to fix problems (17%) and Cost of maintaining technology (14%), (see table 7).

Being smart with respect to internet usage has its own consequences and one major risk associated with this is cyberattacks. In line with this majority of the small businesses (82%) do collect at least one form of customer information while 18% claimed that they do not collect any form of customer information. But are visitors to the firms' website(s) aware that their data are being collected? To this, 39% did agree that they inform the customers but 26% do not while 32% do not only notify the customers, they also offer the opt-out option for customers who do not want their data stored. In all, 41% of the firms do maintain a customer database while 38% do contact their customers from time to time (via phone, email, or mail) about their information on the firm's website (see table 8). Nonetheless, it should be noted also that from the survey, most small firms are not familiar with data protection rules, and just under half of those that collect website visitor data offer an opt-out.

*Table 7. Challenges Faced with Company's use of Technology*

| Challenges Faced | Percentage |
|---|---|
| Taking appropriate security precautions | 24 |
| Cost of needed upgrades to technology | 17 |
| Time it takes to fix problems | 17 |
| Cost of maintaining technology | 14 |
| Lack of expertise | 9 |
| Breaks in service | 7 |
| Other | 4 |
| Dealing with security breaches | 3 |
| Location of my business (I am in a very rural area) | 3 |
| Response time from external technology support company | 3 |

**Source:** National Small Business Association (2019) Technology and Small Business Survey in the U.S.

*Table 8. Actions Firm most commonly takes with Customers' Information*

| Action | Percentage |
|---|---|
| I maintain a customer database | 41 |
| I contact my customers from time to time (via phone, email or mail) | 38 |
| I collect it | 10 |
| I sell some or all of my customer database with outside companies or individuals | 1 |
| I share some or all of my customer database with outside companies or individuals | 0 |
| I do not collect any customer information | 9 |

Source: National Small Business Association (2019) Technology and Small Business Survey in the U.S.

Table 9 indicates that of those who did not obtain prior approval from customers before collecting, storing, using, or disclosing their personal data, 56% believed that this approval was not required. Other reasons for this included that this process takes too much time; cost too much money and that the approval was not important to them. According to Hiscox (2018) Small Business Cyber Risk Report, which focuses on the responses of US small businesses surveyed as a part of the Hiscox Cyber Readiness Report in 2018, 66% of small businesses are concerned or extremely concerned about cyber security risk but only (52%) of them have a clearly defined strategy around cyber security. Shockingly, only 16 percent of these small businesses are very confident in their cyber security readiness. About 23% of them have a leadership role dedicated to cyber, whereas most (46%) have no defined role at all. Curiously, 65% of small businesses have failed to act following a cyber security incident. Also, less than one-third (32%) of small businesses have conducted phishing experiments to assess employee behavior and readiness in the event of an attack. This notwithstanding, and as reported in Security (2018), a study conducted by the Ponemon Institute, sponsored by Keeper Security, revealed that small businesses increasingly face the same cybersecurity risks as larger companies, but only 28 percent rate their ability to mitigate threats, vulnerabilities, and attacks as "highly effective." Yet nearly half of respondents (47 percent) claim that they have no understanding of how to protect their companies against cyberattacks. In all, Verizon's 2019 Data Breach Investigation report, (as cited in Martins (2019)) showed that 43% of breaches impacted Small and Medium scaled businesses. One possible reason for this is that small businesses tend to neglect this threat of cyberattack relying on the fact that they are small and cannot be attacked. This might look irrational in this era of smart cities with high use of the internet.

*Table 9. Primary reason why prior approval from customers before collecting, storing, using or disclosing their personal data is not Obtained*

| Reason | Percentage |
|---|---|
| Not required | 56 |
| Takes too much time | 1 |
| Costs too much money | 1 |
| Not important to me | 6 |
| Too risky | 1 |
| Other | 35 |

Source: National Small Business Association (2019) Technology and Small Business Survey in the U.S.

A study by BullGuard-commissioned research (BullGuard, 2020) reveals small to medium businesses in the US and UK are at increased risk of data breach and cyber-attack and 43% of SMBs have no cybersecurity defense plan in place. Furthermore, additional data from BullGuard's survey shows that despite nearly one-in-five (18.5%) small businesses experiencing cyber-attacks or data breaches, 60% of those surveyed SMB owners think their businesses are not a likely target of cybercriminals and 50% of SMB owners stated their employees do not receive any cybersecurity training. For those who take precautions, A significant number, 65%, of SMB owners report managing their cybersecurity in-house, but less than 10% say they have a dedicated IT staff member. With respect to solutions that SMEs took in the face of cyber-attack, Heinig, (2020) reported study by Manifest in April 2020 on data safety for small businesses. According to him, Manifest surveyed 383 small business owners and managers who use a mobile app and/or website to connect with customers. More than half of respondents (60%) are female; 40% are male. And Nearly one-fifth of respondents (16%) are ages 18-34; 42% are ages 35-54, and 43% are ages 55 and older. The survey result indicated that small businesses use a range of data security measures to protect their data, including limiting employee access and encryption, and are considering investing in more cybersecurity resources in the future. Precisely, the study found that most small businesses (64%) to devote more resources to cybersecurity in 2020. The cybersecurity measures utilized consist of limiting employee access to user data (46%), data encryption (44%), requiring strong user passwords (34%), and training employees on data safety and best practices (34%). And nearly 1 in 5 small businesses commit more resources to cybersecurity (23%) and could improve the security of customer data storage (20%). This notwithstanding, many small business owners still have the belief that their businesses are too small to attract the interest to hackers. Another study by Nationwide on most small businesses unprepared for cybercriminals as reported by Heinig, (2020) revealed that computer viruses and phishing are the major routes employees compromise small business security. Phishing is a fraudulent attempt to obtain sensitive information such as passwords, usernames, or credit cards. For instance, clicking on a malicious link can make a cybercriminal to control business computers, record employee keystrokes, and access sensitive company and customer information. Other types of attack include trojan horse, hacking, data breach, unpatched software, customer information access and company information access.

## CONCLUSION POLICY RECOMMENDATIONS

In today's technology-reliant marketplace, understanding how small businesses utilize technology is of critical importance not only to policymakers, but to thought leaders in the IT industry. The use of internet and other technology-reliant procedures tend to define how smart a city or business operate and with the ongoing digital transformation, it becomes paramount for the small business to adopt these new forms of technologies, especially the internet and this makes them vulnerable to cyberattacks. But unfortunately, many small businesses think that they are too small to be attacked by cyber attackers. For instance, data from the US National Cyber Security Alliance survey indicate that 83 percent of small businesses have no formal cybersecurity plan while 69 percent have no plan in place at all. As such there is a need for these small businesses to realize the need for them to employ some risk management skills in trying to control and guide against the risk of cyberattack on their businesses.

Based on the aim of this paper, we found that SMEs can utilize these business intelligent tools to help promote their operations, growth, and performance, thereby enhancing the effectiveness of a city being "smart". Though this comes with some obstacles that included the risk and cost of adopting these tools. And in line with is, the following recommendations are made.

- Small businesses should be encouraged to embrace and adopt the use of internet and other technology-reliant procedures that makes them smart in a smart city. The merits of this adoption to them includes it enhances their capability to disseminate, communicate and receive information, minimize some time-consuming tasks through automated functionality and enhance their marketing capacities. This increases their market horizon and encourages more productivity. More specifically, the small businesses can start adopting these technologies including IoT through using Google Assistant and other IoT assistants like Siri for individuals and teams as a way of adding productivity and efficiency to our workdays. According to Brown (2019), this will help these small businesses in saving time especially as it relates to them seek enquires like from a payroll questions, fact-checking, scheduling meetings, changing appointments, and reordering office supplies. It can also enhance better way to control inventory given that the virtual assistant (paywall) can always be tracking what is available and immediately reorder when necessary. Adopting the IoT technologies can also aid cost saving capabilities. For instance, integrating light and temperature controls into the business environment can help lower energy consumption and give significant cost savings as these devices can automatically monitor and regulate when appliances, machines and equipment are switched on and turn especially when not in use.
- One major concern of the small businesses in adopting these technologies is the cost and the security risk involves especially as it relates to cyber-

attacks. A recommendation in this regard is for the small businesses to go into a contract with a third-party managed security service outfit, (Paraskevas and Buhalis, 2002; Spinellis et al., 1999). This will entail getting security services from another company that specializes in IT security. One possible disadvantage of this is that it has the tendency to increase the cost of doing business by these SMEs, thereby drawing much funding from the SMEs constrained budget. In terms of the cost, the government can also grant subsidies, and tax breaks or holidays to small businesses that are interested in adopting these technologies. This will act as incentive for then to embrace it and encourage many who may not have had an interest in adopting these technologies. One important thing here is that the government should find a way of ensuring that those who receive such a subsidy, tax break or holiday uses these for the intended purpose. This can do be sending out inspectors to check on these small businesses in a bid to ensure adoption and compliance.

- Given that majority of SMB owners belief that because they are small, they have zero vulnerabilities and cannot be victims of cyber-attacks, it becomes pertinent for the government and other associated agencies to help in providing more awareness, education and assistance needed by these SMEs on the need for them to recognize importance of putting some security measures in place to curb and/or eliminate any threat of cyber-attack. And they, small businesses, should be made to understand that the threat of cyber-attack is real and should not be ignored. Possible measures that small businesses can utilize include the use of firewalls, antivirus, and endpoint security solutions; monitor computer use, device, and password policies; Email security solutions like anti-phishing solutions, spam filters, email signing certificates; Employee cyber security awareness training; Incident response and disaster recovery plans; Encrypted drives; Current data backups and two-factor authentication as this adds an extra layer of security to passwords that would otherwise be compromised easily (Heinig, 2020). Other measures and techniques to include in a small business cybersecurity plan can include: Setting employee data access guidelines; Audit services and settings for data safety; Install software updates regularly; Establish an exit protocol for churned employees; Develop password protocols with password managers; Back up data periodically and implement antivirus software (Nationwide, "Most Small Businesses Unprepared for Cybercriminals" as reported in Heinig, 2020).

- It is essential to note that education is very crucial and vital in any small business's effort at reducing cyber-attacks once the ICT technologies are adopted by them. This is because when employees are educated and encouraged to participate in cybersecurity training, the business's risk of attack can be considerably reduced. Therefore, small business owner in adopting these technologies should make it a priority in their policy to educate, inspire and train their employees on the matters of cybersecurity and how to avoid possible attacks on their business.

In all the adoption of all these ICT technologies by the small businesses will go a long way to enhance their productivity, and competitiveness by making them smarter. Though the cost may be a bit high initially but in the long run, the small businesses will be better-off, thus, there is a need for more policies that will create more understanding, education, training, adoption, and implementation for these small businesses.

## REFERENCES

Al-Nasrawi, Adams, & El-Zaart. (2015). A Conceptual Multidimensional Model for Assessing Smart Sustainable Cities. *Journal of Information Systems and Technology Management, 12*(3). doi:10.4301/S1807-17752015000300003

Alawadhi, S., Aldama-Nalda, A., Chourabi, H., Gil-Garcia, J. R., Leung, S., Mellouli, S., Nam, T., Pardo, T. A., Scholl, H. J., & Walker, S. (2012). Building Understanding of Smart City Initiatives. *Lecture Notes in Computer Science, 7443*, 40–53. doi:10.1007/978-3-642-33489-4_4

Barrionuevo, J. M., Berrone, P., & Ricart, J. E. (2012). Smart Cities, Sustainable Progress. *IESE Expert Insight, 14*, 50–57. Retrieved from: https://www. researchgate.net/ profile/ Pascual_Berrone/ publication/ 276088190_ Smart_ Cities_ Sustainable_ Progress_ Opportunities_ for_ Urban_ Development/ links/ 563f9a3908ae8d65c0150f53.pdf

Department for Business, Innovation and Skills (BIS). (2013). *Smart Cities Background Paper*. London: Department for Business Innovation and Skills. Retrieved from: https://assets.publishing.service.gov.uk/ government/ uploads/ system/ uploads/ attachment_ data/ file/ 246019/ bis- 13- 1209- smart- cities- background- paper- digital.pdf

Biswas, S. (2020). *How IoT is impacting businesses today*. Accessed on April 14, 2020 and retrieved from: https://keap.com/ business- success- blog/ marketing/ automation/ how- the- internet- of- things- impacts- small- business

Brown, C. (2019). Five ways you should be incorporating IoT in your small business. *Forbes*. Retrieved from: https://www.forbes.com/ sites/ forbestechcouncil/ 2019/ 03/ 15/ five- ways- you- should- be- incorporating- iot- in- your- small- business/ #2e3fc8a7dc58

British Standards Institution (BSI). (2014). *Smart cities framework – Guide to establishing strategies for smart cities and communities, PAS 181*. Retrieved from: https://shop.bsigroup.com/ upload/ 267775/ PAS% 20181% 20(2014).pdf

BullGuard. (2020). *BullGuard: New Study Reveals One in Three SMBs Use Free Consumer Cybersecurity and One in Five Use No Endpoint Security at All.* prnewswire.com

Camp, L. J. (2006). The State of Economics of Information Security. *Information Security Journal, 2*(2). http: //www. is-joumal. org/ VO2102/ 21SJLP189-Camp. pdf

Cedeño, J., Papinniemi, J., Hannola, L., & Donoghue, I. (2018). *Developing Smart Services by Internet of Things in Manufacturing Business.* doi:10.12783/dtetr/ icpr2017/17680

Center for Cities. (2014). *Smart Cities*. Accessed on April 04, 2020 and retrieved from: https://www.centreforcities.org/ reader/ smart-cities/ what-is-a-smart-city/ 1-smart-cities-definitions/

Cisco. (2006). *Designing Network Security*. Cisco Press. Retrieved from: http: // www. Cisco press. com/content/images/I587051176/samplechapter/1587051176c ontent. pdf

Cosgrove, M. (2011). *Smart Cities series: introducing the IBM city operations and management solutions*. IBM.

Dotzler, J. (2018). *5 Ways the Internet of Things (IoT) is Transforming Small Business*. Gordon Flesch Company Inc. Retrieved from: https://www.gflesch.com/ elevity -it- blog/ ways -iot- is-transforming- small- business

Eger, J.M., (2009). Smart Growth, Smart Cities, and the Crisis at the Pump A Worldwide Phenomenon. *I-Ways, 32*(1), 47 –53.

Essays, U. K. (2013). *The History Of Smart Cities Concept Information Technology Essay*. Retrieved from https://www.uniassignment.com/ essay-samples/ information-technology/ the- history -of- smart- cities- concept- information- technology- essay. php? vref=1

Falconer, G., & Mitchell, S. (2012). *Smart City Framework A Systematic Process for Enabling Smart + Connected Communities*. CISCO. Retrieved from: https:// www.cisco.com/ web/ about/ ac79/ docs/ ps/ motm/ Smart- City- Framework.pdf

Giffinger, R., Fertner, C., Kramar, H., Kalasek, R., Pichler-Milanovis, N., & Meijers, E. (2007). *Smart Cities: Ranking of European Medium-Sized Cities*. Vienna, Austria: Centre of Regional Science (SRF), Vienna University of Technology. Retrieved from: http://www.smart-cities.eu/ download/ smart_cities_final_report.pdf

Hamid, B., Jhanjhi, N. Z., Humayun, M., Khan, A., & Alsayat, A. (2019). Cyber Security Issues and Challenges for Smart Cities: A survey. *2019 13th International Conference on Mathematics, Actuarial Science, Computer Science and Statistics (MACS)*, 1-7. 10.1109/MACS48846.2019.9024768

Heinig, I. (2020). Data Safety for Small Businesses: 2020 Cybersecurity Statistics. *The Manifest*. Retrieved from: https://themanifest.com/ mobile-apps/ data- safety- small- businesses- 2020- cybersecurity- statistics

HISCOX. (2018). *2018 HISCOX Small Business Cyber Risk Report*. Retrieved from: https://www.hiscox.com/ documents/ 2018- Hiscox- Small- Business- Cyber- Risk- Report.pdf

International Telecommunication Union. (2014). *Technical Report on Smart Sustainable Cities: An analysis of definitions*. United Nations, International Telecommunication Union (ITU-T), Focus Group on Smart Sustainable Cities (FG-SSC).

Jarvis, D. (2019). Small Businesses, It's Time to Ride the IoT Wave. *IoT Business News*. Retrieved from: https://iotbusinessnews.com/ 2019/ 11/ 14/ 30269- small- businesses -its- time -to- ride-the- iot-wave/

Jones, N., & Matt Graham, C. (2020, January). Can the IoT Help Small Businesses? *Bulletin of Science, Technology & Society*, *38*(1), 3–12. Advance online publication. doi:10.1177/0270467620902365

Keap Business Success Blog. (2020). *How IoT is impacting businesses today*. Accessed on April 14, 2020 and retrieved from: https://keap.com/ business- success- blog/ marketing/ automation/ how -the- internet -of- things- impacts- small- business

Kourtit, Nijkamp, & Arribas. (2012). Smart Cities in Perspective – A Comparative European Study by Means of Self-organizing Maps. *Innovation: The European Journal of Social Science Research, 25*(2), 229–246.

Maffeo, L. (2019). *Should your small business invest in the Internet of Things?* Retrieved from: https://blog.capterra.com/ should- your- small- business- invest -in-the- internet -of- things/#1

Mahizhnan, A. (1999). Smart Cities: The Singapore Case. *Cities, 16*(1), 13–18. doi:10.1016/S0264-2751(98)00050-X

Martins, A. (2019). Cyberattacks and Your Small Business: A Primer for Cybersecurity. *Business News Daily.* https://www.businessnewsdaily.com/8231-small-business-cybersecurity-guide.html

Moeuf, A., Pellerin, R., Lamouri, S., Tamayo-Giraldo, S., & Barbaray, R. (2018). The industrial management of SMEs in the era of Industry 4.0. *International Journal of Production Research, 56*(3), 1118–1136. doi:10.1080/00207543.2017.1372647

Muente-Kunigami & Mulas. (2015). *Building smarter cities.* World Bank Brief.

Nam, T., & Pardo, T. A. (2011). Conceptualizing smart city with dimensions of technology, people, and institutions. *Proceedings of the 12th Annual International Digital Government Research Conference: Digital government innovation in challenging times, 282 – 291.* 10.1145/2037556.2037602

National Small Business Association (NABA). (2019). *National 2019 Technology & Small Business Survey.* Retrieved from: https://nsba.biz/wp-content/uploads/2019/06/ Technology-Survey-2019.pdf

Nichols, R. M. (2020). How Small Businesses Benefit from the IoT. *IOT Feature News.* Retrieved from: https://www.iotevolutionworld.com/iot/articles/445643-how-small-businesses-benefit-from-iot.htm#

Park, E., Del Pobil, A. P., & Kwon, S. J. (2018). The Role of Internet of Things (IoT) in Smart Cities: Technology Roadmap-oriented Approaches. *Sustainability, 10*(10), 1388. doi:10.3390u10051388

Samih, H. (2019). Smart cities and internet of things. *Journal of Information Technology Case and Application Research, 21*(1), 3-12. doi:10.1080/15228053. 2019.1587572

Schaffers, Ratti, & Komninos. (2012). Special Issue on Smart Applications for Smart Cities – New Approaches to Innovation: Guest Editors' Introduction. *Journal of Theoretical and Applied Electronic Commerce Research, 7*(3). doi:10.4067/ S0718-18762012000300005

Security. (2018). *Nearly 70 Percent of SMBs Experience Cyber Attacks*. Accessed April 04, 2020 from: https://www.securitymagazine.com/articles/89586-nearly-70-percent-of-smbs-experience-cyber-attacks

Simić, M., Vucetic, M., Kee, G.H., & Stanković, M. (2019). *Big Data and Development of Smart City*. doi:10.15308/Sinteza-2019-581-588

Spors, K. (2014). How the 'Internet of Things' Will Revolutionize Small Business. *American Express*. Retrieved from: https://www.americanexpress.com/ en-us/ business/trends-and-insights/ articles/ how-the-internet-of-things-will-revolutionize-small-business/

Stojkoska, B.R., & Trivodaliev, K. (2017). *A review of Internet of Things for smart home: Challenges and solutions*. doi:10.1016/j.jclepro.2016.10.006

Tableau.com. (n.d.). *What is business intelligence? Your guide to BI and why its matters*. Retrieved from: https://www.tableau.com/learn/articles/business-intelligence

Thuzar, M. (2011). *Urbanization in South East Asia: Developing Smart Cities for the Future?* Regional Outlook.

Chapter 9
# Review of the Role of the Internet of Things (IoT) on the Consumer Market:
## Focusing on Smart Tourism, Healthcare, and Retailing

**Yong Kyu Lee**
*York College, City University of New York, USA*

## ABSTRACT

*This chapter reviews the internet of things (IoT) as a key component of a smart city and how it is applied to consumers' daily lives and business. The IoT is a part of information and communication technology (ICT) and is considered a powerful means to improve consumers' quality of life. The "thing" could be any object which has internet capability, such as wearable devices and smart TVs/phones/speakers. Several studies have identified driving factors that have led consumers to adopting them, but also concerns of consumers' resistance to IoT devices. The three major fields of application of IoT technologies were selected to review the role of the IoT in consumers' daily lives and business.*

## INTRODUCTION

A smart city has been defined in different ways by different researchers and specialists (Eremia et al., 2017). Even though there is no unified definition of a smart city, smart city concepts include a social system and technology. The only differences lie in some concepts focusing more on social inclusion and others focusing more

DOI: 10.4018/978-1-7998-5326-8.ch009

on information and communications technology (Deakin, 2013; Kopackova & Libalova, 2017). Six areas—people, government, economy, mobility, environment, and living—have been identified as part of most smart city models (Anthopoulos et al., 2016; Zubizarreta et al., 2015).

Regardless of how a smart city is defined, it represents that information and communication technology is likely to coordinate a city's social components (e.g., people, environment, government, etc.) to improve citizens' quality of life as well as the efficiency of the city services (Anthopoulos et al., 2016; Vicini et al., 2012). Especially, it has been considered that the Internet of things (IoT) is one of the important infrastructures in a smart city because it interconnects the people and things at anytime, anyplace, with anything and anyone (Jin et al., 2014; Park et al., 2018; Piro et al., 2014).

Therefore, it is worthwhile to understand how the IoT has been applied to people's everyday lives in the development of a smart city concept. More specifically, this chapter reviews the role of the IoT on consumers' daily lives and business in three major areas—smart tourism, healthcare, and retailing—because it is one of the powerful means that contributes significant changes in smart cities.

## BACKGROUND

### Definitions and Characteristics of the IoT

It is known that the IoT, "allows people and things to be connected anytime, anyplace, with anything and anyone ideally using any path/network and any service" (Guillemin & Friess 2009, p. 8). The IoT uses technologies of radio-frequency identification (RFID), wireless sensor network (WSN), and 4G/5G mobile communication to identify, locate, track, monitor, and manage smart objects (Mingjun et al., 2012). The "things" are smart objects that are able to be connected to other devices and communicate with them in real time. They could be typical internet-enabled consumer devices, such as home appliances, smart phones/TVs/speakers, wearable devices, vehicles, lights/switches, and so on.

Within the definition of the IoT, three main system-level characteristics have been identified (Miorandi et al., 2012, p. 1502):

1) *Anything communicates*: smart things have the ability to wirelessly communicate among themselves, and form ad hoc networks of interconnected objects.
2) *Anything is identified*: smart things are identified with a digital name and the relationships among things can be specified in the digital domain whenever physical interconnection cannot be established.

3) *Anything interacts*: smart things can interact with the local environment through sensing and actuation whenever present.

This IoT is a complex and sociotechnical system comprised of physical, technological, and socioeconomic environments. In the physical environment, people and things are linked and interacted together with a ubiquitous wireless network. The technological environment includes hardware, software, networking, integrated platforms, technical standards, and data. The socioeconomic environment focuses more on stakeholders, such as entrepreneurs, business leaders, government, consumers, and so on (Krotov, 2017). Table 1 (Krotov, 2017, p. 834) summarizes elements of IoT.

The connectivity of the IoT leads to several types of interaction: 1) consumers can interact directly with the devices; 2) the devices can interact directly with each other; 3) consumers can interact with each other through the devices; and 4) the devices can interact with the physical world (Hoffman & Novak, 2015). This internet capability of the IoT not only makes consumers easily control devices but also changes company–customer relationships (Balmer & Yen, 2017).

## Adoption of the IoT

Even though current consumers are not likely to quickly adopt this revolutionary technology, such as a smart-home device (e.g., internet-connected appliances, home-monitoring systems, speakers, or lighting) (Woodside & Sood, 2016), the IoT market is estimated to be worth $3 trillion with over 27 billion IoT internet connections to be in place by 2025 (Meyer, 2016). With such a rate of expansion and spread of its impact on consumers' daily lives, the acceptance and use of IoT technology is an area that has become necessary to investigate. Researchers have attempted to identify the driving factors that have led consumers to adopt the IoT technology (e.g., Balaji et al., 2018; Gao & Bai, 2014; Pazvant & Faiz, 2018). For example, Gao and Bai (2014) identified factors that affected the acceptance of the IoT adopting the technology acceptance model (TAM) as a theoretical base. First, the IoT is likely to be accepted when users think it is very useful to facilitating their daily lives (perceived usefulness). Second, the use of the IoT technology should be easy to use (perceived ease of use). Third, users' adoption of the IoT is also affected by social influence, such as peers, family, and the media (social influence). Fourth, users are highly motivated to adopt the IoT technology when it is enjoyable and fun to use (perceived enjoyment). Fifth, the acceptance of the IoT increases as users believe that they know how to use it (perceived behavioral control). Pazvant and Faiz (2018) also used TAM as a theoretical model and demonstrated that behavioral intention to use the IoT is influenced by perceived usefulness, ease of use, and attitude.

*Table 1. Elements of the IoT*

| | | |
|---|---|---|
| **Technological Environment** | Hardware | Various wireless devices (e.g., wireless laptop computers, smart phones, RFID tags, wireless censors, RFID readers) used to connect to human and non-human objects on the IoT and enable communication and interaction among these objects via a ubiquitous wireless network. |
| | Software | Front-end software applications developed to create value for a particular group of customers and various utility applications (e.g., middleware or server-side software) supporting execution of end-user IoT apps. |
| | Networking | Various networking technologies and hardware enabling wireless communication among IoT nodes and connecting these nodes to the internet. |
| | Integrated platforms | An integrated, cloud-based platform (e.g., Microsoft Azure) that enables integration and seamless interoperability of various hardware, software, and networking elements of the IoT. |
| | Standards | Various technical and operational standards outlining the design of various IoT elements and ensuring their interoperability. Standards are developed by industry associations. |
| | Data | Massive volumes of data generated by IoT nodes constantly broadcasting their properties via the network (e.g., a temperature sensor broadcasting the room temperature every two minutes) or by engaging in transaction with other IoT nodes. |
| **Physical Environment** | Human objects | People directly interacting with the IoT with the help of various wireless devices (e.g., laptop computers, smartphones, RFID tags, health sensors). |
| | Non-human objects | Physical objects (e.g., cars, fruits, packages) and animals that can connect and communicate via a network. |
| | Physical surrounding | The physical space (e.g., room, building, park, city) or a physical substance (e.g., air, water, soil) that human and non-human objects are embedded in or interact with. |
| **Socio-Economic Environment** | Consumers | Individual consumers or organizations targeted by specific IoT applications. |
| | Legislative bodies | Organizations responsible for formulating, disseminating, and enforcing various laws and regulations related to IoT. |
| | Industry associations | Various organizations comprising for-profit companies and non-profit institutions responsible for setting standards and guidelines that facilitate IoT adoption and ensure interoperability of IoT technological elements and security of the overall IoT infrastructure. |
| | Consumer privacy groups | Formal and information organizations advocating for consumer rights and protection consumers of IoT applications and related technology from security and privacy violations. |
| | Entrepreneurs | Entrepreneurs and leaders of existing businesses or non-profit organizations engaging in entrepreneurship and intrapreneurship using IoT. |

Source: (Krotov, 2017)

However, there are concerns about consumers' adoption of the IoT as it is expected that the growth of the adoption rate is strong in the long-term. A 2016 Accenture digital consumer survey (which polled 28,000 consumers in 28 countries on the use of consumer technology) reported that price, security, and ease of use are barriers that prevent consumers from adopting the IoT devices and services. Of the consumers, 62% responded that IoT devices are too expensive and 47% were concerned about privacy and security, such as data breaches and hacker attacks. In addition, 61% of consumers experienced challenges (e.g., too complicated to use) when using a new IoT device (Björnsjö et al., 2016). Mani and Chouk (2017) also investigated factors of consumers' resistance to IoT devices and identified several barriers. If consumers perceive that smart products are not useful (perceived usefulness) or not unique/different (perceived novelty), consumer resistance to smart products is high. High prices are also a barrier (perceived price). In addition, if consumers are concerned about privacy (privacy concerns) or their ability to use (self-efficacy), they are more likely to face high resistance to adoption. These identified barriers inform companies that they must fix them to ignite the growth of adoption rate and offer positive experiences.

## APPLICATION FIELDS OF IoT

It has been discussed that the IoT has a positive effect on consumers and companies. From the consumers' view, IoT could boost efficiency, convenience, and quality of consumers' living by empowering them to control products. From the companies' view, they could learn consumer behavior, preferences, and influences by accumulating consumer-related information through devices and individuals who connect to internet via such devices (Balmer & Yen, 2017). Because the IoT technologies have been given wide attention, there is large number of applications in many areas, such as transportation and logistics (e.g., assisted driving), healthcare (e.g., tracking, data collection), smart-environment (e.g., home, office, smart gym), and personal and social domains (e.g., social networking). The quality of consumers' lives would be improved by these applications (Atzori et al., 2010). Table 2 (Woodside & Sood, 2017, p. 100) shows several products as examples that are closely-linked to consumers' daily lives.

### Smart Tourism Destination and IoT

In this section, smart tourism is discussed as an application to the IoT: 1) smart tourism is one of the industries that has been most transformed by IoT technology (Atzori et al., 2010; Chiappa & Baggio, 2015); 2) the IoT is a core network able to realize smart tourism (Wu, 2017); and 3) smart tourism is one of the most important factors in constructing a smart city (Tripathy et al., 2018).

*Table 2. IoT application*

| Thing (Object) | Description |
| --- | --- |
| Inhaler | Connects an asthma inhaler to a mobile phone. System provides insight from crowdsourcing user data predicting inhaler usage |
| Mobile social | Mobile phone uses internal sensors for position determination and appends social media pictures and videos creating personal stories, e.g., social media—Snapchat |
| Lock | Remote door locking from a mobile phone controlled via the internet. In hotels, the lock usage from mobile phones bypasses receptionists for quick check-in |
| Light | Lighting systems controllable from phone applications, as well as external triggers, e.g., if the weather is rainy the application will be set in light blue |
| Taxi | A phone application directs a taxi directly to the requestor. The payment for the ride is cashless, e.g., ride-sharing services—Uber, Lyft, etc. |
| Payment reader | A small credit card reader plugs into the mobile phone allowing businesses the opportunity to conduct business anywhere |
| Mood tracker | Smartwatch monitors mood and heart rate recommend interventions for managing stress |
| Commerce button | Pressing a button initiates ordering of a single preprogrammed item via Wi-Fi. The button normally resides with existing household supplies, including soap powder, e.g., Amazon dash |
| Beacon | Sensors transmit location and offers to mobile phone users. Devices are capable of integration within store mannequins or shelving |
| Video doorbell | Sharable video of events captured upon doorbell ringing and neighborhood level viewing as 'next door TV' |
| Smart glasses | An innovative "pick-by-vision" allowing hands-free ordering |
| Shopping bag | Once customers place items in a bag it calculates the total and commences with auto checkout |
| Umbrella | A connected umbrella sends an alert if it is left behind. A novel feature is a built-in weather station providing alerts to the community |
| Drone | Unmanned aerial vehicle with the ability to fly maintaining payloads of sensors, including video cameras and to carry packages |
| Robot | Character-driven social robot for acting as a family assistant—helpful for seniors, adults, teens, and kids in the home |
| Signage | A digital signage solution for shopping centers, restaurants, and schools using digital television and a centrally-controlled set of top boxes with scheduled play out of the messages and/or advertising |

Source: (Woodside & Sood, 2017)

Tourist destinations offer an integrated experience to consumers (e.g., tourists) through a combination of touristic products and services. Even though travelers select destinations based on geographical regions (e.g., country, island, town), they also select areas under their motivation for the trip (e.g., purpose of visit, past experience). As tourism destinations, successful ones have six core resources known as the six A's:

1) Attractions (e.g., natural, artificial, cultural place)
2) Accessibility (e.g., transportation system)
3) Amenities (e.g., accommodation, tourist services)
4) Available packages (e.g., service bundles)
5) Activities (e.g., festivals)
6) Ancillary services (e.g., banks, hospitals) (Buhalis, 2000)

As emerging technologies, such as information communication technologies, influence travel and tourism (Atzori et al., 2010; Soteriades & Avgeli, 2007), smartness has been required in tourism destinations (Buhalis & Amaranggana, 2014). Because a place where this smartness is deployed is considered a smart city, the development of a smart city could positively affect the formation of smart tourism destinations. From a tourism context, smartness creates an environment where various stakeholders (e.g., tourists, tourism organizations, governments, and local residents/communities) are interconnected through a technological platform, and information related to tourism activities can be exchanged in real time (Buhalis & Amaranggana, 2014). Guo et al. (2014) and Wang et al. (2016) note that smart tourism is supported by four core information technologies: IoT, mobile communication, cloud computing, and artificial intelligence technologies. Table 3 (Kaur & Kaur, 2016, p. 358) shows the various technologies deployed in order to provide smart tourism services, such as mobile communication (e.g., web and mobile services), cloud computing, the IoT, and Big Data analysis. In addition, Nitti et al. (2017) proposed the IoT as the core element of building smart tourism in the smart city.

*Table 3. Ideas for smart tourism*

| Smart Tourism Ideas |
| --- |
| Use of sensors, cameras, and smart phones |
| Use of Big Data to analyze information |
| Collaboration of web and mobile services |
| Use of cloud services and the IoT |
| Use of touch screens for easy interaction |
| Better assistance to tourists through mobile tours and apps |

Source: (Kaur & Kaur, 2016)

## Geo-Location Technologies and IoT

In a smart tourism destination system, IoT-connected devices enable tourists to immediately access any travel information (e.g., food, accommodation, attractions, shopping, entertainment, and other related information) as well as any form of information (e.g., text, photos, audio, video, and other forms) while they are traveling. These devices allow them to effectively plan trips, explore the destination, and make a better decision for travel; thus, it brings enhanced tourism experiences and the satisfaction of tourism to tourists.

IoT technologies can be deployed in the accommodation industry to provide integrated services to tourists. Automated door locks, thermostats, light switches, TV, telephones, and other devices could be connected to a common network so that guests could have personalized experiences in a smart guest room. Table 4 (Car et al., 2019, p. 170–171) shows several solutions and examples of IoT in the hospitality industry.

Brennan et al. (2018) investigated how foreign tourists use smartphone applications while visiting South Korea. Tourists were likely to use smartphones and applications to book accommodations, search for attractions/information, shop online, navigate downtown streets on foot or by car, and interact with others. They also like to share their experiences with family and friends through social media. South Korea, a smart tourism destination, provides tourists with a variety of personalized mobile application services to improve foreign tourists' experience and maximize enjoyment while traveling. In addition, New York City provides free services like high-speed public Wi-Fi, phone calls to anywhere in the U.S., device charging, and a touchscreen tablets for access to maps and city services through Links, a communication network kiosk. There are more than 2,200 Links installed in NYC (Shah et al., 2019). Local people, as well as tourists visiting in New York City, enjoy these free services.

## Big Data Analysis and IoT

The development of the IoT has helped providers collect and analyze data from IoT sensors, and generate results. Especially, real-time internet connectivity in smart tourism makes it possible to generate the huge amount of Big Data available from tourists. For example, tourism enterprises and practitioners (e.g., travel agencies, hotels, and transportations) can use the IoT as a powerful network channel to capture tourist interest, identify tourism hotspots, and so on. Gajdošík (2019) discussed how to collect large volumes of data available from tourists while they are traveling because a data-driven approach is a promising way to understand tourists' behavior. During the stay at the destination, data could be collected from various sources. For example, social media provide valuable information, such as comments,

*Table 4. The IoT contributions to the hospitality industry*

| Solution | Application/Example |
|---|---|
| Personalized hotel rooms | The Hilton and Marriott have experimented with slightly different takes on the "connected room" concept, where users are able to control many of the room's features from their mobile phone or from a provided tablet. In addition, over time, the IoT platforms could memorize a guest's specific comfort preferences, such as temperature, lights, TV channels and shades, and automatically set up the room for their next stay. Hotels can automatically send electronic key cards to guests' smartphones, allowing them to check-in without anyone's assistance. |
| Voice-based interaction | *Amazon Alexa* enables the guest to use voice-controls on different smart home devices. It is basically a guest's personal butler who never tires of fulfilling their needs. Alexa can be configured by hospitality providers to allow guests to control and adjust in-room devices, such as lights, thermostats, blinds, and TVs. |
| Integration with mobile | *Fast check-in*: Starwood and Hilton, for example, already offer an option of checking in via a mobile gadget instead of spending time at the front desk. *Control device*: All functions performed by several remote controls, key cards, and switches are now controlled by one click of a button on a mobile device. |
| Body area sensors | *Wireless medical sensor* technology further expands the scope of data collection by providing detailed data about organs and systems within the body. For example, service providers can filter out high carbohydrate and sugary meal options for diabetic guests, high cholesterol meal options for patients with heart disease, etc. |
| Inventory management | The IoT will change the way hotels manage their inventories. IoT-implemented systems will keep record of the inventory and manage the changes in them automatically. |
| Location-based information | The ability to send SMS about menu items at the restaurant when guests are close by or advertising gym services when they are near the gym. It may also mean sending up-to-date information about local transport links or nearby attractions. |
| "Flic": a wireless button | With "Flic", guests could notify housekeepers about issues with the press of a button. Ordering services and sending automated messages are facilitated, e.g., when someone calls reception to ask for more towels or coffee. |
| Building automation and monitoring | In-room monitoring systems can be used to detect whether a room is occupied or unoccupied so as to schedule housekeeping services. |

Source: (Car, Stifanich & Šimunić, 2019)

reviews, photos, and videos. Destinations' and hotels' websites also generate more specific data, such as transaction data from hotel reservations. Sensors embedded throughout destination environment are other sources. RFID or Wi-Fi hotspots can monitor tourists' behavior and measure the density of crowds during their stay at a destination. Many attractions (e.g., theme parks) already use an RFID-based wristband as one of the IoT technologies. It can be used to grant guests access to their attractions, rooms, and other services, and pay for purchases without carrying wallets and so on. Service providers collect and analyze the huge amount of data from guests to plan marketing strategies and improve their services and efficiency. Del Vecchio et al. (2018) discussed how big data can create value for stakeholders at a smart tourism destination, focusing on social media data (e.g., posts, tweet/

retweets, comments, replies, photo, and video) published on event organizers' official websites, Instagram, Facebook, and Twitter. Applying a multiple-case study analysis, this research suggests that social Big Data analysis improves managers and promoters' decision-making processes, enhances tourists' experiences, develops new business models and service offerings, and builds strong relationships between customers and stakeholders.

The amount of data generated by connected IoT devices allows travel agencies and attractions to develop new travel routes and customized marketing activities, enhance tourists' experiences, and create new product and service offerings. They can also respond quickly to tourists' comments and complaints by monitoring tourists' activities in real-time so that they have a greater chance of satisfying tourists' needs and wants. Governments can use data collected by websites, social media, mobile devices, and wearables to monitor tourist activities and supervise the operation of tourism enterprises and practitioners. This may allow governments to effectively manage the tourist market.

## Smart Healthcare and IoT

As people are concerned about their health and willing to seek good-quality treatment regardless of the distance from their home, the importance of the IoT technologies in the healthcare industry is emphasized (MIMOS Berhad, 2014). In the healthcare industry, the Internet of health things (IoHT) integrates the physical and digital worlds through smart objects that communicate with other objects or people. IoHT can be used as a tool to improve access to health, quality of care, and consumer experience (Andrews et al., 2017). For example, patients' health conditions (e.g., cardiac, mental, and behavioral health) can be monitored remotely and regularly by IoHT even though they are not in the hospital. The interconnection between smart objects allows medical centers to gather data available on monitoring patient activities in their living environments, prevent falls in an emergency, and quickly respond to health deterioration when needed. Service providers can effectively offer wellness and prevention services to patients and customers through wearables. Wearables offer the opportunity to track and monitor tourists' daily activities, such as steps taken, stairs climbed, duration and quality of sleep, pulse or heart rate, and calories consumed and burned. The collected data from wearables provide personalized analysis and advice to empower them to live a healthier life.

Wearable activity trackers are very useful for older adults—especially those who have never used them—because wearables enable them to focus on and increase their level of physical activity (Kononova et al., 2019). In addition, there are situations where people cannot easily move from their source location to their healthcare destination (e.g., a medical center) due to a special health condition.

For those people, Geographical Routing for Mobile Tourists (GRMT) has been developed based on the interconnectivity of the IoT technologies, such as tourists' wearables and smartphones, cellular networks, healthcare centers, and databases (e.g., a geographical and transportation database, a healthcare database, and a tourism location database). This approach offers an appropriate route to the nearest healthcare center even when tourists have an emergency condition (Almobaideen et al., 2017).

## Retailing and IoT

As shown in table 5 (Grewal et al., 2020, p. 100), many retailers have been adopting IoT technologies to enhance customers' shopping experiences. Because the IoT technology enables customers to interact with retailers in real-time while they are shopping at the store, they can make more informed decisions and receive more customized and up-to-date offers.

In a retailing context, smartphones play a large role in the IoT because shoppers can use their smartphone to interact with IoT devices. For example, customized in-store experiences (e.g., personalized promotion) are provided to customers who enter the store having retail applications through location-based beacon technology (Gregory, 2015). Smart shelves also use this proximity-based beacon communication to send personalized product-related marketing messages (e.g., discounts, targeted advertisements) and a helpful reminder to shoppers' mobile phone applications (Inman & Nikolova, 2017). Scan-and-go technology allows customers to scan items via their smartphone while shopping, checking out, and paying in the retailer's application (e.g., Sam's club) (Inman & Nikolova, 2017). In Amazon Go stores, customers scan their smartphones at the store entrance, pick up the products they want, and pay without scanning them at the check-out (Grewal et al., 2020; Grewal et al., 2017). In addition, customers' shopping information (e.g., their movements through a store) is collected by sensors and used to provide them with an enhanced in-store shopping experience by improving store layout and merchandise placement (Gregory, 2015).

While customers are shopping at the retailer, the interaction with the IoT retail technology influences their perceived value of using IoT. For example, by interacting with smart shopping cars, customers receive shopping-related information in real-time (e.g., information on product location, information related to products), which results in enjoying a personalized shopping experience (Balaji & Roy, 2017). When the IoT is attractive and easy to use, and provides advanced features and functions, consumers are more likely to perceive it with high shopping value through IoT and continue to use the IoT (Adapa et al., 2020; Balaji & Roy, 2017). Moreover, consumers with a high perceived value of using smart retail technology are likely to efficiently complete their shopping goals; thus, they are more likely to have loyalty to a store (Adapa et al., 2020).

*Table 5. In-store technology examples in a retailing context*

| Retailers | Summary of In-Store Technology |
|---|---|
| Amazon 4-star; Fry's | Digital price tags at Amazon 4-Star stores are updated based on Amazon.com prices and display different prices for Prime members. At Fry's, digital price tags also feature video advertisements, coupons, and nutritional information; stores can instantly change prices and activate promotions to undercut competitors. |
| Kroger; Stop & Shop | Self-checkout using mobile or handheld scanners that allow consumers to scan groceries as they shop, bag them instantly, and leave the store after paying at a self-checkout lane; options to pay through the scanners will exist in the future. |
| Amazon Go Store | Grab and go options that require consumers to scan their smartphones upon entry; they can then grab items and walk out without needing to check out because AI and cameras capture what consumers purchase and charge their account. |
| IKEA; Kate Spade | Augmented reality at IKEA is now offered at select stores: consumers can upload pictures of their room and virtually place IKEA furniture in it to create a desired look. At Kate Spade, consumers can create custom Kate Spade handbags using an in-store augmented reality display that senses which bag the consumer has picked up, then be offered various options from which to choose to express personality (e.g., straps, flaps, bag charms). |
| Geissler Grocery | In-store kiosks list recipe ideas, promotions, and information; consumers can review the deals and recipes to find ones that meet their needs. |
| Sephora | Social augmented reality that allows consumers to take pictures of themselves and then try on cosmetics and receive suggestions, both from the application and from friends with whom the consumers share the pictures on social media. |
| Rebecca Minkoff | Smart mirrors in dressing rooms allow shoppers to adjust the lighting and contact sales associates to obtain other desired products. Consumers can also see the items they are trying on in different colors or accessorize with various items to create unique looks. |
| Marriott & Dominos | Disembodied robots, such as Alexa, can turn on lights, provide information in response to requests from Marriott hotel guests, or else allow consumers to order pizza from Domino's through a voice-activated assistant. |
| Lowes | Embodied customer service robots, such as the LoweBot, roam stores to allow consumers to interact with it and receive answers to their questions. |

Source: (Grewal, Noble, Rogevveen, & Nordfalt, 2020)

## Challenges Faced by the IoT World

While the IoT provides consumers with several benefits, such as personalized and enhanced customer experiences, its challenges should not be overlooked. Crucially, security and privacy have been identified as the major concerns for consumers regardless of applications to which the IoT technology is applied (Acquity group, 2014; Al-Momani et al., 2016; Maple, 2017; Nord et al., 2019).

Cremer et al. (2017) addressed the overlooked areas of the dark side of IoT, focusing on the negative aspects of the IoT on marketing practices. Information misuse and privacy issues were highlighted as the IoT providers' behaviors for its own benefits rather than those of the customers. Because the IoT empowers firms to monitor customers' everyday lives through the IoT devices (e.g., wearable exercise units, smart devices), they are likely to collect as much information about customers as possible. However, such powerful knowledge does allow firms to overpower customers and this detailed information could be used in ways of which they do not approve or of which they are not aware. In addition, customers' sensitive and personal information may be used in unwanted and intrusive ways, such as pop-up ads or unsolicited emails, offering various unwanted services.

With respect to the issues of security, people are concerned about whether personal information is exposed by hacks and data breaches because the IoT devices usually collect and store their personal information as well as monitor their activities (Acquity group, 2014; Al-Momani et al., 2016; Maple, 2017; Nord et al., 2019). Therefore, data protection from unauthorized persons and the confidentiality of consumers' personal information have to be guaranteed so that customers perceived privacy risk is reduced (Sicari et al., 2015). The IoT service providers have to clearly communicate what data is being collected and for what it is going to be used (e.g., the consent of the consumer to use their data) (Maple, 2017). In addition, more secure mechanisms to authenticate, identify, and authorize legitimate users should be provided along with data anonymity and confidentiality in order to keep unauthorized users from accessing these data (Maple, 2017; Sicari et al., 2015)

## CONCLUSION

The purpose of this chapter is to provide insight into the role of the IoT on consumers' daily lives and business by reviewing its fields of application because the IoT is instrumental to the successful implementation of a smart city (Jin et al., 2014). Especially, smart tourism, healthcare, and retail are discussed to learn what benefits consumers and entrepreneurs get from the IoT technologies. These application fields are closely connected to the development of the smart city and their markets increase with the IoT technologies (Adapa et al. 2020; Andrews et al., 2017; MIMOS Berhad, 2014). The IoT offers many advantages, such as efficient operation, reduced cost, increased productivity, more satisfied customers, and differentiated/customized services. Through the IoT concept and its application, it is expected that the IoT technologies can be applied to any consumer market to enhance consumers' satisfaction and quality of life, and have numerous business opportunities. However, the negative aspects of the IoT also have been discussed. Cremer et al. (2017) highlighted the situations where the IoT providers intentionally exploit their customers in unfair ways for their own benefits. For example, privacy violations occur because they access customers' data, including sensitive and personal information collected by the IoT device. In addition, they may use customers' data not for customer satisfaction but for their own profit. Therefore, the IoT needs to find ways to overcome obstacles and challenges in the process of implementing IoT. This chapter will be helpful for researchers and practitioners to understand the huge role of IoT, especially in a consumer market.

## REFERENCES

Acquity Group. (2014). *Internet of Health Things: The Future of Consumer Adoption.* Accenture Report.

Al-Momani, A. M., Mahmoud, M. A., & Ahmad, M. S. (2016). Modeling the adoption of internet of things services: A conceptual framework. *International Journal of Applied Research, 2*(5), 361–367.

Andrews, K., M., Hsii, P., & Porritt, A. (2017). *Internet of Health Things Survey.* Accenture Report.

Anthopoulos, L., Janssen, M., & Weerakkody, V. (2016). A Unified Smart City Model (USCM) for smart city conceptualization and benchmarking. In Smart Cities and Smart Spaces: Concepts, Methodologies, Tools, and Applications (pp. 247-264). IGI Global.

Atzori, L., Iera, A., & Morabito, G. (2010). The internet of things: A survey. *Computer Networks, 54*(15), 2787–2805. doi:10.1016/j.comnet.2010.05.010

Balaji, M. S., & Roy, S. K. (2017). Value co-creation with Internet of things technology in the retail industry. *Journal of Marketing Management, 33*(1-2), 7–31. doi:10.10 80/0267257X.2016.1217914

Balaji, M. S., Roy, S. K., Sengupta, A., & Chong, A. (2018). User acceptance of IoT applications in retail industry. In Technology Adoption and Social Issues: Concepts, Methodologies, Tools, and Applications (pp. 1331-1352). IGI Global. doi:10.4018/978-1-5225-5201-7.ch061

Balmer, J. M., & Yen, D. A. (2017). The Internet of total corporate communications, quaternary corporate communications and the corporate marketing Internet revolution. *Journal of Marketing Management, 33*(1-2), 131–144. doi:10.1080/02 67257X.2016.1255440

Berhad, M. I. M. O. S. (2014). *IoT Idea Book, Kuala Lumpur, Malaysia.* Retrieved January 2, 2020, from http://www.mimos.my/wp-content/uploads/2016/01/IoT-Idea-Book-Experiential-Travel-and-Tourism.pdf

Björnsjö, A., Viglino, M., & Lovati, G. (2016). *Igniting Growth in Consumer Technology.* Accenture Report.

Brennan, B. S., Koo, C., & Bae, K. M. (2018). Smart Tourism: A Study of Mobile Application Use by Tourists Visiting South Korea. *Asia-pacific Journal of Multimedia Services Convergent with Art, Humanities, and Sociology, 8*(10), 1–9.

Buhalis, D. (2000). Marketing the competitive destination of the future. *Tourism Management, 21*(1), 97–116. doi:10.1016/S0261-5177(99)00095-3

Car, T., Stifanich, L. P., & Šimunić, M. (2019). Internet of Things (IoT) in Tourism and Hospitality: Opportunities and Challenges. *Tourism in Southern and Eastern Europe, 5,* 163–175. doi:10.20867/tosee.05.42

Davis, F. D. (1989). Perceived usefulness, perceived ease of use, and user acceptance of information technology. *Management Information Systems Quarterly, 13*(3), 319–340. doi:10.2307/249008

De Cremer, D., Nguyen, B., & Simkin, L. (2017). The integrity challenge of the Internet-of-Things (IoT): On understanding its dark side. *Journal of Marketing Management, 33*(1-2), 145–158. doi:10.1080/0267257X.2016.1247517

Deakin, M. (Ed.). (2013). *Smart cities: governing, modelling and analysing the transition.* Routledge. doi:10.4324/9780203076224

Del Chiappa, G., & Baggio, R. (2015). Knowledge transfer in smart tourism destinations: Analyzing the effects of a network structure. *Journal of Destination Marketing & Management, 4*(3), 145–150. doi:10.1016/j.jdmm.2015.02.001

Del Vecchio, P., Mele, G., Ndou, V., & Secundo, G. (2018). Creating value from social big data: Implications for smart tourism destinations. *Information Processing & Management, 54*(5), 847–860. doi:10.1016/j.ipm.2017.10.006

Eremia, M., Toma, L., & Sanduleac, M. (2017). The smart city concept in the 21st century. *Procedia Engineering, 181,* 12–19. doi:10.1016/j.proeng.2017.02.357

Gajdošík, T. (2019). Big Data Analytics in Smart Tourism Destinations. A New Tool for Destination Management Organizations? In *Smart Tourism as a Driver for Culture and Sustainability* (pp. 15–33). Springer. doi:10.1007/978-3-030-03910-3_2

Gao, L., & Bai, X. (2014). A unified perspective on the factors influencing consumer acceptance of internet of things technology. *Asia Pacific Journal of Marketing and Logistics, 26*(2), 211–231. doi:10.1108/APJML-06-2013-0061

Gregory, J. (2015). *The Internet of Things: revolutionizing the retail industry.* Accenture Strategy.

Grewal, D., Noble, S. M., Roggeveen, A. L., & Nordfalt, J. (2020). The future of in-store technology. *Journal of the Academy of Marketing Science, 48*(1), 96–113. doi:10.100711747-019-00697-z

Grewal, D., Roggeveen, A. L., & Nordfält, J. (2017). The future of retailing. *Journal of Retailing, 93*(1), 1–6. doi:10.1016/j.jretai.2016.12.008

Guillemin, P., & Friess, P. (2009). *Internet of things strategic research roadmap.* The Cluster of European Research Projects, Tech. Rep.

Guo, Y., Liu, H., & Chai, Y. (2014). The embedding convergence of smart cities and tourism internet of things in China: An advance perspective. *Advances in Hospitality and Tourism Research, 2*(1), 54–69.

HoffmanD. L.NovakT. (2015). Emergent experience and the connected consumer in the smart home assemblage and the internet of things. Available at SSRN 2648786. doi:10.2139srn.2648786

Inman, J. J., & Nikolova, H. (2017). Shopper-facing retail technology: A retailer adoption decision framework incorporating shopper attitudes and privacy concerns. *Journal of Retailing, 93*(1), 7–28. doi:10.1016/j.jretai.2016.12.006

Jin, J., Gubbi, J., Marusic, S., & Palaniswami, M. (2014). An information framework for creating a smart city through internet of things. *IEEE Internet of Things Journal, 1*(2), 112–121. doi:10.1109/JIOT.2013.2296516

Kaur, K., & Kaur, R. (2016). Internet of things to promote tourism: An insight into smart tourism. *International Journal of Recent Trends in Engineering & Research, 2*(4), 357–361.

Kononova, A., Li, L., Kamp, K., Bowen, M., Rikard, R. V., Cotten, S., & Peng, W. (2019). The Use of Wearable Activity Trackers among Older Adults: Focus Group Study of Tracker Perceptions, Motivators, and Barriers in the Maintenance Stage of Behavior Change. *JMIR mHealth and uHealth, 7*(4), e9832. doi:10.2196/mhealth.9832 PMID:30950807

Kopackova, H., & Libalova, P. (2017, July). Smart city concept as socio-technical system. In *2017 International Conference on Information and Digital Technologies (IDT)* (pp. 198-205). IEEE. 10.1109/DT.2017.8024297

Krotov, V. (2017). The Internet of Things and new business opportunities. *Business Horizons, 60*(6), 831–841. doi:10.1016/j.bushor.2017.07.009

Mani, Z., & Chouk, I. (2017). Drivers of consumers' resistance to smart products. *Journal of Marketing Management, 33*(1-2), 76–97. doi:10.1080/026725 7X.2016.1245212

Maple, C. (2017). Security and privacy in the internet of things. *Journal of Cyber Policy, 2*(2), 155–184. doi:10.1080/23738871.2017.1366536

Meyer, D. (2016). Why Smartphones Are Bringing Down Internet-of-Things Revenue Forecasts. *Fortune.* https://fortune.com/2016/08/04/smartphones-iot-revenue-machina/

Mingjun, W., Zhen, Y., Wei, Z., Xishang, D., Xiaofei, Y., Chenggang, S., & Jinghai, H. (2012, October). A research on experimental system for Internet of things major and application project. In *2012 3rd International Conference on System Science, Engineering Design and Manufacturing Informatization* (Vol. 1, pp. 261-263). IEEE. 10.1109/ICSSEM.2012.6340722

Miorandi, D., Sicari, S., De Pellegrini, F., & Chlamtac, I. (2012). Internet of things: Vision, applications and research challenges. *Ad Hoc Networks, 10*(7), 1497–1516. doi:10.1016/j.adhoc.2012.02.016

Nitti, M., Pilloni, V., Giusto, D., & Popescu, V. (2017). Iot architecture for a sustainable tourism application in a smart city environment. *Mobile Information Systems.*

Nord, J. H., Koohang, A., & Paliszkiewicz, J. (2019). The Internet of Things: Review and theoretical framework. *Expert Systems with Applications, 133*, 97–108. doi:10.1016/j.eswa.2019.05.014

Park, E., Del Pobil, A. P., & Kwon, S. J. (2018). The role of Internet of Things (IoT) in smart cities: Technology roadmap-oriented approaches. *Sustainability, 10*(5), 1388. doi:10.3390u10051388

Pazvant, E., & Faiz, E. (2018). Evaluation of the intention of using products with internet of things within the context of technology acceptance model. *Journal of Management, Marketing and Logistics*, 41-54.

Piro, G., Cianci, I., Grieco, L. A., Boggia, G., & Camarda, P. (2014). Information centric services in smart cities. *Journal of Systems and Software, 88*, 169–188. doi:10.1016/j.jss.2013.10.029

Shah, J., Kothari, J., & Doshi, N. (2019). A Survey of Smart City infrastructure via Case study on New York. *Procedia Computer Science, 160*, 702–705. doi:10.1016/j. procs.2019.11.024

Sicari, S., Rizzardi, A., Grieco, L. A., & Coen-Porisini, A. (2015). Security, privacy and trust in Internet of Things: The road ahead. *Computer Networks, 76*, 146–164. doi:10.1016/j.comnet.2014.11.008

Soteriades, M. D., & Avgeli, V. A. (2007). Promoting tourism destinations: a strategic marketing approach. *Turizam: međunarodni znanstveno-stručni časopis, 55*(3), 335-345.

Tripathy, A. K., Tripathy, P. K., Ray, N. K., & Mohanty, S. P. (2018). iTour: The future of smart tourism: An IoT framework for the independent mobility of tourists in smart cities. *IEEE Consumer Electronics Magazine, 7*(3), 32–37. doi:10.1109/MCE.2018.2797758

Vicini, S., Bellini, S., & Sanna, A. (2012, May). How to co-create Internet of things-enabled services for smarter cities. In *The First International Conference on Smart Systems, Devices and Technologies* (pp. 55-61). Academic Press.

Wang, X., Li, X. R., Zhen, F., & Zhang, J. (2016). How smart is your tourist attraction?: Measuring tourist preferences of smart tourism attractions via a FCEM-AHP and IPA approach. *Tourism Management, 54*, 309–320. doi:10.1016/j.tourman.2015.12.003

Woodside, A. G., & Sood, S. (2017). Vignettes in the two-step arrival of the internet of things and its reshaping of marketing management's service-dominant logic. *Journal of Marketing Management, 33*(1-2), 98–110. doi:10.1080/0267257X.2016.1246748

Wu, X. (2017). Smart tourism based on internet of things. *Revista de la Facultad de Ingeniería, 32*(10), 66–170.

Zubizarreta, I., Seravalli, A., & Arrizabalaga, S. (2015). Smart city concept: What it is and what it should be. *Journal of Urban Planning and Development, 142*(1), 04015005. doi:10.1061/(ASCE)UP.1943-5444.0000282

## KEY TERMS AND DEFINITIONS

**Big Data:** A large quantity of data engendered by interconnected Internet of things in real time.

**Information and Communication Technology:** Technology that interconnects all forms of communication, enabling users to access, process, and store information, as well as share it with other users.

**Internet of Things (IoT):** Any object/device that is connected to other ones via the internet to communicate and exchange information.

**Smart City:** An urban area that uses information and communication technology to improve the quality of citizen's life and efficiently manage public services.

**Smart Healthcare:** A healthcare system that enables patients and doctors to communicate with each other and remotely exchange information monitored, collected, and analyzed from patients' daily activities via the IoT.

**Smart Tourism Destination:** A place built on the principles of a smart city and satisfies the needs and tastes of tourists through information and communication technology.

# Compilation of References

Acquity Group. (2014). *Internet of Health Things: The Future of Consumer Adoption*. Accenture Report.

Adegun, O. B. (2011). Shelter and the future African city. *The Built & Human Environment Review.*, *4*(2), 33–40.

Agarwala, N., & Chaudhary, R. D. (2019). China's Policy on Science and Technology: Implications for the Next Industrial Transition. *India Quarterly*, *75*(2), 206–227. doi:10.1177/0974928419841786

Agranoff, R. (2006). Inside Collaborative Networks: Ten Lessons for Public Managers. *Public Administration Review*, *66*(1), 56–65. doi:10.1111/j.1540-6210.2006.00666.x

Agranoff, R., & McGuire, M. (2003). *Collaborative Public Management: New Strategies for Local Governments*. Georgetown University Press.

Ajao, A. (2019). *Electric scooters and micro-mobility: Here's everything you need to know*. https://www.forbes.com/sites/adeyemiajao/2019/02/01/everything-you-want-to-know-about-scooters-and-micro-mobility/#4e7112cc5de6

Aksoy, A. (2019). *Martı e-scooter experience review*. https://medium.com/@ardaksoy/vaka-analizi-mart%C4%B1-elektrikli-scooter-kiralama-deneyimi-i%CC%87ncelemesi-kullan%C4%B1c%C4%B1-g%C3%B6z%C3%BCnden-2-f16961053530

Alawadhi, S., Aldama-Nalda, A., Chourabi, H., Gil-Garcia, J. R., Leung, S., Mellouli, S., ... Walker, S. (2012, September). Building understanding of smart city initiatives. In *International conference on electronic government* (pp. 40-53). Springer. 10.1007/978-3-642-33489-4_4

Albino, V., Berardi, U., & Dangelico, R. M. (2015). Smart cities: Definitions, dimensions, performance, and initiatives. *Journal of Urban Technology*, *22*(1), 3–21. doi:10.1080/1063073 2.2014.942092

Al-Momani, A. M., Mahmoud, M. A., & Ahmad, M. S. (2016). Modeling the adoption of internet of things services: A conceptual framework. *International Journal of Applied Research*, *2*(5), 361–367.

Al-Nasrawi, Adams, & El-Zaart. (2015). A Conceptual Multidimensional Model for Assessing Smart Sustainable Cities. *Journal of Information Systems and Technology Management*, *12*(3). doi:10.4301/S1807-17752015000300003

Alonso, R. G., & Lippez-De Castro, S. (2016). Technology helps, people make: A smart city governance framework grounded in deliberative democracy. In J. R. Gil-Garcia, T. A. Pardo, & T. Nam (Eds.), *Smarter as the new Urban Agenda* (pp. 333–347). Springer International. doi:10.1007/978-3-319-17620-8_18

Aluko, O. (2010). Rule of law, planning and sustainable development in Nigeria. *Journal of Sustainable Development in Africa, 12*(7), 88–95.

Álvarez, R., Duarte, F., AlRadwan, A., Sit, M., & Ratti, C. (2017). Re-Imagining Streetlight Infrastructure as a Digital Urban Platform. *Journal of Urban Technology, 24*(2), 1–14. doi:10.1 080/10630732.2017.1285084

Andersen, R. (2020). *The Panopticon Is Already Here.* Retrieved 6 August 2020, from https://www.theatlantic.com/magazine/archive/2020/09/china-ai-surveillance/614197/

Andrews, K., M., Hsii, P., & Porritt, A. (2017). *Internet of Health Things Survey.* Accenture Report.

Ansell, C. (2012). Collaborative governance. In The Oxford handbook of governance. Oxford University Press.

Ansell, C. (2000). The networked polity: Regional development in Western Europe. *Governance: An International Journal of Policy, Administration and Institutions, 13*(2), 279–291. doi:10.1111/0952-1895.00136

Ansell, C., & Gash, A. (2008). Collaborative Governance in Theory and Practice. *Journal of Public Administration Theory and Practice, 18*(4), 543–571. doi:10.1093/jopart/mum032

Anthopoulos, L., Janssen, M., & Weerakkody, V. (2016). A Unified Smart City Model (USCM) for smart city conceptualization and benchmarking. In Smart Cities and Smart Spaces: Concepts, Methodologies, Tools, and Applications (pp. 247-264). IGI Global.

Anton, R. (2018). *Intelligent communication and patterning in smart cities.* Assistive Technologies in Smart Cities. Https. doi:10.5772/intechopen.79629

Arndt, W. H., Drews, F., Hertel, M., Langer, V. & Wiedenhöft, E. (2019). *Integration of shared mobility approaches in Sustainable Urban Mobility Planning.* German Institute of Urban Affairs (Difu).

Arora, R., Parashar, A., & Transforming, C. C. I. (2013). Secure user data in cloud computing using encryption algorithms. *International Journal of Engineering Research and Applications, 3*(4), 1922–1926.

Aspin, D. N., & Chapman, J. D. (2012). Toward a philosophy of lifelong learning. In *Second International Handbook of Lifelong Learning* (pp. 3–35). doi:10.1007/978-94-007-2360-3_1

Asubonteng. (2011). *The Potential for PPP in Ethiopia.* Addis Ababa Chamber of Commerce and Sectoral Associations. Retrieved from http://www.ethiopianchamber.com/Data/Sites/1/psd-hub-publications/the-potentialfor-public-private-partnership-(ppp)-in-ethiopia.pdf

Ateş, M., & Önder, D. E. (2019). The Concept of 'Smart City' and Criticism within the Context of its Transforming Meaning. *Megaron, 14*(1). https://austintexas.gov/department/shared-mobility-services

Atzori, L., Iera, A., & Morabito, G. (2010). The internet of things: A survey. *Computer Networks, 54*(15), 2787–2805. doi:10.1016/j.comnet.2010.05.010

Balaji, M. S., Roy, S. K., Sengupta, A., & Chong, A. (2018). User acceptance of IoT applications in retail industry. In Technology Adoption and Social Issues: Concepts, Methodologies, Tools, and Applications (pp. 1331-1352). IGI Global. doi:10.4018/978-1-5225-5201-7.ch061

Balaji, M. S., & Roy, S. K. (2017). Value co-creation with Internet of things technology in the retail industry. *Journal of Marketing Management, 33*(1-2), 7–31. doi:10.1080/0267257X.2016.1217914

Balmer, J. M., & Yen, D. A. (2017). The Internet of total corporate communications, quaternary corporate communications and the corporate marketing Internet revolution. *Journal of Marketing Management, 33*(1-2), 131–144. doi:10.1080/0267257X.2016.1255440

Baltac, V. (2019). Smart cities—A view of societal aspects. *Smart Cities, 2*(4), 538–548. doi:10.3390martcities2040033

Barlow, M., & Levy Bencheton, C. (2019). *Smart cities, smart future: Showcasing tomorrow.* Wiley.

Barriga, J. J., Sulca, J., León, J. L., Ulloa, A., Portero, D., Andrade, R., & Yoo, S. G. (2019). Smart Parking: A Literature Review from the Technological Perspective. *Applied Sciences (Basel, Switzerland), 9*(21), 4569. doi:10.3390/app9214569

Barrionuevo, J. M., Berrone, P., & Ricart, J. E. (2012). Smart Cities, Sustainable Progress. *IESE Expert Insight, 14*, 50–57. Retrieved from: https://www.researchgate.net/ profile/ Pascual_Berrone/ publication/ 276088190_ Smart_ Cities_ Sustainable_ Progress_ Opportunities_ for_ Urban_ Development/ links/ 563f9a3908ae8d65c0150f53.pdf

Bassi, A. (2016). Looking at smart cities with an historical perspective. *Designing, Developing, and Facilitating Smart Cities*, 3–15. doi:10.1007/978-3-319-44924-1_1

Batty, M. (2018). Artificial intelligence and smart cities. *Environment and Planning. B, Urban Analytics and City Science, 45*(1), 3–6. doi:10.1177/2399808317751169

Becker, G. (1964). *Human capital: A theoretical and empirical analysis with special reference to education.* University of Chicago Press.

Benbouzid, B. (2019). To predict and to manage. Predictive policing in the United States. *Big Data & Society, 6*(1). doi:10.1177/2053951719861703

Beom-Su, K., HoSung, P., Kyong Hoon, K., Daniel, G., & Ki-Il, K. (2017). *A Survey on Real-Time Communications in Wireless Sensor Networks.* doi:10.1155/2017/1864847

Berhad, M. I. M. O. S. (2014). *IoT Idea Book, Kuala Lumpur, Malaysia.* Retrieved January 2, 2020, from http://www.mimos.my/wp-content/uploads/2016/01/IoT-Idea-Book-Experiential-Travel-and-Tourism.pdf

Bevir, M., & Richards, D. (2009). Decentering policy networks: A theoretical agenda. *Public Administration, 87*(1), 3–14. doi:10.1111/j.1467-9299.2008.01736.x

Bezançon, X. (2004). *2000 ans d'histoire du partenariat public-privé . Pour la réalisation des équipements et services collectifs.* Paris: Presses de l'ENPC.

Biao, I. (2013). The place of transformative learning in the building of learning cities in Africa. *Journal of Adult and Continuing Education, 19*(1), 3–16. doi:10.7227/JACE.19.1.2

Biswas, S. (2020). *How IoT is impacting businesses today.* Accessed on April 14, 2020 and retrieved from: https://keap.com/ business- success- blog/ marketing/ automation/ how- the- internet- of- things- impacts- small- business

Björnsjö, A., Viglino, M., & Lovati, G. (2016). *Igniting Growth in Consumer Technology.* Accenture Report.

Boehm, J. E., Evans, H. M., Jillavenkatesa, A., Nadal, M. E., Przybocki, M. A., Witherell, P. W., & Zangmeister, R. A. (2019). *2018 National Institute of Standards and Technology Environmental Scan.* NIST Publications.

Bogason, P., & Toonen, T. A. (1998). Introduction: Networks in public administration. *Public Administration, 76*(2), 205–227. doi:10.1111/1467-9299.00098

Bolívar, M. P. R., & Meijer, A. J. (2016). Smart governance: Using a literature review and empirical analysis to build a research model. *Social Science Computer Review, 34*(6), 673–692. doi:10.1177/0894439315611088

Booth, M. (2006). Public engagement and practical wisdom. In S. Paulin (Ed.), *Introduction: Communities Voices: Creating Sustainable Spaces.* University of Western Australia Press.

Borkowska, K., & Osborne, M. (2018). Locating the fourth helix: Rethinking the role of civil society in developing smart learning cities. *International Review of Education, 64*(3), 355–372. doi:10.100711159-018-9723-0

Borowiec, S. (2016). *AlphaGo seals 4-1 victory over Go grandmaster Lee Sedol.* Retrieved 4 August 2020, from https://www.theguardian.com/technology/2016/mar/15/googles-alphago-seals-4-1-victory-over-grandmaster-lee-sedol

Boshier, R. W. (2005). Lifelong learning. In L. English (Ed.), *International encyclopedia of adult education* (pp. 373–378). Palgrave Macmillan.

Boshier, R. W. (2018). Learning cities: Fake news or the real deal? *International Journal of Lifelong Education, 37*(4), 419–434. Advance online publication. doi:10.1080/02601370.2018.1491900

Boswell, J., Niemeyer, S., & Hendriks, C. M. (2013). Julia Gillard's Citizens' Assembly Proposal for Australia: A Deliberative Democratic Analysis. *Australian Journal of Political Science, 48*(2), 164–178. doi:10.1080/10361146.2013.786675

Brennan, B. S., Koo, C., & Bae, K. M. (2018). Smart Tourism: A Study of Mobile Application Use by Tourists Visiting South Korea. *Asia-pacific Journal of Multimedia Services Convergent with Art, Humanities, and Sociology*, *8*(10), 1–9.

British Standards Institution (BSI). (2014). *Smart cities framework – Guide to establishing strategies for smart cities and communities, PAS 181*. Retrieved from: https://shop.bsigroup.com/ upload/ 267775/ PAS% 20181% 20(2014).pdf

Brown, C. (2019). Five ways you should be incorporating IoT in your small business. *Forbes*. Retrieved from: https://www.forbes.com/ sites/ forbestechcouncil/ 2019/ 03/ 15/ five- ways- you-should- be- incorporating- iot- in- your- small- business/ #2e3fc8a7dc58

Brundage, M., Avin, S., Clark, J., Toner, H., Eckersley, P., Garfinkel, B., . . . Anderson, H. (2018). *The malicious use of artificial intelligence: Forecasting, prevention, and mitigation.* arXiv preprint arXiv:1802.07228.

Bryson, J. M., Crosby, B. C., & Bloomberg, L. (2014). Public value governance: Moving beyond traditional public administration and the new public management. *Public Administration Review*, *74*(4), 445–456. doi:10.1111/puar.12238

Bryson, J. M., Crosby, B. C., & Stone, M. M. (2006). The Design and Implementation of Cross-Sector Collaborations: Propositions from the Literature. *Public Administration Review*, *66*(1), 44–55. doi:10.1111/j.1540-6210.2006.00665.x

Buhalis, D. (2000). Marketing the competitive destination of the future. *Tourism Management*, *21*(1), 97–116. doi:10.1016/S0261-5177(99)00095-3

BullGuard. (2020). *BullGuard: New Study Reveals One in Three SMBs Use Free Consumer Cybersecurity and One in Five Use No Endpoint Security at All.* prnewswire.com

Byrd, B. (2014). *Modernizing Public Parking To Improve Transportation And Strengthen Democracy In New York City.* White Paper By Senior Fellow For Economic Development Columbia University. Available from http://rooseveltforward.org/wp-content/uploads/2015/10/BritByrd.WhitePaper.Web_.pdf

Camp, L. J. (2006). The State of Economics of Information Security. *Information Security Journal*, *2*(2). http: //www. is-joumal. org/ VO2102/ 21SJLP189-Camp. pdf

Canadian Council for Public Private Partnerships. (2008). *Public Sector Accounting for Public Private Partnership Transactions in Canada.* Retrieved on 21st Jan 2013 from: https://www.pppcouncil.ca/pdf/pppfinance-072008.pdf

Canadian Council on Learning (CLI). (2010). *The 2010 Composite Learning Index: Five years of measuring Canada's progress in lifelong learning.* Retrieved from www.cli-ica.ca

Cappon, P., & Laughlin, J. (2013). Canada's composite learning index: A path towards learning communities. *International Review of Education*, *59*(4), 505–519. doi:10.100711159-013-9374-0

Carrignon, D. (2019). *Connected and autonomous vehicles, electric scooters and their implications for road network design* [Conference presentation]. European Transport Conference, Dublin, Ireland.

Car, T., Stifanich, L. P., & Šimunić, M. (2019). Internet of Things (IoT) in Tourism and Hospitality: Opportunities and Challenges. *Tourism in Southern and Eastern Europe*, *5*, 163–175. doi:10.20867/tosee.05.42

Carter, L., Kaga, R., & da Rosa, A. (2014). *Public-Private Partnerships: A reference guide version 2: WB*. ADB and Inter-American Development Bank.

Castelnovo, W., Misuraca, G., & Savoldelli, A. (2016). Smart cities governance: The need for a holistic approach to assessing urban participatory policy making. *Social Science Computer Review*, *34*(6), 724–739. doi:10.1177/0894439315611103

Cave, D., Hoffman, S., Joske, A., Ryan, F., & Thomas, E. (2019). *Mapping China's Tech Giants*. Australian Strategic Policy Institute. Retrieved from https://www.aspi.org.au/ report/ mapping – chinas – tech - giants? __ cf _ chl _ jschl _ tk __ = 5e6a d821 deb6 f569 3dd2 7937 3dc9 c27d 693d 65df – 1595 6919 65 – 0 – AVGn cFsE 7rKN JriV C4Hz Amaf 7x94 wZQx GYX8 4hXZ zKYa yARB ez - vK1V 3094 75FB 6q3R zJB2 NMY _ Udrm 2u1O rIDz jN9j bNri xNVI RW7T YTv0 spl7 kBAK 8mlRJ _ QUNN zNRy O8a0 Fhgy RuJL 6dkg 1SoA BwOq Ay0o LexV HvLe aEGY Llsw XbtP TSEh GcMa oMMV ucfC h0Ht cuCO vixh 2H9h vN _ t9sO m1JF tkrx – OTJU 82H0 QpJ1 0I86 aGPr EGbK GJ1K qdKL ZPUv l _ YDCvm _ iSgA fHfH6 _ - 23dY 53x9 ucOa E1eS OGUx W0dN agu2 NyGe iWDt _ gV-AQ

Cavelty, M. D., & Sute, M. (2009). Public–Private Partnerships are no silver bullet: An expanded governance model for Critical Infrastructure Protection. *International Journal of Critical Infrastructure Protection*, *4*(2), 179–187. doi:10.1016/j.ijcip.2009.08.006

Cedeño, J., Papinniemi, J., Hannola, L., & Donoghue, I. (2018). *Developing Smart Services by Internet of Things in Manufacturing Business*. doi:10.12783/dtetr/icpr2017/17680

Center for Cities. (2014). *Smart Cities*. Accessed on April 04, 2020 and retrieved from: https:// www.centreforcities.org/ reader/ smart-cities/ what-is-a-smart-city/ 1-smart-cities-definitions/

Charalabidis, Y., Koussouris, S., Lampathaki, F., & Misuraca, G. (2012). ICT for governance and policy modelling: Visionary directions and research paths. In Y. Charalabidis & S. Koussouris (Eds.), *Empowering Open and Collaborative Governance* (pp. 263–282). Springer. doi:10.1007/978-3-642-27219-6_14

Chickering, A. W. (1977). *Experience and learning: An introduction to experiential learning*. Change Magazine Press.

Choi, I., & Yang, B. C. (2012). Comparing the characteristics of lifelong learning cities in Korea and Japan: A historical sociological approach. *KEDI Journal of Educational Policy*, 183–202. http://eng.kedi.re.kr

Chourabi, H., Nam, T., Walker, S., Gil-Garcia, J. R., Mellouli, S., Nahon, K., . . . Scholl, H. J. (2012, January). Understanding smart cities: An integrative framework. In *2012 45th Hawaii international conference on system sciences* (pp. 2289-2297). IEEE.

Chourabi, H. (2012). Understanding smart cities: An integrative framework. In *45th Hawaii International Conference on System Sciences*. IEEE Computer Society. 10.1109/HICSS.2012.615

Chun, S. A., Luna-Reyes, L. F., & Sandoval-Almazán, R. (2012). Collaborative e-government. *Transforming Government: People. Process and Policy, 6*(1), 5–12. doi:10.1108/17506161211214868

Cisco. (2006). *Designing Network Security*. Cisco Press. Retrieved from: http: //www. Cisco press. com/content/images/I587051176/samplechapter/1587051176content. pdf

Cobb, J. (2013). *Leading the learning revolution: The expert's guide to capitalizing on the exploding lifelong education market* [Kindle version]. Retrieved from Amazon.com.

Cockerell, I. (2019). *Inside China's Massive Surveillance Operation*. Retrieved 6 August 2020, from https://www.wired.com/story/inside-chinas-massive-surveillance-operation/

Compagnon, S. (2019). *Les trottinettes électriques entrent dans le Code de la route*. https://www. leparisien.fr/amp/societe/les-trottinettes-entrent-dans-le-code-de-la-route-24-10-2019-8179773. php?__twitter_impression=true

Conti, D. D. M., Guevara, A. J. D. H., Heinrichs, H., Silva, L. F. D., Quaresma, C. C., & Beté, T. D. S. (2019). Collaborative governance towards cities sustainability transition. *Urbe. Revista Brasileira de Gestão Urbana*, 11.

Cooper, T. L., Bryer, T. A., & Meek, J. W. (2006). Citizen-Centered Collaborative Public Management. *Public Administration Review, 66*(1), 76–88. doi:10.1111/j.1540-6210.2006.00668.x

Cosgrove, M. (2011). *Smart Cities series: introducing the IBM city operations and management solutions*. IBM.

Cruz, C. O., & Sarmento, J. M. (2017). Reforming traditional PPP models to cope with the challenges of smart cities. *Competition and Regulation in Network Industries, 18*(1-2), 94–114. doi:10.1177/1783591717734794

Cuzzillo, T., & Cuzzillo, T. (2018, March 28). *Who pays for smart cities?* https://www.datadoodle. com/2018/04/12/who-pays-for-smart-cities/

Dace, H. (2020). *China's Tech Landscape: A Primer*. Retrieved 5 August 2020, from https:// institute.global/policy/chinas-tech-landscape-primer

Davis, F. D. (1989). Perceived usefulness, perceived ease of use, and user acceptance of information technology. *Management Information Systems Quarterly, 13*(3), 319–340. doi:10.2307/249008

De Cremer, D., Nguyen, B., & Simkin, L. (2017). The integrity challenge of the Internet-of-Things (IoT): On understanding its dark side. *Journal of Marketing Management, 33*(1-2), 145–158. do i:10.1080/0267257X.2016.1247517

Deakin, M. (Ed.). (2013). *Smart cities: governing, modelling and analysing the transition*. Routledge. doi:10.4324/9780203076224

Del Chiappa, G., & Baggio, R. (2015). Knowledge transfer in smart tourism destinations: Analyzing the effects of a network structure. *Journal of Destination Marketing & Management,* *4*(3), 145–150. doi:10.1016/j.jdmm.2015.02.001

Del Vecchio, P., Mele, G., Ndou, V., & Secundo, G. (2018). Creating value from social big data: Implications for smart tourism destinations. *Information Processing & Management, 54*(5), 847–860. doi:10.1016/j.ipm.2017.10.006

Department for Business, Innovation and Skills (BIS). (2013). *Smart Cities Background Paper.* London: Department for Business Innovation and Skills. Retrieved from: https://assets.publishing. service.gov.uk/ government/ uploads/ system/ uploads/ attachment_ data/ file/ 246019/ bis- 13- 1209- smart- cities- background- paper- digital.pdf

Devas, N. (2001). Does city governance matter for the urban poor? *International Planning Studies,* *6*(4), 393–408. doi:10.1080/13563470120092395

Dhanoa, J. (2020). *Will e-scooters form vital part of travel post Covid-19 restrictions in the region?* https://gulfbusiness.com/will-e-scooters-form-vital-part-of-travel-post-covid-19-restrictions-in-the-region/

Dillon, T., Wu, C., & Chang, E. (2010, April). Cloud computing: issues and challenges. In *2010 24th IEEE international conference on advanced information networking and applications* (pp. 27-33). IEEE. 10.1109/AINA.2010.187

Dirks, S., & Keeling, M. (2009). *A vision of smarter cities: How cities can lead the way into a prosperous and sustainable future.* IBM Global Business Services.

Dollery, B. (2012). *Catalyzing the renewal of local infrastructure in regional communities: The case for Local Infrastructure Australia.* Regional Australia Institute. Retrieved from: http://www. regionalaustralia.org.au/wp-content/uploads/2013/06/RAI-Renewal-of-Local-Infrastructure-in-Regional-Australia.pdf

Donahue, J. (2004). On collaborative governance. *Corporate social responsibility initiative Working Paper, 2.*

Donahue, J. D., & Zeckhauser, R. (2011). *Collaborative Governance: Private Roles for Public Goals in Turbulent Times.* Princeton University Press. doi:10.1515/9781400838103

Dosi, G. (1982). Technological paradigms and technological trajectories: A suggested interpretation of the determinants and directions of technical change. *Research Policy, 11*(3), 147–162. doi:10.1016/0048-7333(82)90016-6

Dotzler, J. (2018). *5 Ways the Internet of Things (IoT) is Transforming Small Business.* Gordon Flesch Company Inc. Retrieved from: https://www.gflesch.com/ elevity -it- blog/ ways -iot- is-transforming- small- business

Duarte, F., Ratti, C. (2016), Smart cities, big data, Internet of Things. *IEEE Standards University Magazine, 6*(4).

Eastman. (2015). *Big Data and Predictive Analytics: On the Cybersecurity Front Line.* IDC Whitepaper.

Eccarius, T., & Lu, C. C. (2020). Adoption intentions for micro-mobility–Insights from electric scooter sharing in Taiwan. *Transportation Research Part D, Transport and Environment, 84,* 102327. doi:10.1016/j.trd.2020.102327

Eckert, T., Preisinger-Kleine, R., Fartusnic, C., Houston, M., Juceviciené, P., Dillon, B., & … . (2012). *Quality in developing learning cities and regions: A guide for practitioners and stakeholders.* Ludwig Maximilian University.

Ecobuild website. (n.d.). *Smart city definition and applications in our country.* https://www.ecobuild.com.tr/post/ak%C4%B1ll%C4%B1-%C5%9Fehir-tan%C4%B1m%C4%B1-ve-%C3%BClkemizdeki-uygulamalar#:~:text=D%C3%BCnyada%20ge%C3%A7erli%20ak%C4%B1ll%C4%B1%20%C5%9Fehircilik%20tan%C4%B1mlar%C4%B1,%C3%87evre%2C%20Finans%20ve%20Ekonomi%20%C5%9Feklindedir

Efron, S., Schwindt, K., & Haskel, E. (2020). *Security Risks of China's Investments in Israel.* Retrieved 6 June 2020, from https://www.rand.org/pubs/research_reports/RR3176.html

Eger, J.M., (2009). Smart Growth, Smart Cities, and the Crisis at the Pump A Worldwide Phenomenon. *I-Ways, 32*(1), 47 –53.

Ellis, P., & Roberts, M. (2015). *Leveraging urbanization in South Asia: Managing spatial transformation for prosperity and livability.* The World Bank.

Emerson, K., & Nabatchi, T. (2015). *Collaborative governance regimes.* Georgetown University Press.

Emerson, K., Nabatchi, T., & Balogh, S. (2012). An integrative framework for collaborative governance. *Journal of Public Administration: Research and Theory, 22*(1), 1–29. doi:10.1093/jopart/mur011

EPALE. (2015). *Electronic platform for adult learning in Europe.* Retrieved from https://ec.europa.eu/epale

Eremia, M., Toma, L., & Sanduleac, M. (2017). The Smart City Concept in the 21st Century. *Procedia Engineering, 181,* 12–19. doi:10.1016/j.proeng.2017.02.357

Essays, U. K. (2013). *The History Of Smart Cities Concept Information Technology Essay.* Retrieved from https://www.uniassignment.com/ essay-samples/ information-technology/ the-history -of- smart- cities- concept- information- technology- essay.php? vref=1

European Commission. (2000). *A memorandum on lifelong learning SEC 1832.* Retrieved from https://arhiv.acs.si/dokumenti/Memorandum_on_Lifelong_Learning.pdf

Evans, J. R., & Mathur, A. (2005). The value of online surveys. *Internet Research, 15*(2), 195–219. doi:10.1108/10662240510590360

Facer, K., & Buchczyk, M. (2019). Towards a research agenda for the 'actually existing' learning city. *Oxford Review of Education*, *45*(2), 151–167. doi:10.1080/03054985.2018.1551990

Falconer, G., & Mitchell, S. (2012). *Smart City Framework A Systematic Process for Enabling Smart + Connected Communities*. CISCO. Retrieved from: https://www.cisco.com/ web/ about/ ac79/ docs/ ps/ motm/ Smart- City- Framework.pdf

Falkner, N. (2017, May 10). A smart city is more than international ratings: A smart city works for you. So what do you want? *The Advertiser*. https://www.adelaidenow.com.au/

Fenwick, T. (2000). Experiential learning: A review of the five contemporary perspectives of cognition. *Adult Education Quarterly*, *50*(4), 243–272. doi:10.1177/07417130022087035

Florida, R. (2002). *The rise of the creative class: And how it's transforming work, leisure, community and everyday life*. Basic Books.

Florini, A., & Pauli, M. (2018). Collaborative governance for the sustainable development goals. *Asia & the Pacific Policy Studies*, *5*(3), 583–598. doi:10.1002/app5.252

Food and Agriculture Organizations (FAO). (2017). *The 2030 agenda and the sustainable development goals: the challenge for aquaculture development and management*. UN.

Forster, J. (2016). Global sports governance and corruption. *Palgrave Communications*, *2*(1), 15048. doi:10.1057/palcomms.2015.48

Fowler, F. J. Jr. (2013). *Survey research methods*. Sage Publications.

Frederickson, H. G. (1999). The repositioning of American Public Administration. *PS, Political Science & Politics*, *32*(4), 701–712. doi:10.1017/S1049096500056547

Frey, C., & Osborne, M. (2020). *China Won't Win the Race for AI Dominance*. Retrieved 2 August 2020, from https://www.foreignaffairs.com/articles/united-states/2020-06-19/china-wont-win-race-ai-dominance

Fuller, S. (2018). Social democracy and neoliberalism: Beyond sibling rivalry. *Global Policy*, 10–23.

Fung, A., & Wright, E. (2001). Deepening democracy: Innovations in empowered participatory governance. *Politics & Society*, *29*(1), 5–41. doi:10.1177/0032329201029001002

Furco, A. (1996). Service-learning: A balanced approach to experiential education. In B. Taylor (Ed.), *Expanding boundaries: Serving and learning* (pp. 2-5). Retrieved from California State University-Fresno State website: http://www.csufresno.edu/ facultysl/documents/ ABalancedApproach.pdf

Gajdošík, T. (2019). Big Data Analytics in Smart Tourism Destinations. A New Tool for Destination Management Organizations? In *Smart Tourism as a Driver for Culture and Sustainability* (pp. 15–33). Springer. doi:10.1007/978-3-030-03910-3_2

Ganti, R. K., & Lei, H. (2011). Mobile crowdsensing: Current state and future challenges. *IEEE Communications Magazine*, *49*(11), 32–39. doi:10.1109/MCOM.2011.6069707

Gantz, J. F., & Reinsel, D. (2012) The Digital Universe in 2020: Big Data, Bigger Digital Shadows, and Biggest Growth in the Far East Available from: https://www.emc.com/leadership/digital-universe/2012iview/index.htm

Gao, L., & Bai, X. (2014). A unified perspective on the factors influencing consumer acceptance of internet of things technology. *Asia Pacific Journal of Marketing and Logistics, 26*(2), 211–231. doi:10.1108/APJML-06-2013-0061

Gassmann, O., Böhm, J., & Palmié, M. (2019). The future of cities and the concept of smart cities. *Smart Cities, 3–4*, 3–4. Advance online publication. doi:10.1108/978-1-78769-613-620191007

Gautam, S. (2018). *Benefits of Smart Parking: How Smart Parking Reduces Traffic.* https://www.parking-net.com/parking-industry-blog/get-my-parking/how-smart-parking-reduces-traffic#:~:text=Smart%20parking%20can%20reduce%20traffic,can%20help%20drivers%20locate%20spots

Gerlak, A. K., Lubell, M., & Heikkila, T. (2013). The Promise and Performance of Collaborative Governance. In S. Kamieniecki & M. E. Kraft (Eds.), *The Oxford Handbook of US Environmental Policy* (p. 413). Oxford University Press.

Gewirtz, J. (2019). *China's Long March to Technological Supremacy.* Retrieved 1 June 2020, from https://www.foreignaffairs.com/articles/china/2019-08-27/chinas-long-march-technological-supremacy

Giffinger, R., Fertner, C., Kramar, H., Kalasek, R., Pichler-Milanovis, N., & Meijers, E. (2007). *Smart Cities: Ranking of European Medium-Sized Cities.* Vienna, Austria: Centre of Regional Science (SRF), Vienna University of Technology. Retrieved from: http://www.smart-cities.eu/download/ smart_cities_final_report.pdf

Giffinger, R., Fertner, C., Kramar, H., Kalasek, R., Pichler-Milanovic, N., & Meijers, E. (2018). *Smart cities–Ranking of European medium-sized cities.* Centre of Regional Science.

Gil-Garcia, J. R., Pardo, T. A., & Nam, T. (2015). What makes a city smart? Identifying core components and proposing an integrative and comprehensive conceptualization. *Information Polity, 20*(1), 61–87. doi:10.3233/IP-150354

Gollagher, M., & Hartz-Karp, J. (2013). The Role of Deliberative Collaborative Governance in Achieving Sustainable Cities. *Sustainability, 5*(6), 2343–2366. https://www.mdpi.com/2071-1050/5/6/2343. doi:10.3390u5062343

Gössling, S. (2020). Integrating e-scooters in urban transportation: Problems, policies, and the prospect of system change. *Transportation Research Part D, Transport and Environment, 79*, 102230. doi:10.1016/j.trd.2020.102230

Gregory, J. (2015). *The Internet of Things: revolutionizing the retail industry.* Accenture Strategy.

Grewal, D., Noble, S. M., Roggeveen, A. L., & Nordfalt, J. (2020). The future of in-store technology. *Journal of the Academy of Marketing Science, 48*(1), 96–113. doi:10.100711747-019-00697-z

Grewal, D., Roggeveen, A. L., & Nordfält, J. (2017). The future of retailing. *Journal of Retailing*, *93*(1), 1–6. doi:10.1016/j.jretai.2016.12.008

Guillemin, P., & Friess, P. (2009). *Internet of things strategic research roadmap*. The Cluster of European Research Projects, Tech. Rep.

Guo, J., Lynch, L., & Isaac Mitchell, I. (2019). *Shared mobility in the city of Saint Paul*. The University of Minnesota.

Guo, Y., Liu, H., & Chai, Y. (2014). The embedding convergence of smart cities and tourism internet of things in China: An advance perspective. *Advances in Hospitality and Tourism Research*, *2*(1), 54–69.

Haberler Website. (n.d.). *The Istanbul Metropolitan Municipality e-scooter rules*. https://www.haberler.com/ibb-harekete-gecti-elektrikli-scooter-larda-13476754-haberi/

Habitat, U. N. (2013a). *Why the world needs an urban sustainable development goal?* Author.

Habitat, U. N. (2013b). *State of the world's cities 2012/2013: Prosperity of cities*. Routledge.

Haenlein, M., & Kaplan, A. (2019). A brief history of artificial intelligence: On the past, present, and future of artificial intelligence. *California Management Review*, *61*(4), 5–14. doi:10.1177/0008125619864925

Halcomb, E. J., & Davidson, P. M. (2006). Is verbatim transcription of interview data always necessary? *Applied Nursing Research*, *19*(1), 38–42. doi:10.1016/j.apnr.2005.06.001 PMID:16455440

Hale, K. (2020). *Amazon, Microsoft & IBM Slightly Social Distancing From The $8 Billion Facial Recognition Market*. Retrieved 2 August 2020, from https://www.forbes.com/sites/korihale/2020/06/15/amazon-microsoft--ibm-slightly-social-distancing-from-the-8-billion-facial-recognition-market/#41b125474a9a

Hamid, B., Jhanjhi, N. Z., Humayun, M., Khan, A., & Alsayat, A. (2019). Cyber Security Issues and Challenges for Smart Cities: A survey. *2019 13th International Conference on Mathematics, Actuarial Science, Computer Science and Statistics (MACS)*, 1-7. 10.1109/MACS48846.2019.9024768

Hardt, C., & Bogenberger, K. (2019). Usage of e-scooters in urban environments. *Transportation Research Procedia*, *37*, 155–162. doi:10.1016/j.trpro.2018.12.178

Harsono, H. (2020). *China's Surveillance Technology Is Keeping Tabs on Populations Around the World*. Retrieved 2 August 2020, from https://thediplomat.com/2020/06/chinas-surveillance-technology-is-keeping-tabs-on-populations-around-the-world/

Hawkins, A. J. (2020). *Electric scooter-sharing grinds to a halt in response to the COVID-19 pandemic*. https://www.theverge.com/2020/3/20/21188119/electric-scooter-coronavirus-bird-lime-spin-suspend-bikes

Healey, P. (2003). Collaborative Planning in Perspective. *Planning Theory, 2*(2), 101–123. doi:10.1177/14730952030022002

Hecht, G., & Allen, M. T. (2001). *Technologies of power*. MIT Press.

Heidegger, M. (1954). The question concerning technology. *Technology and values: Essential readings, 99*, 113.

Heinig, I. (2020). Data Safety for Small Businesses: 2020 Cybersecurity Statistics. *The Manifest*. Retrieved from: https://themanifest.com/ mobile-apps/ data- safety- small- businesses- 2020- cybersecurity- statistics

Hendriks, C. M. (2011). *The politics of public deliberation: Citizen Engagement and interest advocacy*. Palgrave Macmillan. doi:10.1057/9780230347564

Hibbler, D., & Scott, L. (2015). Role of leisure in humanizing learning cities. In L. Scott (Ed.), *Learning Cities for Adult Learners* (pp. 73–82)., doi:10.1002/ace.20124

Hillman, J., & McCalpin, M. (2019). *Watching Huawei's "Safe Cities"*. Retrieved 6 August 2020, from https://www.csis.org/analysis/watching-huaweis-safe-cities

HISCOX. (2018). *2018 HISCOX Small Business Cyber Risk Report*. Retrieved from: https://www.hiscox.com/ documents/ 2018- Hiscox- Small- Business- Cyber- Risk- Report.pdf

Hix, S. (1998). The study of the European Union II: The 'new governance' agenda and its rival. *Journal of European Public Policy, 5*(1), 38–65. doi:10.1080/13501768880000031

Hodge, G., & Greve, C. (2011). Theorizing Public-Private Partnership Success: A Market Based Alternative to Government? *Public Management Research Conference, 1*, 1-23. Retrieved from: http://openarchive.cbs.dk/bitstream/handle/10398/8573/Greve_2011_c.pdf?sequence=1

HoffmanD. L.NovakT. (2015). Emergent experience and the connected consumer in the smart home assemblage and the internet of things. Available at SSRN 2648786. doi:10.2139srn.2648786

Holford, J., & Jarvis, P. (2000). The learning society. In A. L. Wilson & E. R. Hayes (Eds.), *Handbook of Adult and Continuing Education* (pp. 643–659). Jossey-Bass.

Homeland Security Research. (2013). *China Safe Cities Technologies and Markets 2013-2022 Report - Cumulative 2013-2022 $138 Billion | Homeland Security Market Research*. Retrieved 6 August 2020, from https://homelandsecurityresearch.com/reports/china-safe-cities-technologies-and-markets/

Hood, C. (1995). The New Public Management in the 1980s: Variations on: A Theme. *Accounting, Organizations and Society, 20*(2/3), 93–109. doi:10.1016/0361-3682(93)E0001-W

Hop website. (n.d.). https://hoplagit.com/

Horrigan, J. B. (2016, March). *Lifelong learning and technology*. Retrieved from https://www.pewresearch.org/

Hughes, T. P. (1993). *Networks of power: electrification in Western society, 1880-1930*. JHU Press.

Hutter, G. (2016). Collaborative governance and rare floods in urban regions–Dealing with uncertainty and surprise. *Environmental Science & Policy*, *55*, 302–308. doi:10.1016/j. envsci.2015.07.028

Hvistendahl, M. (2020). *How a Chinese AI Giant Made Chatting—and Surveillance—Easy.* Retrieved 6 August 2020, from https://www.wired.com/ story/ iflytek – china – ai – giant – voice – chatting - surveillance/ ?bxid = 5cec 2712 3f92 a45b 30f0 d63d & cndid = 5508 6070 & esrc = bounce X & source = EDT _ WIR _ NEWS LETTER _ 0 _ DAILY _ ZZ & utm _ brand = wired & utm _ campaign = aud – dev & utm _ mailing = WIR _ Daily _ 051820 & utm _ medium = email & utm _ source = nl & utm _ term = list1 _ p4

Ibold, S., Medimorec, N., Wagner, A., & Peruzzo, J. (2020). *The COVID-19 outbreak and implications to sustainable urban mobility – some observations.* https://www.transformative-mobility.org/news/ the-covid-19-outbreak-and-implications-to-public-transport-some-observations

Ibrahim H. E. (2017). Car Parking Problem in Urban Areas, Causes and Solutions 1st International Conference on Towards a Better Quality of Life. Available at https://ssrn.com/abstract=3163473 doi:10.2139srn.3163473

IMF. (2005). *The IMF's Approach to Promoting Good Governance and Combating Corruption—A Guide.* Available at: www.imf.org/external/np/gov/guide/eng/index.htm

Inman, J. J., & Nikolova, H. (2017). Shopper-facing retail technology: A retailer adoption decision framework incorporating shopper attitudes and privacy concerns. *Journal of Retailing*, *93*(1), 7–28. doi:10.1016/j.jretai.2016.12.006

Innes, J. E., & Booher, D. E. (1999). Consensus Building and Complex Adaptive Systems: A Framework for Evaluating Collaborative Planning. *Journal of the American Planning Association*, *65*(4), 412–423. doi:10.1080/01944369908976071

International Telecommunication Union. (2014). *Technical Report on Smart Sustainable Cities: An analysis of definitions.* United Nations, International Telecommunication Union (ITU-T), Focus Group on Smart Sustainable Cities (FG-SSC).

International Telecommunication Union. (2014). *World Telecommunication Development Conference (WTDC-14).* Final Report; International Telecommunication Union.

Iossa, E., & Martimort, D. (2015). The simple microeconomics of public-private partnerships. *Journal of Public Economic Theory*, *17*(1), 4–48. doi:10.1111/jpet.12114

Islam, M. S. (2017). Governance and Development. In A. Farazmand (Ed.), *Global Encyclopedia of Public Administration, Public Policy, and Governance.* Springer., doi:10.1007/978-3-319-31816-5_1990-1

James, E. (2019). Smart cities: The future of urban development. *Forbes.* https://www.forbes.com/ sites/jamesellsmoor/2019/05/19/smart-cities-the-future-of-urban-development/#72a774662f90

Jarvis, D. (2019). Small Businesses, It's Time to Ride the IoT Wave. *IoT Business News*. Retrieved from: https://iotbusinessnews.com/ 2019/ 11/ 14/ 30269- small- businesses -its- time -to- ride- the- iot-wave/

Jarvis, P. (2004). *Adult education and lifelong learning: Theory and practice* (3rd ed.). RoutledgeFalmer. doi:10.4324/9780203561560

Jia, X., Feng, Q., Fan, T., & Lei, Q. (2012). RFID technology and its applications in the Internet of Things (IoT). *2012 2nd International Conference on Consumer Electronics, Communications and Networks (CECNet)*, 1282-1285. 10.1109/CECNet.2012.6201508

Jing, Y. (2015). Governing China. In *21ˢᵗ century: The Road to Collaborative Governance in China*. New York: Palgrave Macmillan.

Jin, J., Gubbi, J., Marusic, S., & Palaniswami, M. (2014). An information framework for creating a smart city through the Internet of things. *IEEE Internet of Things Journal*, *1*(2), 112–121. doi:10.1109/JIOT.2013.2296516

Jomo, C. Sharma, & Platz. (2016). *Public-Private Partnerships and the 2030 Agenda for Sustainable Development: Fit for purpose?* UN Working Paper No. 148. United Nations, Department of Economic and Social Affairs.

Jones, N., & Matt Graham, C. (2020, January). Can the IoT Help Small Businesses? *Bulletin of Science, Technology & Society*, *38*(1), 3–12. Advance online publication. doi:10.1177/0270467620902365

Juniper Research. (2018) Smart Cities – What's In It For Citizens? Available from: https://newsroom. intel.com/wp-content/uploads/sites/11/2018/03/smart-cities-whats-in-it-for-citizens.pdf

Kaur, K., & Kaur, R. (2016). Internet of things to promote tourism: An insight into smart tourism. *International Journal of Recent Trends in Engineering & Research*, *2*(4), 357–361.

Keap Business Success Blog. (2020). *How IoT is impacting businesses today*. Accessed on April 14, 2020 and retrieved from: https://keap.com/ business- success- blog/ marketing/ automation/ how -the- internet -of- things- impacts- small- business

Kearns, P. (2012). Learning cities as healthy green cities: Building sustainable opportunity cities. *Australian Journal of Adult Learning*, *52*(2), 368–391.

Kennedy, A. (2019). *How can cities get a handle on electric scooters?* https://dirt.asla. org/2019/01/16/how-can-cities-get-a-handle-on-electric-scooters/

KGM website. (n.d.). https://www.kgm.gov.tr/sayfalar/kgm/sitetr/trafik/kanunyonetmelikler.aspx

Khalifa, E. (2019). Smart cities: Opportunities, challenges, and security threats. *Journal of Strategic Innovation and Sustainability*, *14*(3), 2019–2079.

Khanna, A., & Anand, R. (2016, January). IoT based smart parking system. In *2016 International Conference on Internet of Things and Applications (IOTA)* (pp. 266-270). IEEE. 10.1109/ IOTA.2016.7562735

Kharkovyna, O. (2020). *Smart Cities: Applications of Artificial Intelligence in Urban Management*. Retrieved 5 August 2020, from https://towardsdatascience.com/smart-cities-applications-of-artificial-intelligence-in-urban-management-c445c414c8eb

Kim, E., Gardner, D., Deshpande, S., Contu, R., Kish, D., & Canales, C. (2018). *Forecast Analysis: Information Security, Worldwide, 2Q18 Update*. Gartner Research.

Kitchin, R. (2015). Making sense of smart cities: Addressing present shortcomings. *Cambridge Journal of Regions, Economy and Society*, 8(1), 131–136. doi:10.1093/cjres/rsu027

Klopfenstein, L. C., Delpriori, S., Polidori, P., Sergiacomi, A., Marcozzi, M., Boardman, D., Parfitt, P., & Bogliolo, A. (2019). Mobile crowdsensing for road sustainability: Exploitability of publicly-sourced data. *International Review of Applied Economics*, 1–22.

Kolb, D. A. (1984). *Experiential learning: Experience as the source of learning and development*. Prentice Hall.

Kononova, A., Li, L., Kamp, K., Bowen, M., Rikard, R. V., Cotten, S., & Peng, W. (2019). The Use of Wearable Activity Trackers among Older Adults: Focus Group Study of Tracker Perceptions, Motivators, and Barriers in the Maintenance Stage of Behavior Change. *JMIR mHealth and uHealth*, 7(4), e9832. doi:10.2196/mhealth.9832 PMID:30950807

Kooiman, J. (Ed.). (1993). *Modern governance: New government-society interactions*. Sage.

Kooiman, J., Bavinck, M., Chuenpagdee, R., Mahon, R., & Pullin, R. (2008). Interactive governance and governability: An introduction. *The Journal of Transdisciplinary Environmental Studies*, 7(1), 1–11.

Kopackova, H., & Libalova, P. (2017, July). Smart city concept as socio-technical system. In *2017 International Conference on Information and Digital Technologies (IDT)* (pp. 198-205). IEEE. 10.1109/DT.2017.8024297

Kostrzewska, M., & Macikowski, B. (2017). Towards hybrid urban mobility: Kick scooter as a means of individual transport in the city. *IOP Conference Series. Materials Science and Engineering*, 245, 052073. doi:10.1088/1757-899X/245/5/052073

Kourtit, Nijkamp, & Arribas. (2012). Smart Cities in Perspective – A Comparative European Study by Means of Self-organizing Maps. *Innovation: The European Journal of Social Science Research*, 25(2), 229–246.

KPMG International Cooperative. (2012). *A Swiss entity*. Available online: https://home.kpmg.com/us/en/home.html

Kranzberg, M. (1986). Technology and History:" Kranzberg's Laws. *Technology and Culture*, 27(3), 544–560. doi:10.2307/3105385

Krotov, V. (2017). The Internet of Things and new business opportunities. *Business Horizons*, 60(6), 831–841. doi:10.1016/j.bushor.2017.07.009

Kumar, T. V. (2020). Smart living for smart cities. In *Smart Living for Smart Cities* (pp. 3–70). Springer.

Lane, J. (2000). *New public management*. Routledge.

Lea, R. J. (2017). *Smart cities: An overview of the technology trends driving smart cities*. Retrieved 5 August 2020, from https://www.researchgate.net/publication/326099991_Smart_Cities_An_Overview_of_the_Technology_Trends_Driving_Smart_Cities

Leach, W. D. (2006). Collaborative Public Management And Democracy: Evidence From Western Watershed Partnerships. *Public Administration Review, 66*(s1), 100–110. doi:10.1111/j.1540-6210.2006.00670.x

Lee, J. H., & Hancock, M. G. (2012). Toward a Framework for Smart Cities: A Comparison of Seoul, San Francisco and Amsterdam. *Stanford Program on Regions of Innovation and Entrepreneurship, 1*(1), 1-22. https://sprie.gsb.stanford.edu/people/Jung-hoon_Lee/

Lee, I., & Lee, K. (2015). The Internet of Things (IoT): Applications, investments, and challenges for enterprises. *Business Horizons, 58*(4), 431–440. doi:10.1016/j.bushor.2015.03.008

Lee, J., Strickland, C., & Bienemann, J. (2017). *Reducing greenhouse gas emissions attributed to the building sector in New York City. American Society of Civil Engineers. International Conference on Sustainable Infrastructure*, New York, NY. 10.1061/9780784481202.031

Lee, M., & Jan, S. K. (2017). Lifelong learning policy discourses on international organisations since 2000: A kaleidoscope or merely fragments? In *The Palgrave International Handbook on Adult and Lifelong Education and Learning* (pp. 375–396). doi:10.1057/987-137-55783-4

Leftwich, A. (1994). Governance, the State and the Politics of Development. *Development and Change, 25*(2), 363–386. doi:10.1111/j.1467-7660.1994.tb00519.x

Leon, N. (2011). Complex city systems: Understanding how large technical systems innovation arises in cities. *IBM Journal of Research and Development, 55*(1.2), 16-1.

Leva website. (n.d.). *New French e-scooter rules.* https://leva-eu.com/2019/10/31/new-french-e-scooter-rules/

Lewis, M. (2002). *Risk Management in Public-Private Partnerships*. Working Paper. School of International Business, University of South Australia.

Li, C., Hao, X., & Nanchen, J. (2013). Transforming Beijing into a learning city: Practices and challenges. *International Journal of Continuing Education and Lifelong Learning, 6*(1), 37–54.

Lime website. (n.d.). https://www.li.me/tr/

Lin, T., Rivano, H., & Le Mouel, F. (2017). A Survey of Smart Parking Solutions. *IEEE Transactions on Intelligent Transportation Systems, 18*(12), 3229–3253. doi:10.1109/TITS.2017.2685143

Liu, S., Zhang, P., Wang, Z., Liu, W., & Tan, J. (2016). Measuring the sustainable urbanization potential of cities in Northeast China. *Journal of Geographical Sciences, 26*(5), 549–567. doi:10.100711442-016-1285-0

Longworth, N. (1999). Making lifelong learning work: Learning cities for a learning century. Sterling, VA: Kogan Page.

Macaulay, T. (2020). *US joins G7 AI alliance to counter China's influence.* Retrieved 6 June 2020, from https://sup.news/us-joins-g7-ai-alliance-to-counter-chinas-influence-2/

Maffeo, L. (2019). *Should your small business invest in the Internet of Things?* Retrieved from: https://blog.capterra.com/ should- your- small- business- invest -in-the- internet -of- things/#1

Magnette, P. (2003). European governance and civic participation: Beyond elitist citizenship? *Political Studies, 51*(1), 144–160. doi:10.1111/1467-9248.00417

Mahizhnan, A. (1999). Smart Cities: The Singapore Case. *Cities, 16*(1), 13–18. doi:10.1016/S0264-2751(98)00050-X

Mani, Z., & Chouk, I. (2017). Drivers of consumers' resistance to smart products. *Journal of Marketing Management, 33*(1-2), 76–97. doi:10.1080/0267257X.2016.1245212

Maple, C. (2017). Security and privacy in the internet of things. *Journal of Cyber Policy, 2*(2), 155–184. doi:10.1080/23738871.2017.1366536

Margerum, R. (2011). *Beyond Consensus: Improving Collaborative Planning and Management* (MA thesis). MIT Press.

Marsick, V. J., Watkins, K. E., Scully-Russ, E., & Nicolaides, A. (2016). Rethinking informal and incidental learning in terms of complexity and the social context. *Journal of Adult Learning, Knowledge and Innovation, 1*(1). Retrieved from https://akademiai.com/doi/abs/10.1556/2059.01.2016.003

Martin, I. (1987). Community education: Toward a theoretical analysis. In G. Allen, J. Bastiani, I. Martin, & K. Richards (Eds.), *Community education: An agenda for educational reform* (pp. 9–32). Open University Press.

Martins, A. (2019). Cyberattacks and Your Small Business: A Primer for Cybersecurity. *Business News Daily.* https://www.businessnewsdaily.com/8231-small-business-cybersecurity-guide.html

Mayer, M., Carpes, M., & Knoblich, R. (2014). The global politics of science and technology: An introduction. In *The Global Politics of Science and Technology-Vol. 1* (pp. 1–35). Springer. doi:10.1007/978-3-642-55007-2_1

McCarney, R., Halfani, M., & Rodriquez, A. (1995). Towards an Understanding of Governance: The Emergence of an idea and its implications for Urban research in Developing countries in Urban Research in the Developing World. In Perspectives on the City (pp. 91-141). Toronto: Centre for Urban and Community studies, University of Toronto.

McKenzie, G. (2019). Spatiotemporal comparative analysis of scooter-share and bike-share usage patterns in Washington, DC. *Journal of Transport Geography*, *78*, 19–28. doi:10.1016/j.jtrangeo.2019.05.007

McLaren, D., & Agyeman, J. (2015). *Sharing cities: A case for Truly smart and sustainable cities*. Massachusetts Institute of Technology.

Meijer, A. (2016). Smart city governance: A local emergent perspective. In *Smarter as the new urban agenda* (pp. 73–85). Springer. doi:10.1007/978-3-319-17620-8_4

Meijer, A., & Bolívar, M. P. R. (2016). Governing the smart city: A review of the literature on smart urban governance. *International Review of Administrative Sciences*, *82*(2), 392–408. doi:10.1177/0020852314564308

Merriam, S. B., Caffarella, R. S., & Baumgartner, L. (2007). *Learning in adulthood: A comprehensive guide* (3rd ed.). Jossey-Bass.

Meyer, D. (2016). Why Smartphones Are Bringing Down Internet-of-Things Revenue Forecasts. *Fortune.* https://fortune.com/2016/08/04/smartphones-iot-revenue-machina/

Michell, N. (2016, November 23). *New York awarded 2016 Best Smart City*. https://cities-today.com/new-york-awarded-2016-best-smart-city/

Mingjun, W., Zhen, Y., Wei, Z., Xishang, D., Xiaofei, Y., Chenggang, S., & Jinghai, H. (2012, October). A research on experimental system for Internet of things major and application project. In *2012 3rd International Conference on System Science, Engineering Design and Manufacturing Informatization* (Vol. 1, pp. 261-263). IEEE. 10.1109/ICSSEM.2012.6340722

Minsky, M., & Papert, S. A. (2017). *Perceptrons: An introduction to computational geometry*. MIT Press. doi:10.7551/mitpress/11301.001.0001

Miorandi, D., Sicari, S., De Pellegrini, F., & Chlamtac, I. (2012). Internet of things: Vision, applications and research challenges. *Ad Hoc Networks*, *10*(7), 1497–1516. doi:10.1016/j.adhoc.2012.02.016

Moeuf, A., Pellerin, R., Lamouri, S., Tamayo-Giraldo, S., & Barbaray, R. (2018). The industrial management of SMEs in the era of Industry 4.0. *International Journal of Production Research*, *56*(3), 1118–1136. doi:10.1080/00207543.2017.1372647

Mohanty, S. P., Choppali, U., & Kougianos, E. (2016). Everything you wanted to know about smart cities: The internet of things is the backbone. *IEEE Consumer Electronics Magazine*, *5*(3), 60–70.

Moreau, H., de Jamblinne de Meux, L., Zeller, V., D'Ans, P., Ruwet, C., & Achten, W. M. (2020). Dockless e-scooter: A green solution for mobility? Comparative case study between dockless e-scooters, displaced transport, and personal e-scooters. *Sustainability*, *12*(5), 1803. doi:10.3390u12051803

Morgan, S. (2020). Cybercrime To Cost The World $10.5 Trillion Annually By 2025 Cybercrime Magazine. Available from: https://cybersecurityventures.com/hackerpocalypse-cybercrime-report-2016/

Mozur, P., & Krolik, A. (2019). *A Surveillance Net Blankets China's Cities, Giving Police Vast Powers.* Retrieved 6 August 2020, from https://www.nytimes.com/2019/12/17/technology/china-surveillance.html

Muente-Kunigami & Mulas. (2015). *Building smarter cities.* World Bank Brief.

Nam, T., & Pardo, T. A. (2011, June). Conceptualizing smart city with dimensions of technology, people, and institutions. In *Proceedings of the 12th annual international digital government research conference: digital government innovation in challenging times* (pp. 282-291). 10.1145/2037556.2037602

National Small Business Association (NABA). (2019). *National 2019 Technology & Small Business Survey.* Retrieved from: https://nsba.biz/wp-content/uploads/2019/06/Technology-Survey-2019.pdf

Navarathna, P. J., & Malagi, V. P. (2018). Artificial intelligence in smart city analysis. In *2018 International Conference on Smart Systems and Inventive Technology (ICSSIT)* (pp. 44-47). IEEE. 10.1109/ICSSIT.2018.8748476

Neirotti, P., De Marco, A., Cagliano, A. C., Mangano, G., & Scorrano, F. (2014). Current trends in Smart City initiatives: Some stylized facts. *Cities (London, England), 38*, 25–36. doi:10.1016/j.cities.2013.12.010

Newig, J., Pahl-Wostl, C., & Sigel, K. (2005). The role of public participation in managing uncertainty in the implementation of the Water Framework Directive. *European Environment, 15*(6), 333–343. doi:10.1002/eet.398

NewVantage Partners Releases 5th Annual Big Data Executive Survey for 2017 (2017) Big Data Business Impact: Achieving Business Results through Innovation and Disruption. *Business Wire*

Nichols, R. M. (2020). How Small Businesses Benefit from the IoT. *IOT Feature News.* Retrieved from: https://www.iotevolutionworld.com/iot/articles/445643-how-small-businesses-benefit-from-iot.htm#

Nicoll, K., & Fejes, A. (2008). Mobilising Foucault in the studies of lifelong learning. In A. Fejes & K. Nicoll (Eds.), *Foucault and Lifelong Learning* (pp. 1–18). Routledge.

Nijkamp, P., & Kourtit, K. (2013). The New Urban Europe: Global challenges and local responses in the urban century. *European Planning Studies, 21*(3), 291–315. doi:10.1080/09654313.2012.716243

Nitti, M., Pilloni, V., Giusto, D., & Popescu, V. (2017). Iot architecture for a sustainable tourism application in a smart city environment. *Mobile Information Systems.*

Noh, A. (2012). Collaborative Public Management: Where Have We Been and Where Are We Going? *American Review of Public Administration, 42*(5), 507–522. doi:10.1177/0275074012445780

Nord, J. H., Koohang, A., & Paliszkiewicz, J. (2019). The Internet of Things: Review and theoretical framework. *Expert Systems with Applications, 133*, 97–108. doi:10.1016/j.eswa.2019.05.014

OECD. (2005). *Promoting adult learning*. OECD.

Olsen, J. K. B., Pedersen, S. A., & Hendricks, V. F. (2012). *A Companion to the Philosophy of Technology*. John Wiley & Sons.

Osborne, M., Kearns, P., & Yang, J. (2013). Learning cities: Developing inclusive, prosperous and sustainable urban communities. *International Review of Education*, *59*(4), 409–423. doi:10.100711159-013-9384-y

Özdemir, V., & Hekim, N. (2018). Birth of Industry 5.0: Making sense of big data with artificial intelligence, "the Internet of Things" and next-generation technology policy. *OMICS: A Journal of Integrative Biology*, *22*(1), 65–76. doi:10.1089/omi.2017.0194 PMID:29293405

Pala, Z., & Inanc, N. (2007, September). *Smart parking applications using RFID technology. In 2007 1st Annual RFID Eurasia*. IEEE.

Palm website. (n.d.). *Palm e-scooter*. https://letspalm.com/

Papuççiyan, A. (2019). *E-scooter sharing at the university: Palm*. https://webrazzi.com/2019/07/22/universitelerde-hizmet-veren-elektrikli-scooter-paylasim-girisimi-palm/

Papuççiyan, A. (2019). *E-scooter sharing in Ankara: HOP!* https://webrazzi.com/2019/12/13/ankara-merkezli-elektrikli-scooter-paylasim-girisimi-hop/

Pardo, T. A., Gil-Garcia, J. R., & Luna-Reyes, L. F. (2010). Collaborative governance and cross boundary information sharing: Envisioning a networked and it-enabled public administration. In R. O'Leary, D. M. Van Slyke, & S. Kim (Eds.), *The future of public administration around the world: The Minnow brook perspective* (pp. 129–139). Georgetown University Press.

Park, E., Del Pobil, A. P., & Kwon, S. J. (2018). The Role of Internet of Things (IoT) in Smart Cities: Technology Roadmap-oriented Approaches. *Sustainability*, *10*(10), 1388. doi:10.3390u10051388

Park, S. H., & Han, K. (2018). Methodologic guide for evaluating clinical performance and effect of artificial intelligence technology for medical diagnosis and prediction. *Radiology*, *286*(3), 800–809. doi:10.1148/radiol.2017171920 PMID:29309734

Partnerships British Columbia. (2003). *An Introduction to Public Private Partnerships. Update June 2003*. Partnerships British Columbia.

Pateman, C. (2012). Participatory democracy revisited. *Perspectives on Politics*, *10*(1), 7–19. doi:10.1017/S1537592711004877

Pavlova, M. (2018). Fostering inclusive, sustainable economic growth and 'green' skills development in learning cities through partnerships. *International Review of Education*, *64*(3), 339–354. doi:10.100711159-018-9718-x

Pazvant, E., & Faiz, E. (2018). Evaluation of the intention of using products with internet of things within the context of technology acceptance model. *Journal of Management, Marketing and Logistics*, 41-54.

Pereira, G. V., Parycek, P., Falco, E., & Kleinhans, R. (2018). Smart governance in the context of smart cities: A literature review. *Information Polity*, *23*(2), 143–162. Advance online publication. doi:10.3233/IP-170067

Pérez-Delhoyo, R., Andújar-Montoya, M. D., Mora, H., & Gilart-Iglesias, V. (2018). Citizen participation in urban planning-management processes: Assessing urban accessibility in smart cities. *Proceedings of the 7th International Conference on Smart Cities and Green ICT Systems*. 10.5220/0006704202060213

Pierce, G., & Shoup, D. (2013). Getting the prices right: An evaluation of pricing parking by demand in San Francisco. *Journal of the American Planning Association*, *79*(1), 67–81. doi:10.1080/01944363.2013.787307

Pierre, J. (1999). Models of urban governance: The institutional dimension of urban politics. *Urban Affairs Review*, *34*(3), 372–396. doi:10.1177/10780879922183988

Piro, G., Cianci, I., Grieco, L. A., Boggia, G., & Camarda, P. (2014). Information centric services in smart cities. *Journal of Systems and Software*, *88*, 169–188. doi:10.1016/j.jss.2013.10.029

Pise, P. D., & Uke, N. J. (2016). Efficient security framework for sensitive data sharing and privacy preserving on big-data and cloud platforms. *In Proceedings of the International Conference on Internet of things and Cloud Computing* (pp. 1-5).

Plotnikof, M. (2015). *Challenges of Collaborative Governance: An Organizational Discourse Study of Public Managers' Struggles with Collaboration across the Daycare Area*. Academic Press.

Rao, N.J. (2015). Cybersecurity: Issues and Challenges. *CSI Communications, 39*.

Regmi, K. D. (2017). Habermas, lifeworld and rationality: Towards a comprehensive model of lifelong learning. *International Journal of Lifelong Education*, *36*(6), 679–695. doi:10.1080/02601370.2017.1377776

Report, D. (1996). Learning: The treasure within. Report to UNESCO of the International Commission on Education for the Twenty-first Century. UNESCO Publishing.

Report, F. (1972). *Learning to be: The world of education today and tomorrow*. UNESCO.

Rhodes, R. A. W. (1997). *Understanding governance: Policy networks, governance reflexivity and accountability*. Open University Press.

Richards, N. M., & King, J. H. (2013). Three paradoxes of big data. *Stan. L. Rev. Online*, *66*, 41.

Riggs, W., & Kawashima, M. (2020). *Exploring Best Practice for Municipal E-Scooter Policy in the United States* [Conference presentation]. 99th Annual Meeting of the Transportation Research Board, Washington, DC.

Roehrich, J. K., Lewis, M. A., & George, G. (2014). Are Public-Private Partnerships a Healthy Option? A systematic Literature Review. *Social Science & Medicine*, *113*, 110–119. doi:10.1016/j.socscimed.2014.03.037 PMID:24861412

Roll, I., & Wylie, R. (2016). Evolution and revolution in artificial intelligence in education. *International Journal of Artificial Intelligence in Education, 26*(2), 582–599. doi:10.100740593-016-0110-3

Rosenblatt, F. (1960). Perceptron simulation experiments. *Proceedings of the IRE, 48*(3), 301–309. doi:10.1109/JRPROC.1960.287598

Rotuna, C. I., Cirnu, C. E., & Gheorghita, A. (2017). Implementing Smart City Solutions: Smart City Map and City Drop. *Life (Chicago, Ill.), 28*, 313–327.

Rouhani, O. M., Geddes, R. R., Gao, H. O., & Bel, G. (2016). Social welfare analysis of investment public–private partnership approaches for transportation projects. *Transportation Research Part A, Policy and Practice, 88*, 86–103. doi:10.1016/j.tra.2015.11.003

Roumboutsos, A. (2015). Public private partnerships in transport infrastructure. *International Review (Steubenville, Ohio)*.

Rubin, E. (2019). *Not just for fun: The role of e-scooters in urban planning.* https://www.leoweekly.com/2019/12/not-just-for-fun-the-role-of-e-scooters-in-urban-planning/

Sagiroglu, S., & Sinanc, D. (2013). *May. Big data: A review. In 2013 international conference on collaboration technologies and systems (CTS).* IEEE.

Samih, H. (2019). Smart cities and internet of things. *Journal of Information Technology Case and Application Research, 21*(1), 3-12. doi:10.1080/15228053.2019.1587572

Satterthwaite, D. (2007). *The transition to a predominantly urban world and its underpinnings* (No. 4). Academic Press.

Savas, E. S. (1982). *Privatizing the Public Sector: How to Shrink Government.* Chatham House Publishers.

Schaffers, Ratti, & Komninos. (2012). Special Issue on Smart Applications for Smart Cities – New Approaches to Innovation: Guest Editors' Introduction. *Journal of Theoretical and Applied Electronic Commerce Research, 7*(3). doi:10.4067/S0718-18762012000300005

Scholl, H. J., & Scholl, M. C. (2014). Smart governance: A roadmap for research and practice. *Conference 2014 Proceedings.* Available at: https://www.ideals.illinois.edu/bitstream/handle/2142/47408/060_ready.pdf?sequence=2

Schuler, D. (2016). Smart cities + smart citizens = civic intelligence? *Human Smart Cities,* 41–60. doi:10.1007/978-3-319-33024-2_3

Scott, L. (2012). *Engaged-learning: Community engagement classifications at U.S. land-grant institutions* (Unpublished doctoral dissertation). Teachers College, Columbia University, New York, NY.

Scott, L. (2015). Learning cities for all: Directions to a new adult education and learning movement. In L. Scott (Ed.), *Learning Cities for Adult Learners* (pp. 83–94). doi:10.1002/ace.20125

Scott, L., Mizzi, R. C., & Merriweather, L. R. (2021). Philosophical foundations of adult and continuing education. In T. Rocco, M. Smith, R. Mizzi, L. Merriweather, & J. Hawley (Eds.), *The Handbook of Adult and Continuing Education* (2020 Edition, pp. 11–21). Stylus.

Scott, T. (2015). Does collaboration make any difference? Linking collaborative governance to environmental outcomes. *Journal of Policy Analysis and Management*, *34*(3), 537–566. doi:10.1002/pam.21836

Security. (2018). *Nearly 70 Percent of SMBs Experience Cyber Attacks*. Accessed April 04, 2020 from: https://www.securitymagazine.com/articles/89586-nearly-70-percent-of-smbs-experience-cyber-attacks

Selin, S., & Chevez, D. (1995). Developing A Collaborative Model for Environmental Planning and Management. *Environmental Management*, *19*(2), 189–195. doi:10.1007/BF02471990

Serim website. (n.d.). *Serim e-scooter.* http://www.serim.com.tr/Urunlerimiz/Elektrikli-Scooter-Paylasim-Platformu-3-3075

Shahbaz, A. (2018). *The Rise of Digital Authoritarianism*. Retrieved 2 August 2020, from https://freedomhouse.org/report/freedom-net/2018/rise-digital-authoritarianism

Shah, J., Kothari, J., & Doshi, N. (2019). A Survey of Smart City infrastructure via Case study on New York. *Procedia Computer Science*, *160*, 702–705. doi:10.1016/j.procs.2019.11.024

Sha, K., Yang, T. A., Wei, W., & Davari, S. (2020). A survey of edge computing-based designs for IoT security. *Digital Communications and Networks*, *6*(2), 195–202. doi:10.1016/j.dcan.2019.08.006

Shelton, T., & Lodato, T. (2018). From smart cities to smart citizens? *Creating Smart Cities*, 144–154. doi:10.4324/9781351182409-11

Shoup, D. C. (2006). Cruising for parking. *Transport Policy*, *13*(6), 479–486. doi:10.1016/j.tranpol.2006.05.005

Siano, P., Shahrour, I., & Vergura, S. (2018). Introducing *Smart Cities*: A transdisciplinary journal on the science and technology of smart cities. *Smart Cities*, *1*(1), 1–3. doi:10.3390martcities1010001

Sicari, S., Rizzardi, A., Grieco, L. A., & Coen-Porisini, A. (2015). Security, privacy and trust in Internet of Things: The road ahead. *Computer Networks*, *76*, 146–164. doi:10.1016/j.comnet.2014.11.008

Silvia, C. (2011). Collaborative Governance Concepts for Successful Network Leadership. *State & Local Government Review*, *43*(1), 66–71. doi:10.1177/0160323X11400211

Simić, M., Vucetic, M., Kee, G.H., & Stanković, M. (2019). *Big Data and Development of Smart City*. doi:10.15308/Sinteza-2019-581-588

Smart City New York. (n.d.). *Cooperation to Innovation*. https://mobility.here.com/smart-city-new-york-cooperation-innovation

Smith, A. (1776). *The wealth of nations*. Methuen & Co., Ltd.

Smith, C. S., & Schwieterman, J. P. (2018). *E-scooter scenarios: evaluating the potential mobility benefits of shared dockless scooters in Chicago.* Chaddick Institute For Metropolitan Development At Depaul University.

SMOF. (2012). Public Private Partnership Handbook, Version 2. Singapore: SMOF.

Soteriades, M. D., & Avgeli, V. A. (2007). Promoting tourism destinations: a strategic marketing approach. *Turizam: međunarodni znanstveno-stručni časopis, 55*(3), 335-345.

Sözcü Website. *Legal regulations about e-scooters.* https://www.sozcu.com.tr/2020/ekonomi/elektrikli-scooterlar-icin-yasal-duzenleme-cagrisi-5929626/

Spiro, N. P. (2006). *A Competitive Model for Technology and City Planning: The Synergy of a Digital Urban Grid, a Wireless Cloud and Digital Architecture.* Ubiquitous City.

Spors, K. (2014). How the 'Internet of Things' Will Revolutionize Small Business. *American Express.* Retrieved from: https://www.americanexpress.com/en-us/business/trends-and-insights/articles/how-the-internet-of-things-will-revolutionize-small-business/

Stojkoska, B.R., & Trivodaliev, K. (2017). *A review of Internet of Things for smart home: Challenges and solutions.* doi:10.1016/j.jclepro.2016.10.006

Su, K., Li, J., & Fu, H. (2011, September). Smart city and the applications. In *2011 international conference on electronics, communications, and control (ICECC)* (pp. 1028-1031). IEEE.

Sun, Y., Song, H., Jara, A. J., & Bie, R. (2016). Internet of things and big data analytics for smart and connected communities. *IEEE Access: Practical Innovations, Open Solutions, 4,* 766–773. doi:10.1109/ACCESS.2016.2529723

Suqi, F. (2020). *A Space for Parking in the Future of Mobility.* City Tech Collaborative. Available at: https://www.citytech.org/a-space-for-parking-in-the-future-of-mobility

Tableau.com. (n.d.). *What is business intelligence? Your guide to BI and why its matters.* Retrieved from: https://www.tableau.com/learn/articles/business-intelligence

Tang, S. Y., & Mazmanian, D. A. (2010). *Understanding Collaborative Governance from the Structural Choice-Politics.* IAD, and Transaction Cost Perspectives.

TBB website. (n.d.). https://www.tbb.gov.tr/

Testoni, C., & Boeri, A. (2015). Smart Governance: Urban regeneration and integration policies in Europe. Turin and Malmö case studies. *International Journal of Scientific and Engineering Research, 6*(3), 527–533.

The Local France website. (2019). *Speed limits and no sharing: These are the new laws on electric scooters in France.* https://www.thelocal.fr/20191025/speed-limits-and-no-sharing-these-are-the-new-laws-on-electric-scooters-in-france

Thomas, A. M. (1991). *Beyond education: A new perspective on society's management of learning.* Jossey-Bass.

Thuzar, M. (2011). *Urbanization in South East Asia: Developing Smart Cities for the Future?* Regional Outlook.

Tight, M. (2001). *Key concepts in adult education and training.* RoutledgeFarmer.

Tobias, M. (2018). *How New York is becoming a smart city.* https://www.ny-engineers.com/blog/how-new-york-is-becoming-a-smart-city

Torfing, J. B., Peters, G., Pierre, J., & Sorensen, E. (2012). *Interactive Governance: Advancing the Paradigm.* Oxford University Press. doi:10.1093/acprof:oso/9780199596751.001.0001

Toutkoushian, R. K., & Paulsen, M. B. (2016). *Economics of higher education: Background, concepts, and applications.* Springer Nature. doi:10.1007/978-94-017-7506-9

Traupman, J. C. (1995). *The new college Latin & English dictionary.* Bantam.

Tripathy, A. K., Tripathy, P. K., Ray, N. K., & Mohanty, S. P. (2018). iTour: The future of smart tourism: An IoT framework for the independent mobility of tourists in smart cities. *IEEE Consumer Electronics Magazine, 7*(3), 32–37. doi:10.1109/MCE.2018.2797758

U. S. Department of Health, Education, and Welfare. (1978). *Lifelong learning and public policy.* Washington, DC: U.S. Government Printing Office.

Ulibarri, N. (2019). Collaborative governance: A tool to manage scientific, administrative, and strategic uncertainties in environmental management? *Ecology and Society, 24*(2), 15. doi:10.5751/ES-10962-240215

UN. (2012). World urbanization prospects: the 2011 Revision. New York, NY: UN.

UN. (2015). *Critical Milestones towards a coherent, efficient and inclusive follow up and review of the 2030 Development Agenda for SDGs.* United Nations.

UN. (2015). *Transforming our world: the 2030 Agenda for Sustainable Development.* Accessed from: https://sustainabledevelopment.un.org/post2015/transformingourworld

UN. (2017). *The new urban agenda.* Retrieved from: https://habitat3.org/wp-content/uploads/NUA-English.pdf

UNDP. (1997). *Governance for Sustainable Human Development.* United Nations Development Program.

UNDP. (2015). *Prospects of Public- private Partnership (PPP) in Ethiopia.* Development brief, NO. 1/2015. UNDP.

UN-ESCAP. (2011). *A Guidebook on Public-Private Partnership in Infrastructure.* Author.

UNESCO. (2016). *Learning, sharing and collaborating: Portraits of participating cities of the first members' meeting of the UNESCO Global Network of Learning Cities* [Report]. UNESCO Institute for Lifelong Learning.

UN-Habitat. (2004). *Urban Governance Index: Conceptual Foundation and Field Test Report.* United Nations Habitat.

UN-Habitat. (2012). *Enhancing urban safety and security: Global report on human settlements 2007.* Routledge.

UN-Habitat. (2013). *Water and sanitation in the world's cities: Local action for global goals.* Routledge.

United Nations Human Settlements Programme. (2010). *The State of African Cities 2010: Governance, Inequality and Urban Land Markets.* UN-Habitat.

United Nations. (2011). *World urbanization prospects: The 2011 revision.* Available at: https://www.un.org/en/development/desa/publications/world-urbanization-prospects-the-2011-revision.html

Urio, P. (2010). *Public - Private Partnerships: Success and Failure Factors for in Transition Countries.* University Press of America.

Usher, R., Bryant, I., & Johnston, R. (1997). *Adult education and the postmodern challenge: Learning beyond the limits.* Routledge.

Valdes-Cotera, R., Wang, M., & Lunardon, K. (2018). Realising lifelong learning for all: Governance and partnerships in building sustainable learning cities. *International Review of Education, 64*(3), 287–293. doi:10.100711159-018-9722-1

Van Buuren, A., Edelenbos, J., & Klijn, E. H. (2007). Interactive governance in the Netherlands: The case of the Scheldt Estuary. In *Democratic network governance in Europe.* Palgrave Macmillan. doi:10.1057/9780230596283_8

Vicini, S., Bellini, S., & Sanna, A. (2012, May). How to co-create Internet of things-enabled services for smarter cities. In *The First International Conference on Smart Systems, Devices and Technologies* (pp. 55-61). Academic Press.

Virilio, P. (2010). *Grey ecology* (D. Burk, Trans.). Atropos Press.

Vishnubhotla, R., Rao, P. S., Ladha, A., Kadiyala, S., Narmada, A., Ronanki, B., & Illapakurthi, S. (2010). ZigBee based multi-level parking vacancy monitoring system. In *2010 IEEE International Conference on Electro/Information Technology* (pp. 1-4). IEEE. 10.1109/EIT.2010.5612133

Wain, K. (2000). *The learning society in a postmodern world: The education crisis.* Peter Lang.

Walters, S. (2005). Learning region. In International encyclopedia of adult education (pp. 360–362). New York, NY: Palgrave Macmillan.

Wang, X., Li, X. R., Zhen, F., & Zhang, J. (2016). How smart is your tourist attraction?: Measuring tourist preferences of smart tourism attractions via a FCEM-AHP and IPA approach. *Tourism Management, 54,* 309–320. doi:10.1016/j.tourman.2015.12.003

Wang, Y. P., & Kintrea, K. (2019). Sustainable, healthy and learning cities and neighbourhoods. *Environment & Urbanization Asia, 10*(2), 146–150. doi:10.1177/0975425319859129

Weber, M. (2015). *The Role of Good Governance in Sustainable Development*. Accessed from https://www.wri.org/blog/2015/02/qa-mark-robinson-role-good-governance-sustainable-development

Weil, S. W., & McGill, I. (1989). A framework for making sense of experiential learning. In S. Weil & I. McGill (Eds.), *Making sense of experiential learning: Diversity in theory and practice* (pp. 3–24). Society for Research into Higher Education & Open University Press.

Weiss, T. (2000). Governance, Good Governance and Global Governance: Conceptual and Actual Challenges. *Third World Quarterly, 21*(5), 795–814. doi:10.1080/713701075

West, D., & Allen, J. (2020). *Turning point* (1st ed.). Brookings Institution Press.

Weymouth, R. & Hartz-Karp, J. (2015). Deliberative collaborative governance as a democratic reform to resolve wicked problems and improve trust. *Journal of Economic and Social Policy, 17*(1), 4.

White, C. (2019). *Chinese Companies Use Zimbabweans As Guinea Pigs To Identify Black Faces: Report*. Retrieved 6 June 2020, from https://nationalinterest.org/blog/buzz/chinese-companies-use-zimbabweans-guinea-pigs-identify-black-faces-report-101447

White, J. (1997). *Education and the end of work: A new philosophy of work and learning*. Cassell.

Wong, S. (2002, April). *Learning cities: Building 21st Century communities through lifelong learning*. Travelling Scholarship [Report]. Victoria, Australia: Department of Employment, Training and Tertiary Education of the Victorian Government.

Woodside, A. G., & Sood, S. (2017). Vignettes in the two-step arrival of the internet of things and its reshaping of marketing management's service-dominant logic. *Journal of Marketing Management, 33*(1-2), 98–110. doi:10.1080/0267257X.2016.1246748

World Bank Institute. (2012). *Public-Private Partnerships - Reference Guide Version 1.0*. WB.

World Bank. (2011). Learning for all: Investing in people's knowledge and skills to promote development. In World Bank Group Education Strategy 2020. Washington, DC: World Bank.

World Bank. (2016). *International Bank for Reconstruction and Development (IBRD) & International Development Association (IDA)*. Retrieved from: https://blogs.worldbank.org/sustainablecities/category/regions/south-asia

World Commission on Environment and Development (WCED). (1987). *Our Common Future*. Oxford University Press.

Wright, K.B. (2005). Researching Internet-based populations: Advantages and disadvantages of online survey research, online questionnaire authoring software packages, and web survey services. *Journal of Computer-Mediated Communication, 10*(3).

Wu, D., Hoenig, H., & Dormido, H. (2019). *Who's Winning the Tech Cold War? A China vs. U.S. Scoreboard.* Retrieved 2 August 2020, from https://www.bloomberg.com/graphics/2019-us-china-who-is-winning-the-tech-war/

Wu, X. (2017). Smart tourism based on internet of things. *Revista de la Facultad de Ingeniería*, *32*(10), 66–170.

Xu, L. M. C. M. L., & Afsarmanesh, H. (2012). *Collaborative networks in the internet of services.* Available at: https://scholar.google.com/scholar?hl=en&as_sdt=0%2C5&q=Collaborative+Net works+in+the+Internet+of+Services&btnG=

Yadavalli, A., Kim, R., McFarland, C., & Rainwater, B. (2020). *State of the Cities.* National League of Cities. Retrieved from https://www.nlc.org/sites/default/files/users/user57221/NLC_StateOfTheCities2020.pdf

Yalçıner Ercoşkun, Ö. (2016). Ultimate ICT Network in Turkey For Smart Cities. *Planlama Dergisi, 26*(2), 130–146.

Yang, J. (2012). An overview of building learning cities as a strategy for promoting lifelong learning. *Journal of Adult and Continuing Education, 18*(2), 97–113. doi:10.7227/JACE.18.2.8

Yohanes, H. (2017). Assessment of Challenges and Prospects of Good Governance in Eastern Zone of Tigray: The case of Adigrat City Administration. *Journal of Citizenship and Morality, 1*(1), 83–99.

Yorks, L., & Scott, L. (2014). Lifelong tools for the learner, educator, and worker. In V. C. X. Wang (Ed.), *Handbook of Research on Technologies for Improving the 21st Century Workforce: Tools for Lifelong Learning* (pp. 42–55). IGI Global.

Zadek, S. (2006). *The logic of collaborative governance.* Harvard Kennedy School of Government Working Paper, No. 14.

Zhang, J., Hua, X. S., Huang, J., Shen, X., Chen, J., Zhou, Q., Fu, Z., & Zhao, Y. (2019). City brain: Practice of large-scale artificial intelligence in the<? show [AQ="" ID=" Q1]"?> real world. *IET Smart Cities, 1*(1), 28–37. doi:10.1049/iet-smc.2019.0034

Zubizarreta, I., Seravalli, A., & Arrizabalaga, S. (2015). Smart city concept: What it is and what it should be. *Journal of Urban Planning and Development, 142*(1), 04015005. doi:10.1061/(ASCE)UP.1943-5444.0000282

# About the Contributors

**Lloyd Amaghionyeodiwe** is a Certified Fraud Examiner (CFE) and a Certified Internal Controls Auditor (CICA) who has several years of experience as a lecturer/ professor, researcher, analyst, economist and consultant. He served as a reviewer for many journals and has a good research record with many publications to his credit. His current research interests include Finance, Small Business Mgt & IT, and Economics with more focus on Public Sector & Health Economics.

**Ozge Ercoskun** is a professor in the City and Regional Planning Department of the Gazi University, Ankara, Turkey. She graduated from the City and Regional Planning Department of the Istanbul Technical University in 1998. She completed her master's studies in the Geodetic and Geographic Information Technologies Department of the METU in 2002. She got her Ph.D. degree from the City and Regional Planning Department of the Gazi University in 2007. She has attended several national and international congresses; summer schools and workshops related to ecological urban planning and geographic information systems. She has written 4 books and more than 100 papers on sustainable urban design and ecological and smart urban planning, resilient cities, sustainable transportation and geographic information technologies. She was an editor of a book and she published 6 book chapters from IGI Global. She worked as a researcher in many national and institutional projects. She has awards about sustainability and urban growth, sustainable tourism.

**Betül Ertoy Sarışık** is a lecturer at Ankara Hacı Bayram Veli University. She graduated from the City and Regional Planning Department of the Karadeniz Technical University in 2012. She got her master degree from the Traffic Planning of the Gazi University in 2018. She is attending Ph. D. degree in the City and Regional Planning Department of the Gazi University.

**Yong Kyu Lee** is an Assistant Professor of Marketing in the Department of Business and Economics at York College, the City University of New York, United States. He received his PhD degree from Virginia Tech. His current research interest lies in consumer behavior including goal pursuit, categorization and assortment size, and social media.

**Eda Özlü** between 2006 and 2010, she received her bachelor's degree in Black Sea Technical University City and Regional Planning department. She completed her graduate education in 2014 with her thesis titled "Rural Settlement Action Plan Creation Process: The Experience of Trabzon / Salacik Village" in the field of city and regional planning. She is currently continuing his doctorate education in city and regional planning; she is preparing a doctoral thesis on "Intra-urban Residential Mobility and Reflections on the City". Since 2012, she has been working as a research assistant at Karadeniz Technical University, City and Regional Planning Department.

**Leodis Scott**, is an Assistant Professor of Educational Leadership and DePaul University-Chicago; Adjunct Professor of Adult Learning and Leadership at Columbia University-Teachers College-New York; Board Chair/President at LearnLong Institute for Education and Learning Research (LIFR). Scott received his Doctor of Education (Ed.D.) from Columbia University-Teacher College. His interests include learning cities, analytic philosophy of adult continuing education, and lifelong learning policy.

**Gedifew Sewenet Yigzaw** is a senior lecturer in the department of Governance and Development Studies, Bahir Dar University, Ethiopia. He got a Master of Arts Degree in Governance and Development Studies (specialization: Governance Studies) from Hawassa University, Ethiopia. He is an experienced lecturer, social science advisor, and researcher with a solid curiosity in governance and institutional reform, public service delivery, e-governance and ICT, migration and displacement, regional integration, security, conflict resolution, leadership, public policy, democracy and democratization, media ethics, and development. He is dedicated to strong work commitment, time management, building team work, communication skills, leadership and academic excellence. He has conducted research works and community services, and published academic works in the international reputable peer-reviewed journals, including Scopus indexed journals. He reviewed and examined many research works (i.e., manuscripts, book chapter, MA theses) across the globe. He is excellent in English and a native speaker, writer and reader of Amharic, an Ethiopian language.

# Index

## A

artificial intelligence 91-92, 95-98, 101, 103-106, 118, 125, 134-136, 186

## B

big data 91, 102, 107-112, 114-115, 118-124, 127-128, 134-136, 156, 160, 164, 179, 186-189, 194, 197

## C

cloud computing 112-113, 117-118, 120, 123, 138, 141, 144, 152, 160-161, 166-168, 186
collaboration 1, 3-4, 6-7, 9-12, 16, 19-20, 22-24, 31-32, 34, 40, 92, 113, 119, 122-123, 164
collaborative governance 1, 3-13, 22-29, 31-35
communication 7-9, 37, 40, 58, 61, 69, 85, 97, 109, 112, 114, 130, 135, 138, 141, 144-145, 150, 154-156, 160-161, 180-181, 186-187, 190, 197-198
consumers 57, 157, 163-164, 180-185, 190-192, 196
cyberattack 155, 158, 171, 173

## D

development 1-3, 7, 10-20, 22-30, 33-35, 40, 56, 67, 69-70, 72, 74-79, 83-84, 88, 90-96, 98, 101, 105, 108-109, 112-113, 117, 119, 125-132, 135-136, 138,

141, 144-145, 148, 152-153, 157, 160, 165, 175, 179, 181, 186-187, 192, 197
Dockless E-Scooter 36, 66-67

## E

efficiency 7, 11, 13, 19, 61, 97, 113, 125-126, 130-131, 134, 141-142, 144, 152, 155-156, 162-165, 173, 181, 184, 188
e-scooter providers 37-38, 45, 47, 52, 60-61, 63, 67

## G

goals 1, 5, 11-13, 15-16, 18, 23, 27-28, 33, 35, 70, 75, 109-110, 157, 160, 190
governance 1-13, 16-20, 22-35, 69, 83, 85, 90, 92, 97, 101, 111, 156, 158

## H

Hybrid System Charging 67

## I

innovation 4, 8, 12, 14, 21-22, 30, 40, 58, 79, 88, 92, 94, 98-99, 101-102, 105, 110, 123, 125, 130, 132, 135-137, 144-145, 158, 162, 175, 177-178
Internet of Things (IoT) 95, 97, 107, 138, 153, 156, 161, 163, 176, 178, 180-181, 194, 196-197

# L

large technical systems 91-95, 101-102, 105
learning cities 68-72, 74-76, 79-90
learning society 69, 74, 76, 85, 87, 90
lifelong learning 68-74, 76, 78, 80, 82-90
light vehicles 36, 38, 60, 63, 67

# M

micromobility 36-37, 41-43, 51-52, 56-57,
    61-63, 67
mobile application 39, 46, 48, 138, 141,
    148, 152, 187, 194

# P

Permitted Zones 49, 67
policy 1-2, 4-6, 9-13, 17, 19, 23, 25-29, 31-
    32, 34-35, 55, 57, 63, 66, 70-72, 75,
    83, 85-89, 92-94, 96, 98-99, 102-103,
    111, 136, 154, 172, 175, 196
power networks 91, 96, 98

# Q

quality of life 8, 11, 17, 64, 69, 85, 108,
    125-131, 135, 138, 149-150, 152-153,
    155-156, 158, 160, 180-181, 192

# R

Retailing 180-181, 190-191, 195
risk management 30, 155, 173

# S

safety 17, 33, 42-43, 54-56, 59-60, 63, 98,
    101, 109, 117, 125, 128-129, 131, 135,
    150, 156, 172, 174, 177

small businesses 155, 157-158, 161, 163-
    169, 171-175, 177-178
smart cities 1, 3-4, 7-10, 14, 16, 19-20,
    22-24, 26-27, 31, 37, 40, 57, 61, 65,
    67-69, 71, 85-86, 91, 93, 95-98, 100,
    102, 104, 106-107, 109, 111-112,
    114, 117-118, 120-123, 125, 127-137,
    140-142, 146, 155-158, 160-161, 171,
    175-179, 181, 193-197
smart environment 3, 7, 24, 40, 61, 155,
    158, 166
Smart Healthcare 113, 180, 189, 198
smart parking 97, 138, 141, 145-146, 148-
    149, 151-153
smart tourism 180-181, 184, 186-188, 192,
    194-195, 197-198
Smart Tourism Destination 184, 187-188,
    198
stakeholders 2-14, 16-17, 22-24, 34-35,
    41, 54, 61, 87, 98, 128, 150, 182,
    186, 188-189
survey research 152, 154
systems theory 75, 93-94, 101

# T

technology 3, 7-8, 13, 20, 25, 30, 39-40,
    47, 60-61, 68-70, 75, 85, 87, 92-99,
    101-102, 104-105, 108, 111, 122, 124-
    131, 133, 136-140, 142-146, 150-151,
    153-154, 156-158, 161, 163, 165-172,
    175-178, 180-184, 190-191, 193-198
technopolitics 91
traffic management 113, 141, 146

# U

USA 37, 68, 91, 107, 114, 125, 138, 140,
    155, 157, 165, 180

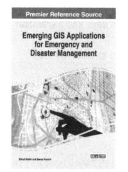
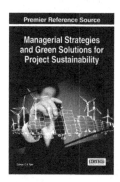

# IGI Global Author Services

Providing a high-quality, affordable, and expeditious service, IGI Global's Author Services enable authors to streamline their publishing process, increase chance of acceptance, and adhere to IGI Global's publication standards.

## Benefits of Author Services:

- **Professional Service:** All our editors, designers, and translators are experts in their field with years of experience and professional certifications.
- **Quality Guarantee & Certificate:** Each order is returned with a quality guarantee and certificate of professional completion.
- **Timeliness:** All editorial orders have a guaranteed return timeframe of 3-5 business days and translation orders are guaranteed in 7-10 business days.
- **Affordable Pricing:** IGI Global Author Services are competitively priced compared to other industry service providers.
- **APC Reimbursement:** IGI Global authors publishing Open Access (OA) will be able to deduct the cost of editing and other IGI Global author services from their OA APC publishing fee.

## Author Services Offered:

**English Language Copy Editing**
Professional, native English language copy editors improve your manuscript's grammar, spelling, punctuation, terminology, semantics, consistency, flow, formatting, and more.

**Scientific & Scholarly Editing**
A Ph.D. level review for qualities such as originality and significance, interest to researchers, level of methodology and analysis, coverage of literature, organization, quality of writing, and strengths and weaknesses.

**Figure, Table, Chart & Equation Conversions**
Work with IGI Global's graphic designers before submission to enhance and design all figures and charts to IGI Global's specific standards for clarity.

**Translation**
Providing 70 language options, including Simplified and Traditional Chinese, Spanish, Arabic, German, French, and more.

## Hear What the Experts Are Saying About IGI Global's Author Services

"Publishing with IGI Global has been *an amazing experience* for me for sharing my research. The *strong academic production* support ensures quality and timely completion." – **Prof. Margaret Niess, Oregon State University, USA**

"The service was *very fast, very thorough, and very helpful* in ensuring our chapter meets the criteria and requirements of the book's editors. I was *quite impressed and happy* with your service." – **Prof. Tom Brinthaupt, Middle Tennessee State University, USA**

www.igi-global.com

Publisher of Peer-Reviewed, Timely, and
Innovative Academic Research Since 1988

## IGI Global's Transformative Open Access (OA) Model:
# How to Turn Your University Library's Database Acquisitions Into a Source of OA Funding

Well in advance of Plan S, IGI Global unveiled their OA Fee Waiver (Read & Publish) Initiative. Under this initiative, librarians who invest in IGI Global's InfoSci-Books and/or InfoSci-Journals databases will be able to subsidize their patrons' OA article processing charges (APCs) when their work is submitted and accepted (after the peer review process) into an IGI Global journal.

## How Does it Work?

**Step 1:** **Library Invests in the InfoSci-Databases:** A library perpetually purchases or subscribes to the InfoSci-Books, InfoSci-Journals, or discipline/subject databases.

**Step 2:** **IGI Global Matches the Library Investment with OA Subsidies Fund:** IGI Global provides a fund to go towards subsidizing the OA APCs for the library's patrons.

**Step 3:** **Patron of the Library is Accepted into IGI Global Journal (After Peer Review):** When a patron's paper is accepted into an IGI Global journal, they option to have their paper published under a traditional publishing model or as OA.

**Step 4:** **IGI Global Will Deduct APC Cost from OA Subsidies Fund:** If the author decides to publish under OA, the OA APC fee will be deducted from the OA subsidies fund.

**Step 5:** **Author's Work Becomes Freely Available:** The patron's work will be freely available under CC BY copyright license, enabling them to share it freely with the academic community.

*Note: This fund will be offered on an annual basis and will renew as the subscription is renewed for each year thereafter. IGI Global will manage the fund and award the APC waivers unless the librarian has a preference as to how the funds should be managed.*

## Hear From the Experts on This Initiative:

"I'm very happy to have been able to make one of my recent research contributions *freely available* along with having access to the *valuable resources* found within IGI Global's InfoSci-Journals database."

– **Prof. Stuart Palmer,**
Deakin University, Australia

"Receiving the support from IGI Global's OA Fee Waiver Initiative *encourages me to continue my research work without any hesitation*."

– **Prof. Wenlong Liu,** College of Economics and Management at Nanjing University of Aeronautics & Astronautics, China